Quality Human Resources Leadership

Quality Human Resources Leadership

A Principal's Handbook

L. David Weller Jr.
Sylvia Weller

The Scarecrow Press, Inc.
Technomic Books
Lanham, Maryland, and London
2000

SCARECROW PRESS, INC.

Published in the United States of America
by Scarecrow Press, Inc.
4720 Boston Way, Lanham, Maryland 20706
www.scarecrowpress.com

4 Pleydell Gardens, Folkestone
Kent CT20 2DN, England

ISBN 1-56676-850-0 (cloth : alk. paper)
Library of Congress Catalog Card No. 99-67272

∞™ The paper used in this publication meets the minimum requirements of American National Standard for Information Sciences—Permanence of Paper for Printed Library Materials, ANSI/NISO Z39.48–1992.
Manufactured in the United States of America.

*To Vicky
with our love*

Quality Human Resources Leadership: A Principal's Handbook is a volume which fuses theory with practice and is designed to assist principals at all levels in their continuous efforts to maximize human potential, promote quality educational outcomes, and practice effective leadership skills. The contents of the volume were conceived out of the twin senses of need and urgency, both from students and colleagues, who called for a work that was practical in scope, was research based in nature, provided case studies, and addressed the more recent responsibilities and demands placed on principals in site-based managed schools.

The contents of this volume originated with our research on *total quality management* as a school reform and restructuring model to infuse shared governance, teacher empowerment, and continuous improvement into schools seeking quality educational outcomes. This research was augmented with our experience as school level and central office level administrators, and our work as consultants, both nationally and internationally, in assisting school principals restructure their schools into site-based managed entities. From these efforts, two overriding truths became evident. First, the substantial increase in site-based managed schools has yielded more authority to the principal to develop and devise mechanisms to produce more effective student results and provide higher-quality programs and levels of teacher performance. Second, many of the newly acquired responsibilities of these site-based school principals were once the prerogative of the director of personnel—a central office position meeting the traditional demands of personnel administration. With the shift in focus of control, principals are now responsible for many of the traditional duties of central office personnel, in general, and the director of personnel, in particular. With increased authority and responsibilities come the need for additional skills and knowledge in the area of human resource management.

Our preparation of this work focused on three questions: (1) What are the essential knowledge and skills necessary for principals to be effective leaders in site-based managed schools? (2) What are the essential knowledge and skills necessary to maximize human potential in site-based managed schools? and (3) What should a handbook contain to provide maximum assistance to principals as they seek to develop human potential to the fullest and strive to achieve quality educational results? This book, therefore, is designed to provide principals with the essential knowledge and skills required of effective human resource leaders. The work provides a new conceptual framework to apply many of the traditional practices of personnel administration, within the context of human resource leadership, in schools practicing shared governance models and seeking effective outcomes.

ACKNOWLEDGMENTS

This work was the result of the combined efforts of the authors and the highly talented, understanding, and demanding editors and publishers at Technomic Publishing Company, Inc. Their valuable suggestions and cooperative assistance were essential in capturing and presenting the full intent of the volume.

Special recognition goes to Donna Bell and Linda Edwards for their valuable assistance in the manuscript preparation and review of the work's style and conformity to standards. Their skills and dedication to quality performance are deeply appreciated. Additional thanks go to LaNelle Davis for her assistance in manuscript coordination and the demands associated with the process. The authors are deeply appreciative of the assistance and professional courtesy extended by practicing principals at site-based managed schools. Their candor and willingness to share freely with the authors their personal experiences and "what works and does not work" in the "real world" of leadership is deeply appreciated and serves to enhance the value of this book.

INTRODUCTION

This volume is designed to prepare school leaders to maximize human potential and to improve their own leadership abilities. The work is arranged to provide the reader with theory, research, and specific examples of how research and theory can be applied in daily practice. Theory and research, if devoid of examples (case studies) of practical application, are often viewed with suspicion by the practitioner. It is only when theory and research can be internalized and viewed as being beneficial to the practitioner that theory and research reap their intended rewards.

The contents and arrangement of this book are presented in three distinct sections with two overarching themes that serve as a template for the contents of the volume. The two themes are (1) the leadership of the principal is the key to establishing a *culture* in the school in which human potential can be maximized and (2) leadership skills and knowledge are necessary to *transform* the *culture* of the school in order to maximize human potential.

Each of the three sections of the book are grouped around these themes. *Section I* focuses on how leadership can transform the culture of the school and it contains two chapters, one on creating a culture to maximize human potential and one on the leadership skills necessary to maximize human potential. *Section II* focuses on methods used by effective principals to transform the culture of their schools and it contains four chapters, one on effective human relations and communication skills; another on effective team building and team work; one on promoting continuous improvement; and one on effective systems of rewards and recognitions. *Section III* presents the knowledge and skills necessary to foster and reinforce the development of human potential.

This section includes five chapters, one on conflict management; one on recruitment, selection, retention, dismissal, and turnover; one on promoting potential through performance appraisal; one on promoting the teacher as leader; and a chapter on maximizing beginning teacher potential. Case studies appear throughout the work to make this book a valuable source of information for the practitioner and to fuse theory and research with practice.

TRANSFORMING THE CULTURE OF SCHOOLS THROUGH LEADERSHIP

CHAPTER 1

Cultural Leadership: Promoting Human Potential

Cultural leadership provides a conceptual framework for understanding the transition from personnel administration (emphasizing worker effectiveness to meet organizational goals) to human resources management (maximizing human potential through more effective use of organizational resources and leadership knowledge and skills). The development of cultural leadership in schools is essential for achieving quality outcomes and maximizing human potential.

CULTURE AND HUMAN RESOURCE LEADERSHIP

The field of human resource management has gained status over the past two decades with its emphasis on maximizing human potential and expanding the traditional functions associated with personnel administration. Although it is not clearly defined in the literature, there is agreement that the nature and purpose of human resource management falls within the rubric of leadership and not of management. It is our contention that *human resource management* should be thought of as *human resource leadership*.

The field of human resource management gradually emerged from federal and state laws, sociopolitical events, court decisions, trends, and theories and research. Current practices include those of traditional personnel administration such as recruiting and hiring, training, compensating, record keeping, and evaluating. But human resource management includes much more. It is leadership, not management, which creates a harmonious community (a culture) where common values, attitudes, and norms are nested within a people-first philosophy, a culture which is dedicated to achieving organizational goals by maximizing the personal and professional development of each employee.

3

Human resource leadership is people positive, people centered, and people valued.

Personnel administration is a more impersonal process, more attuned to effectively and efficiently meeting the goals of the organization, and more consumed by the traditional management duties of record keeping, implementing policy and procedure, organizing, and controlling. Although many of the functions of personnel administration and human resource management overlap, the people-first distinction of human resource management signals a change in philosophy. With this change has dawned an understanding that managing people requires different skills and knowledge than managing policy, procedure, and records. It requires an understanding of human behavior, psychology, and motivation. More importantly, it requires the ability to put this understanding into action through leadership, and the leader who is successful does this through the building and sustaining of culture.

A generic definition containing the essential elements subscribed to by anthropologists, sociologists, and historians is that *culture* is a pattern of meanings derived from traditions, values, norms, beliefs, attitudes, and myths which are held and acted out by a common group of people. Culture becomes the "glue" that holds the community together and represents its true beliefs and convictions. Culture is a reflection of the leader.

Human resource leadership is an interrelated function focusing on serving, caring, facilitating, cooperating, and coordinating. Knezevich (1984) defines educational administration as a "helping profession," one which has "secular ministers" who oversee organizational goals while serving and caring for its employees. Within the context of Knezevich's definition of educational administration, a multidimensional and complex set of tasks, is the leadership function which focuses on caring for and serving employees. It is the leadership aspect which is concerned with maximizing human potential within a culture which stresses the human dimension, the importance of working conditions and relationships, and the motivation and satisfaction of employees.

HISTORICAL OVERVIEW OF PERSONNEL ADMINISTRATION AND HUMAN RESOURCE MANAGEMENT

Personnel administration, defined by Van Zwoll (1964), is "the complex of specific activities directly engaged in by the employing agency . . . to make a pointed effort to secure the greatest possible worker effectiveness consistent with the agency's objectives" (p. 3). Rebore (1982) lists the goals of personnel administration as hiring, retaining, developing, and motivating the staff whereas Webb, Montello, and Norton (1994) relate that personnel administration has been historically and traditionally concerned with performing clerical tasks or jobs someone other than top management or the shop foreman "had to do." Three time periods capture the emergence of personnel administration into human relations management. These are as follows:

(1) The Emergence Period (1890–1930) evidenced the rise of bureaucratic business models and classical organizational theories which stressed coordination, control, production, and organizational efficiency. The rise of labor unions and laws concerning employee rights and benefits contributed greatly to defining the role and responsibilities of personnel administrators.

(2) The Employee Rights and Benefits Period (1930–1970) witnessed the proliferation of social and political pressures for the individual's rights, concern over employee morale and job satisfaction, and the improvement of working conditions. Expansion of federal and state laws regulating management–labor relationships regarding health, fringe, and retirement benefits were coupled with the application of organizational development and leadership theories, with job functions focusing on record keeping, preparing salary schedules, making rating or evaluation reports, keeping personnel and company files, and other assigned clerical duties.

(3) The Human Resource Management Period (1970–present) evidenced the expansion of the importance of cooperative management-labor relations, the role and importance of leadership theory and research, teamwork, communication, consideration for employee personal growth and development, vision and goal setting, and shared governance. Sharing responsibilities, cultivating healthy and productive relationships, emphasizing the importance of organizational culture, and focusing on the importance of the human element are coupled with the concern to achieve organizational efficiency and effectiveness.

Personnel administration's foundation lies in the early theories of organizational development and business management. Sloane (1983) relates that scientific management theories and bureaucratic models dominated organizational structure and management thinking until the early 1950s when a plethora of federal laws and codes significantly affected labor–management relations. Laws ranging from collective bargaining to antidiscrimination to employee retirement packages caused organizations to rewrite policies and change their mental model of employees as a labor force. This change was not a voluntary paradigm shift for management, but a mandated effort, and it enforced new ways of treating and interacting with employees. As a result, personnel administration was designated as the area to frame, implement, and monitor policy designed to meet the requirements set forth by federal legislation.

In education, the advent of collective bargaining during the 1960s drastically altered the field of personnel administration and teachers became involved in the areas of decision making, recruiting, selecting, assigning, and the professional development of teachers (Knezevich, 1984). Teachers now had a voice in policy making regardless of whether administrators were sympathetic to democratic practices or not. The early 1970s witnessed a "new breed" of employees. Less traditional than their counterparts of the 1950s and 1960s, the "new breed" had different values and needs, and traditional dictatorial practices conflicted with their ideas of independence and equality. The fact that they were, in general, more highly educated than previous employees served only to compound the issue. By the 1980s, challenges to authority increased as did absenteeism, militant behavior, and increased demands for equality in the workplace and greater inclusion in the policy-making function. These difficult challenges were relegated to personnel administrators whose training now included public relations techniques and motivational, organizational, and behavioral theories. By the early 1990s, personnel administrators realized that their job descriptions were outdated and that they needed more training in leadership theory, conflict management, and psychology. They began to view themselves as managers of human resources as they became more involved in organizational planning, employee development and training, employee counseling, and the leadership roles required as subsets of these newly expanded responsibilities.

The development of human resource management as a field of study is relatively new and the term *human resource management* is not yet clearly defined. However, the term is more associated with leadership responsibilities than with those of management. Castetter (1996) agrees with Rebore (1991) when he notes that personnel administration, per se, was more focused on achieving the goals of the organization, through control and regulatory means, than it was on maximizing human potential and effectiveness. Human resource management is more of a leadership function than a maintenance one with its emphasis on the individual as a valued professional with unique skills and knowledge which are essential to organizational effectiveness. This new conceptualization of the human resources function calls for knowledge and skills in the areas of motivation and leadership which are essential to maximizing *individual* potential and achieving quality outcomes.

In this context, the *individual* becomes the focal point for promoting organizational effectiveness and efficiency. Effective principals focus on selecting, hiring, and developing individuals who are viewed as valuable additions to an existing faculty constituting skilled and knowledgeable professionals committed to achieving the goals of the school. Webb, Montello, and Norton (1994) relate that effective schools depend on the quality of its teachers for program effectiveness and that human resource management becomes the most important function of principals. Sustaining relationships and maintaining a school's culture to achieve quality outcomes require knowledge and the ability to apply motivational and leadership theories to promote teacher potential to the fullest.

HUMAN RESOURCE LEADERSHIP

Human resource leadership is actualized by providing a satisfying and quality-oriented work environment (Castetter, 1996). Providing this environment incorporates the three essential components of leadership: technical, human, and conceptual. *Technical* aspects are management-type tasks such as enforcing policy and demonstrating efficient use of fiscal and physical resources. *Human* aspects stress the importance of working conditions, job satisfaction, and providing the necessary support for employees to excel. *Conceptual* aspects include building vision, shaping attitudes and norms, and finding new ways to achieve both individual and organizational goals (Katz, 1974). In this context, human resource leadership becomes the most salient function of school administrators because it influences every aspect of schooling and taps the creative energies of school principals.

Human resource leadership, therefore, is a people business with the first concern of principals being to create a culture which enhances the achievement of personal goals. The primary role of the principal becomes that of a leader who enhances the human dimension within a supportive and dedicated work community and causes individual goals to be fused with organizational goals thereby promoting common interests and goals.

Goals of Human Resource Leadership

Generally, the agreed upon goals of human resource leadership are "to attract, develop, retain, and motivate personnel in order to (a) achieve the system's purpose, (b) assist members in satisfying position and group performance standards, (c) maximize personal career development, and (d) reconcile individual and organizational objectives" (Castetter, 1996, p. 5). Goal accomplishment, relates Rebore (1991), demonstrates the effectiveness of human resource leadership with effectiveness resulting from a systematic, structured process which allows individuals and groups to work cooperatively while providing flexibility to respond to internal and external changes or demands. Central to goal achievement are clearly defined vision and mission statements, humanistic leadership, and an on-going evaluation system.

Vision and mission provide the overall direction and foundation for goal development. Weller, Hartley, and Brown (1994) note that vision provides the infrastructure of the organization which includes its governance processes;

policies and priorities; and its values, norms, beliefs, attitudes, and traditions—in essence, the organization's culture. Smith and Piele (1997) maintain that vision is "moral images" of the future and reflects the leader's values, beliefs, and attitudes. Vision liberates the organization to achieve new paradigms, it promotes commitment and energizes people to excel, it establishes standards of excellence, and it provides focus and purpose to work.

Leadership is the essential component in creating organizational vision and goals. Gardner (1964) states that leaders create states of mind, provide direction, and provide a moral unity which is necessary to achieve social and organizational ends. Leaders clearly articulate their values and goals, convince others of their merit, and "lift people out of their petty preoccupations, carry them above conflicts that tear a society apart, and unite them in the pursuit of objectives worthy of their best efforts" (p. 12). Leaders provide a sense of harmony through tacit agreements among subordinates that align their energies toward mutually accepted common goals and ideals. According to Bennis and Nanus (1985), this encompasses the essence of transformational leadership. To them, "the organization finds its greatest expression in the consciousness of a common social responsibility, and that is to translate that vision into a living reality . . . which reflects the community of interests of both leaders and followers" (p. 217).

Transformational leaders excite and energize their followers to dream, envision ideals, and view their work from a different perspective. These leaders challenge others to identify purpose and create a vision and long-term goals that require their collective, creative efforts to accomplish. Bass (1985) relates that transformational leaders inspire and unite their followers in a search of a better future, higher quality outcomes, and higher performance levels. Weller (1998a) maintains that transformational leadership is the keystone to reengineering the school's culture. Reengineering requires the tearing down of existing dysfunctional cultural elements and redesigning a school's culture based on new values, attitudes, beliefs, assumptions, goals, rites, and rituals. Leaders reengineering their school seek quality outcomes and create dissatisfaction with existing conditions by identifying current failures and discontent within the existing culture and then challenging their followers to create a new infrastructure which ensures commitment to newly identified values, beliefs, and assumptions that are jointly developed and shared. In essence, they create a new "moral fabric" that liberates and maximizes human potential. Hoy and Miskel (1996) note that transformational leadership closely describes the "ideal" leader: one who inspires, liberates, and develops high expectations and performance levels in their followers while focusing on people and team work to achieve organizational goals.

Evaluation is an essential part of leadership and goal setting. Schools are learning communities and effective educational program outcomes are the primary goals of schooling. Within the learning community, knowledge management becomes central to quality performance and products. *Knowledge management,* broadly defined, provides processes which promote the continuous development of intellectual ability and the redesign of instructional delivery systems to increase the effectiveness and efficiency of outcomes. Essential to the objectives of knowledge management are *data, information, knowledge,* and *action.* Wilson and Asay (1999) report that *data* are raw facts that are unrelated but abound in daily work. *Information* deals with connecting facts and giving them meaningful relationships. *Knowledge* refers to combining these relationships, making them meaningful, and then *acting* on this body of knowledge to improve existing conditions. Knowledge management serves to optimize and extend our ability to act effectively, think analytically, and improve continuously. Evaluation then becomes the process by which leaders can investigate the effectiveness of knowledge-in-action and determine the degree to which goals are fulfilled.

Leaders view evaluation as the foundation for continuous improvement. Evaluation in Total Quality Management (TQM) schools is looked upon as an opportunity to improve personally and professionally and to strengthen areas of weakness so that more effective student learning results. Formative and summative evaluation procedures are used to collect data and redesign or develop new programs in attempts to yield higher outcomes for teachers and students alike. Weller (1999) relates that principals in TQM schools stress the importance of inquiry and encourage teachers to innovate, try new teaching techniques, develop new instructional materials, and design curricular offerings to improve the outcomes of schooling. In these schools, both formative and summative evaluation is applied to program and teacher evaluation. Evaluation is viewed as a learning and developmental process in which assistance and encouragement to improve are provided through a collaborative, supportive network comprising administrators and peer teachers. The goal to improve continuously, to manage knowledge effectively, and to become a true learning community is realized in schools practicing the quality management principles.

PRODUCTIVE SCHOOL CULTURES

Confusion exists over the terms *climate* and *culture.* School climate describes a school's shared perceptions of its inhabitants, its "morale," and its attitude toward its function as an educational organization. Lunenburg and Ornstein (1996) define school climate as "the environmental quality within the organization . . . and [it] may be referred to as *open, bustling, warm, easy going, informal, cold, impersonal, hostile, rigid,* and *closed"* (p. 74). Climate is a part of a school's culture but *does not* describe or encompass school culture. Moreover, climate is rooted in psychology whereas culture is rooted in history, sociology, and anthropology.

In contrast, *culture* represents the shared beliefs, norms, values, assumptions, and attitudes that telegraph what the organization stands for, its mission, and its expectations. Culture is what the school's inhabitants truly believe and value, and it is reinforced in the way they behave with regularity, both overtly and covertly. Culture is the shared meanings and values that give a sense of community, direction, commitment, and purpose to the organization.

Culture contributes in large measure to a school's effectiveness or ineffectiveness. Deal (1993) refers to culture as those traditions, values, and beliefs that constitute a school's history, which are practiced on a daily basis and contribute to its effectiveness. The school culture guides the actions of principals, teachers, and students based on the common set of beliefs held about the purpose of schooling and the roles each should play. The culture of a school represents the way people behave toward one another, the way they feel about themselves, and the way the job of schooling is performed. Weller (1999) notes that schools have been characterized as "good" or "bad" or "desirable" or "undesirable" based on their culture or the way a school "feels." This "feel" is evident upon first observation and is reinforced in hallways, lunchrooms, and classrooms and in conversations with students, teachers, and administrators. Culture leads one to say, "This is a nice place to work," or "Gee, there is no way I would work here."

Positive, productive school cultures are promoted through reform practices, such as participatory management models, which serve to transform the basic nature and purpose of schooling, a nature which is more social than technical (Deal, 1993). The social aspects of schooling are the values, beliefs, and norms held by the school's population that are practiced daily to achieve the goals of teachers, administrators, and students.

School reform requires the transformation of both the social elements of schooling and the governance structure used to implement and sustain the reform effort. Structural changes are technical changes and do not by themselves significantly affect school effectiveness. Cunningham and Gresso (1993) reported that introducing new structures and conducting "technical tampering" *do not* singularly transform schools into effective educational organizations. Cultural change in schools precedes structural changes which will then naturally evolve from and serve to reinforce the new values, beliefs, and attitudes of the school.

Reengineering is a process used in quality oriented schools to provide a conceptual framework to unlock the existing culture, rethink the context of work, and redesign how work itself is performed. Reengineering allows administrators and teachers to "bridge the gap" between what should be provided and what is actually provided by the school (Weller, 1998b). This holistic process calls for horizontal, nonlinear collaboration to assess core values and beliefs. Through jointly developed vision and goal statements, a new and different set of social characteristics (a new culture) emerges and serves as the foundation for building new cognitive and affective models about the purpose and nature of schooling. *Cultural transformation* refers to building cultural linkages between the vision and goals of the school and its teachers and students. *Cultural linkages,* notes Weller (1998a), are those old traditions, values, attitudes, and beliefs that are closely akin to the new vision and goals and those that are incorporated as part of the school's new social characteristics. The reality that an entirely new set of values and beliefs will emerge is unlikely because many of the old values are central to schooling. The fusing of the old with the new will ease and smooth the school's transition process.

Research supports the importance of key leadership behaviors in transforming a school's culture. Democratic or humanistic leadership characteristics, such as using teacher teams in developing vision and goals, modeling, and reinforcing expected behaviors and holding high expectations for success, facilitate the cultural transformation process (Sergiovanni et al., 1992). Effective leaders, says Etzioni (1988), transform culture by bonding people's values, aspirations, and ideals through the creation of a "commonness" that fosters mutual commitment and allows for personal fulfillment. Allowing followers to take responsibility for their actions and rewarding their achievements as they strive to attain new goals become central to the leadership function. Bennis and Nanus (1985) relate that transformational leaders "energize" their followers to pursue the purpose of culture by helping them align their needs and expectations with those of the organization. Leaders provide clear direction and support and reward behaviors which solidify and perpetuate the values and beliefs of the organization. Leaders, they maintain, provide a *moral compass* for their followers. They set examples and encourage others to meet and excel the ideals and standards that are valued and held in common.

Team work is another salient ingredient in cultural transformation. Cunningham and Gresso (1993) and Weller, Hartley, and Brown (1994) report that effective transformation of school culture requires jointly developed visions and goals to ensure singular purpose and commitment. Time and energy expended in shaping the school's culture provide the vested interest necessary for success. Shared governance flows from initial teacher involvement and allows teachers the latitude to develop school policies and practices necessary to promote the new values and beliefs of the school. New policies, consistent with the new belief system, now provide the infrastructure for new norms, attitudes, traditions, and behaviors essential for the acceptance of a new culture.

Three Levels of School Culture

School culture, reports Schein (1985), has three levels: *artifacts, values* and *beliefs,* and tacit *assumptions.* Lunenberg (1985) adds the *perspective* level that is essential for building a sense of community and shared meaning.

(1) *Artifacts:* Tangible artifacts are language, stories, myths, rituals, cere-monies, and other visible symbols that have value and provide meaning to the school. These artifacts are practiced daily in teacher and student behavior and include compliance to rules and regulations and the type of personal interactions that exists among teachers, students, and administra-tors. The artifacts level is the "feeling" level of the school's culture and it provides outsiders with direct experiences of that culture and creates first impressions.

(2) *Perspectives:* These are the norms, rules, and regulations of the school, which are socially shared and which guide those actions used to solve common problems that confront the school. Perspectives, in a larger sense, provide the overall guidelines for acceptable behavior among students, teachers, and administrators. Perspectives can be considered to be the *moral template* used to guide action and interaction.

(3) *Values and beliefs:* These are the *moral fiber* of the school and provide the direction for daily conduct. Values and beliefs guide classroom learning, are seen in school discipline policies, and are the foundation for the pur-pose of schooling. Values and beliefs are the foundation of the school's vision and mission statements and dominate its philosophy of education.

(4) *Assumptions:* Tacit assumptions are characterized as the "hidden values" and beliefs of the school and are patterns of behavior which emerge over time. Tacit assumptions are beliefs held by teachers and others that govern behavior, expectations, and relationships. They define the boundaries of relationships, guide personal conduct, and may result from conscious or unconscious decisions or choices. Put another way, explicit values and behaviors become implicit over time and guide daily conduct and personal interaction.

Changing School Culture

Changing a school's culture is a difficult and time-consuming task. Culture, the "glue" that holds a community together, provides purpose and reasons for its existence. Change requires providing a new direction, new commitments, and new and better ideals. Cultural change first requires a general feeling of dissatisfaction with existing conditions and outcomes, a knowing that *some-thing is not right.* Second, change requires proactive leadership. Capitalizing on popular discontent, leaders must provide new "mental models" of a better future, encourage new ideals and assumptions, and help others to envision a new purpose for schooling. Third, change of any kind requires a structured, systematic process, which requires systems thinking, broad participation, and clear direction and specific targets for achievement (Conley, 1993; Weller, 1998; West-Burnham, 1993). These achievement targets are best accomplished by designing a change process with incremental steps that are targets in and of themselves, but are sequenced to provide a holistic change model. Weller and West-Burnham found the TQM principles of Deming (1986) to have the essential ingredients for a successful cultural change.

Change brought about by incremental steps and widespread involvement is more effective than holistic change that results from administrative mandates. Lasting change occurs through stages of implementation with widespread cooperation and participation. Lunenburg and Ornstein (1996) point out that in educational change, teachers have to "feel ready" for change, have a desire to change, and be involved in the change process. *Readiness* comes from personal dissatisfaction with existing conditions and results and from a willingness to seek alternatives to existing assumptions and ideals. Conley (1993) notes that effective principals "sense" when cultural change is needed and they provide direction and targets as alternatives to current conditions and outcomes. Principals "excite" teachers about new possibilities and provide realistic scenarios of what *can* be. Deal (1987) defines "readiness" as general teacher dissatisfaction with existing conditions which leaders can detect through watching, listening, interpreting, and intuition. "Management by walking around" best provides principals with this sense of readiness. In TQM schools, principals have relied on teachers who express high levels of frustration with student attitude and performance and who serve as barometers for introducing Deming's theory to effect cultural change (Weller and Hartley, 1994).

Readiness to change, says Deal and Peterson (1990), is facilitated by principals who identify cultural artifacts as major sources of existing problems and call for the re-examination of these values and beliefs within the context of existing social expectations and demands. Bolman and Deal (1991) identify sources of teacher dissatisfaction as lack of input concerning school policy, teacher evaluation practices, instructional and curricular concerns, and conflict between teacher roles and the school's expectations of teacher performance. Teacher dissatisfaction may also stem from hostile and unsafe working conditions, lack of autonomy over decisions that affect their classrooms, inadequate supervisory practices, unclear and less than timely communication from administrators, and ineffective and unimportant staff development programs (Hoy and Miskel, 1996). Lunenburg and Ornstein (1996) add that teacher dissatisfaction results from highly bureaucratic procedures, unclear goals and job descriptions, lack of administrator and parental support, and lack of recognition and reward for their skills, talents, and contributions.

Readiness to change is also facilitated by the school's "power agents," the informal peer leaders in the school who exercise strong influence over their colleagues and play an important role in successfully bringing about cultural change. Change becomes more appealing and meets with less resistance when power agents express discontent and are major figures in the planning and implementation process of change. Weller and Hartley (1994) observed that teachers who are confronted with change will feel threatened by the prospects of change. Change signals a lack of control over professional lives and introduces disequilibrium and uncertainty. The prospect of change conjures up images of instability and the lack of predictability. Teachers feel more secure with "the known," regardless of their discontent with existing conditions, because it provides a sense of security and stability. Teacher power agents serve as a settling and reassuring force to those who see change as chaos and a threat to their daily routine.

Changing the school's culture is neither easily nor quickly accomplished. A variety of factors influence the need for change, but *timing* the change initiative is the most important consideration to maximize the probability of successful change. Conley (1993) and Hoy and Miskel (1996) provide the following indicators for cultural change:

(1) External dissatisfaction from parents, community members, business leaders, and government officials who view the school as ineffective in meeting its goals as an educational organization.

(2) Internal pressures from teachers and students dissatisfied with the overall quality of the curriculum and reputation of the school.

(3) Teachers and parents expressing dissatisfaction with low student test scores, low teacher and student morale, and high rates of student vandalism, absenteeism, and dropout.

(4) Triggering social, economic, or political events, such as increases in population and positive economic conditions, calling for new changes in school programs or policies, or the building of new schools.

Timing cultural change, says Conley (1993) and Weller (1999), is often an intuitive "sense" that change is needed *now* with the need for change becoming the foundation for taking the initiative to change. Systems thinking is central to effective change. Systematic change provides sequential steps that serve as natural conduits connecting change initiatives and allow for a continuous flow of progress toward goal achievement. Compartmentalized or fragmented change often requires repetition and results in wasted effort and time, low morale and frustration, and failure.

A systematic, cultural change model is presented below which represents a fusion of work presented by Dumaine (1990), Bolman and Deal (1991), and Weller (1998a).

(1) Create dissatisfaction with existing conditions and use examples of external and internal dissatisfiers to strengthen the argument for change. Target specific cultural artifacts as root causes for dissatisfaction and call for support in changing to a new set of values and beliefs that more closely embrace current needs or ideals.

(2) Develop a clear set of new images or "mental models" of the future and honestly and realistically describe what is required to achieve these goals. Delineate the steps necessary to accomplish the transition and, most importantly, the shared benefits of the new culture.

(3) Begin to model those values and beliefs included in the images of the future. The leader's behavior is observed and often speaks louder than words.

(4) Amass a cadre of those most eager to change, support their ideas and initiatives, and openly reward and praise their efforts and successes. Success is catching.

(5) Encourage others to support the change initiative and provide moral support and resources to those willing to become members of a "subculture" of the school. Instill an attitude of freedom to fail and to experiment, and reward their efforts and provide a platform for their achievements to be recognized and implemented by others. When success is evident, others will begin to take initiatives to seek rewards and recognition to achieve personal and professional satisfaction.

(6) Adopt a transformation model which includes joint planning and goal setting, wide-scale participation, a support and rewards system, a communication process which provides timely and comprehensive information about the transformation process, and an evaluation system that provides both formative and summative results.

(7) Plan for change by fully understanding the "old culture," realize its strengths and weaknesses, and use its positive aspects to help fuse the old culture with the new. Successful cultural transitions need "bridges" to make the transition easier and to provide a sense of security as the new culture is attempted. Change affects some people more positively and sooner than it affects others. The immediate pay-offs for some will not always be recognized immediately. Principals must clearly address the benefits for *all* teachers and make them understand how their participation plays a vital role in the overall success of the transformation process. Early involvement in planning for the change process is the best way for teachers to understand their new roles and to realize the direct benefits.

(8) Reward and recognize publically when successful accomplishments are achieved. Successful achievements soon become the newly accepted values, beliefs, norms, and assumptions of the new culture.

(9) Be prepared to have new values and beliefs "tested" by members of the organization as change takes place. Challenges, which require the school, its leader, and its teachers to solve problems in ways that are reflective of new values and beliefs, prove that the new culture is more than just empty words.

The following case study depicts an example of a typical challenge with which principals can expect to be confronted.

Principal Wilson was pleased with the progress of the cultural transformation initiative. Teachers, parents, and administrators developed the school's vision and goals and new values and beliefs were identified and accepted. The new shared governance model was designed by teachers and administrators, teams were formed and responsibilities identified, and today was the first meeting of the school's governance council. The council consisted of representatives of teachers from each department, staff member representatives, and parents. The first item on the agenda was to align current school policies with the newly adopted values and belief system.

The meeting was called to order by Mrs. Trend, the elected chair, who was the science department's representative and a veteran teacher of fifteen years. The first agenda item was about to be discussed when Mr. Bates, a teacher of social studies with nine years of teaching experience, asked to present a statement drafted by members of his department. With no objections from the council, Mr. Bates asked the council to support a request that was more aligned with the values and beliefs of the new culture. The request contained the following: "The issue of required teacher attendance at all after-school athletic events contributes to low morale and low job satisfaction. The demands on *personal* time, without compensation time or other rewards, is contrary to the values and beliefs that teachers are professionals, that each person should be treated fairly and without threat of recrimination, and that decisions affecting faculty members will be addressed by the school's council. Therefore, we request the council remove this policy from the list of requirements teachers are "made" to comply with on time which is their own."

The request was a "test" of the new belief system and although Mr. Wilson was committed to the new culture and shared governance, he defended the need for teachers' attendance at athletic events to help "control the crowd" in the interests of safety and order. Mrs. Trend formally expressed her department's dissatisfaction with the after-school attendance policy and opened the meeting for discussion. The general dissatisfaction expressed with the policy led to a motion to create a task force to propose an alternative to the policy as the concern of safety and order was a viable concern. Task force members were appointed with two of the eight task force members coming from the social studies department.

Four weeks later, the task force presented the following proposal: (1) one-fourth of the teacher population had to attend and serve as chaperones for "crowd control" purposes (the original intent for total teacher attendance); (2) teachers were required to sign-up for the athletic events of *choice* before the beginning of each athletic season; (3) teachers who could not attend events, as a result of last minute conflicts, had to find substitutes in their stead; and (4) if any event lacked the required number of teachers needed to chaperone, volunteers would be called for first and, if necessary, teachers would be selected by the principal on a rotating basis.

Allowing teachers to develop and agree on an alternative to a long-standing policy satisfied two objectives. First, appointing a task force and allowing teachers to make decisions about a major job dissatisfier improved morale and resolved an immediate problem. Second, teachers were dissatisfied with their lack of input into school-based decisions and the task force on athletic events was the first in a series of test cases to challenge the principal's commitment to shared governance.

Certain factors serve to reduce the acceptance of change. Weller (1998a, 1999) points out that change can be thwarted by personal selfish reasons, which are natural, survival reactions, and these must be addressed up front by principals expecting cooperation and success in their transformation effort. First, change represents a departure from established routine and security. When a person's security is threatened, the natural instinct is to resist this intrusion with sufficient effort to stop the threat. Overt and covert means are deemed acceptable when threats to economic or job security are feared to be an outcome of change. Second, people want to know up front, "What's in it for me?" Individuals *need* and *want* to know how change will affect them directly and in a positive, personally profitable way. When advantages to their social, economic, and political self-interests are made clear, their willingness to cooperate and to make the change effort successful is gained because change now is in their *own* best self-interests. In each case, it is the responsibility of the principal to make certain that each staff member's primary concerns are adequately addressed. Failure to do so will ensure fragmented cooperation and the use of both overt and covert opposition methods.

Additional resistors to cultural change are discussed by Hoy and Miskel (1996) and by Lunenburg and Ornstein (1996) and include the following:

(1) Fear of the unknown
(2) Fear that change will negatively affect one's economic, social, and political security (both outside and inside the work place)
(3) Fear of an inability to master new knowledge and skills essential for success
(4) Fear of losing power, influence, or prestige

(5) Fear that one's own knowledge or skills will become unimportant or obsolete

Team Work and Cultural Transformation

Change models calling for broad-based participation and team work greatly increase the success of cultural transformation. Broad-based participation allows those affected by change to plan, design, and implement change strategies. Teams provide for uninhibited brainstorming which provides the multiple ideas and perspectives necessary to determine members' core values and beliefs and to assess objectively those existing cultural artifacts that impede new goals and ideals for the school.

Teams also serve as communication *networks* that provide on-going information about the status of the change process and about the ideas and progress of other groups. Networks reduce anxiety and thwart the development of rumors that hinder effective change. Teams, in addition, build grass roots ownership in the change initiative. The investment of time and effort and the infusion of individual ideas build strong and widespread commitment.

Transformation models, which include team work as central to shared governance, sustain teacher commitment and enthusiasm. Owens (1995) states that teachers' primary concerns lie in curriculum and instructional matters. Having direct influence in formulating policies in these areas allows for the sanction of core values and beliefs while providing job satisfaction and autonomy over working conditions.

Weller and Hartley (1994) and Murgatroyd and Morgan (1993) report high teacher morale and self-esteem in TQM schools where teachers are empowered to solve problems affecting classroom performance and where teacher teams address curricular issues and design staff development programs. The educational values of continuous improvement and respect for the rights and dignity of teachers as professionals are nurtured and reinforced through empowered teacher policy-making councils.

Some TQM schools evidence high teacher job satisfaction and increased performance as results of increased responsibility over the school's curricular and instructional programs (Murgatroyd and Morgan, 1993; Weller, 1996). Hackman and Oldham's model (1980) seems to be applicable in these schools. Their model states that three psychological factors are essential to enhance self-motivation: (1) the feeling of being responsible for one's work (having autonomy to solve problems and make decisions about work); (2) the feeling that one's work is meaningful (value and worth of the job are evident to the self and others); and (3) the knowledge of the results of work (continuous feedback regarding the effectiveness of one's performance by peers and supervisors). Works by Hart (1990) and Frase and Matherson (1992) report increased job satisfaction with the use of the Hackman and Oldham model. Team work and shared governance provide the foundation for these positive outcomes.

Hiring Teachers to Support the School's Culture

Teacher selection depends on the employment philosophy of the principal and the available talent pool at the time of hiring. Debate exists as to which hiring practice is best—principal selection or teacher team selection. A combination of the two methods seems to be ideal because the principal is ultimately responsible for making the hiring decisions whereas teacher recommendations provide feedback on important cultural and teaching-related variables. Because principals shoulder the ultimate responsibility for staffing and promoting effective teacher outcomes, many argue that those hired should have similar values, beliefs, assumptions, and philosophical orientations as held by the principal. Others argue for staff diversity and maintain that strength lies in diverse values, beliefs, and philosophical orientations. Faculties with similar cultural beliefs, however, tend to be more cohesive with common values and assumptions promoting greater commitment and collegiality. All these are important factors for promoting school effectiveness and a healthy school culture.

Principals opening new schools can build culture by hiring teachers with values and assumptions compatible with those cultural attributes desired in the school. Deal and Peterson (1990) emphasize the necessity of hiring the "right staff" as essential for creating and sustaining a healthy school culture. When teachers and administrators have conflict over philosophical or value differences, disruption occurs in the educational process which may result in teacher frustration and job dissatisfaction. Deal and Peterson also state that when cultural attributes are universally shared, "socializing" new staff members into the culture is easier and less time consuming. For this reason, they advocate that teachers be a part of the interviewing and hiring process so that new working relationships are built on the solid base of shared values.

REFERENCES

Bass, B. M. 1985. *Leadership and Performance Beyond Expectations.* New York: Free Press.

Bennis, W. and B. Nanus. 1985. *Leaders: The Strategies for Taking Charge.* New York: Harper Collins.

Bolman, L. G. and T. E. Deal. 1991. *Reframing Organizations: Artistry, Choice, and Leadership.* San Francisco: Jossey-Bass.

Castetter, W. B. 1996. *The Human Resource Function in Educational Administration.* Sixth edition. Englewood Cliffs, NJ: Prentice-Hall.

Conley, D. T. 1993. "Road map to restructuring: Policies, practices and the emerging visions of schooling." Eugene, OR: ERIC Clearinghouse on Educational Management.

Cunningham, W. C. and D. W. Gresso. 1993. *Cultural Leadership: The Culture of Excellence in Education.* Needham Heights, MA: Allyn and Bacon.

Deal, T. E. 1987. "The culture of schools," in *Leadership: Examining the Illusion.* L. Sheive and M. Schoenheit, eds. Alexandria, VA: Association for Supervision and Curriculum Development.

Deal, T. E. 1993. "The culture of schools," in M. Sashkin and H. J. Walberg, eds. *Educational Leadership and School Culture.* Berkley, CA: McCutchan.

Deal, T. E. and K. D. Peterson. 1990. *The Principal's Role in Shaping School Culture.* Washington, DC: Office of Educational Research and Improvement.

Deming, W. E. 1986. *Out of the Crisis.* Cambridge, MA: Massachusetts Institute of Technology Press.

Dumaine, B. 1990. "Creating a new culture." *Fortune,* 121:127–131. New York: The Time, Inc. Magazine Company.

Etzioni, A. 1988. *The Moral Dimension: Toward a New Theory of Economics.* New York: The Free Press.

Frase, L. E. and R. R. Matherson. 1992. "Restructuring: Fine tuning the system in Fort McMurray catholic schools." *Challenge,* 29(1):16–22.

Gardner, J. W. 1964. "The antileadership vaccine." *An Annual Report of the Carnegie Corporation.* New York: Carnegie Corporation.

Hackman, J. R. and G. R. Oldham. (1980). *Work Re-design.* Reading, MA: Addison-Wesley.

Hart, A. W. 1990. "Impacts of the school social unit on teacher authority during work redesign." *American Educational Research Journal,* 27(3):503–532.

Hoy, W. K. and C. G. Miskel. 1996. *Educational Administration: Theory, Research, and Practice.* Fifth edition. New York: McGraw-Hill.

Katz, R. L. 1974. "Skills of an effective administrator." *Harvard Business Review,* 52:90–102.

Knezevich, S. J. 1984. *Administration of Public Education: A Source Book for the Leadership and Management of Educational Institutions.* New York: Harper & Row.

Lunenberg, C. C. and A. C. Ornstein. 1996. *Educational Administration: Concepts and Practices.* Second edition. Belmont, CA: Wadsworth Publishing.

Lunenberg, C. C. 1985. "On the feasibility of cultural intervention in organizations," in *Organizational Culture.* P. Frost, L. Moore, M. Lewis, C. C. Lunenberg, and J. Martin (eds), 169–185. Beverly Hills: Sage.

Murgatroyd, S. and C. Morgan. 1993. *Total Quality Management and the School.* Philadelphia, PA: Open University Press.

Owens, R. G. 1995. *Organizational Behavior in Education.* Fifth edition. Needham Heights, MA: Allyn and Bacon.

Rebore, R. W. 1982. *Personnel Administration in Education.* Englewood Cliffs, NJ: Prentice-Hall.

Rebore, R. W. 1991. *Personal Administration in Education: A Management Approach.* Third edition. Englewood Cliffs, NJ: Prentice-Hall.

Schein, E. H. 1985. *Organizational Culture and Leadership.* San Francisco: Jossey-Bass.

Sergiovanni, T. J., M. Burlingame, F. S. Coombs, and P. W. Thurston. 1992. *Educational Governance and Administration.* Boston: Allyn and Bacon.

Sloane, A. A. 1983. *Personnel: Managing Human Resources.* Englewood Cliffs, NJ: Prentice-Hall.

Smith, S. C. and P. K. Piele. 1997. *School Leadership.* Eugene, OR: ERIC Clearinghouse on Educational Management.

Van Zwoll, J. A. 1964. *School Personnel Administration.* New York: Appleton Century Crofts.

Webb, L. D., P. A. Montello, and M. S. Norton. 1994. *Human Resources in Administration: Personnel Issues and Needs in Education.* Second edition. New York: Macmillan.

Weller, L. D. 1996. "Return on quality: A new factor in assessing quality efforts." *International Journal of Educational Management,* 10(1):30–40.

Weller, L. D. 1998a. "Unlocking the culture for quality schools: Reengineering." *International Journal of Educational Management,* 12(6):250–259.

Weller, L. D. 1998b. "Reengineering the schools for quality," in R. Muth and M. Martin, eds. *Toward the Year 2000: Preparing Leaders for Quality Schools: The Sixth Yearbook of the National Council of Professors of Educational Administration,* 69–68. Lancaster, PA: Technomic Publishing.

Weller, L. D. 1999. *Quality Middle School Leadership: Eleven Central Skill Areas.* Lancaster, PA: Technomic Publishing.

Weller, L. D. and S. H. Hartley. 1994. "Total Quality Management and school restructuring: Georgia's approach to educational reform." *Quality Assurance in Education,* 2(2):18–25.

Weller, L. D., S. H. Hartley, and C. L. Brown, 1994. "Principals and TQM: Developing vision." *The Clearing House,* 67(5):298–301.

West-Burnham, J. 1993. *Managing Quality in Schools.* Harlow, England: Longman Group, Ltd.

Wilson, L. T. and D. Asay. 1999. "Putting quality in knowledge management." *Quality Progress,* 32(1):25–31.

CHAPTER 2

Leadership for Maximizing Human Potential

In quality-oriented, high-performing schools, principals excel as managers *and* leaders by maximizing human resource potential. That is, they have the ability to mold a wide array of human resources, which varies in quality and quantity, into organizations that produce quality products and services. Principals have the ability to harness external resources with internal talent to promote effective outcomes for teachers and students alike. Effective principals are conscious of the importance their leadership behavior plays in maximizing human potential, in creating a positive and healthy work environment, and in meeting the needs and expectations of their teachers who represent the most precious resource a school can have.

THE ENIGMA OF LEADERSHIP

"Leadership" has long been a topic of study and discussion. In Plutarch's *Lives,* the behaviors and values of famous ancient Romans are described, along with how their behavior and conduct were emulated as a part of leadership training (Bonner, 1977). Genghis Kahn and Atilla the Hun were great leaders who possessed characteristics that allowed their armies to conquer parts of Asia and Russia, to spread their culture, and to dominate the lives of the conquered. Machiavelli's *The Prince* provides Lorenzo de' Medici with political prescriptions, which entailed clandestine schemes and corrupt officials, on how to be a successful leader in the Italian city states. Leaders, such as Joan of Arc, Thomas Jefferson, Winston Churchill, and Gandhi, have all been studied for their leadership qualities, and their behaviors and values have been taught as leadership characteristics worthy of adoption and practice.

Historical theorists, such as Thomas Carlyle, describe the "Great Man" theory of leadership, which states that leaders are born, not made. Karl Marx and George Hegel maintained that leaders are a product of the social and economic forces of their time. Gardner (1990) believes a more balanced view of leadership is called for. That is, environmental and historical forces create conditions that allow leaders to emerge. Leaders, in turn, affect these events with successful outcomes, leave their mark on history, and are studied for their behavioral characteristics. In explanation, Gardner states that ". . . by the time Martin Luther emerged, the seeds of the Reformation had already sprouted in many places, but no one could argue that the passionate, charismatic priest who nailed his ninety-five theses to the church door was a puppet of history. Historical forces set the stage for him, but once there, he was himself a historical force" (p. 7).

Traits of military, political, and socioeconomic leaders are studied to determine the characteristics of good leaders and to try to capture the necessary skills and behaviors of good leadership. Keegan (1987) finds some merit in this approach, but he also cogently argues that leadership is a phenomena of "the rigors of contextualization" (p. 3). Good leadership can then be interpreted as a result of behavior displayed within the context of the circumstances of the time, which dictates a command of facts, theories, and an understanding of a variety of disciplines to adequately plan for, and then act out, within the context of a diverse milieu. Berman (1982) provides an example of contextualization in the war between America and Vietnam. American leadership failed to understand the context or culture of the Vietnamese. Their strong spirit of nationalism, their agrarian society and values, and their long struggle with society were misunderstood by American leaders with their strategic planning, advanced technology, and superior fire power. In the end, America won the battle but lost the war.

Within the past several decades, over 3,000 empirical articles on leadership have appeared and over 350 definitions of leadership have been printed (Lunenburg and Ornstein, 1996). Studies on leadership effectiveness have examined variables such as the concept and use of power, leader traits, leader behaviors, environmental and personal contingencies, leadership styles, and leadership theories and models. To date, no conclusive, universally accepted findings exist as to what constitutes effective leadership.

Definitions abound in the attempt, however, and a quick examination of several definitions include verbs such as *influence* and *persuade.* Others include *motivate, guide,* and *direct.* Definitions of leadership behavior that come from famous leaders or academics inadequately define its nature or fail to capture the full array of attributes that effective leaders possess. For example, Harry S. Truman defines a leader as "a man who has the ability to get other people to do what they don't want to do and like it" (Brussell, 1988, p. 317). Richard M.

Nixon describes a leader as "one who implements noble ideals and principles with practical accomplishments" (Brussell, 1988, p. 317). Bennis and Nanus (1985) define leadership as "influencing, guiding in direction, course, action, and opinion" (p. 21). Argyris (1976) defines leadership as "effective influence" (p. 227), and Hogan, Curphy, and Hogan (1994) state that "leadership is persuading other people to set aside . . . individual concerns and to pursue a common goal that is important for them and the welfare of the group" (p. 493). Burns (1978) relates that definitions of leadership have different origins and do provide a key for understanding different leaders and their times. Burns points to external factors, such as psychological, sociological, and economic and political theories, as sources for defining leadership, and adds that definitions also come from intellectuals "who seek to grasp, manipulate, reorder, adjust, ponder, theorize, and criticize" (p. 141). Definitions of leadership, therefore, remain countless.

The multitude of definitions of leadership and the research findings on leadership "provide a sliver of insight with each remaining an incomplete and wholly inadequate explanation" (Bennis and Nanus, 1985, p. 4). These definitions reflect fads, academic trends, and political influences and fail to represent a clear picture of reality. Some provide an ideal representation of expected behavior, whereas others partly explain complex behavior through language tainted by perceived notions. What this suggests is that any person's definition of leadership is as valid as another's and that one's definition of leadership is cast within the context of one's frame of reference regarding time, one's sociopolitical and economic experiences, and one's own personality traits.

Compounding the enigma of leadership is the idea that many types of leaders exist. Leaders come in all shapes and sizes and display different leadership traits and styles. They have different personalities and hold different values and assumptions. Leaders range from great historical figures to common, ordinary community members. Teachers are leaders in their schools, in their communities, and in their churches. Family members are leaders and so are government officials and professional people. In short, who is *not* a leader?

What is clear and undisputed is that leaders must have followers—leaders do not exist in isolation. Leaders are a product of their times, their environments, their offices, their followers, and their own values and conceptualization of leadership, and all are essential parts of the leadership puzzle. For leadership to exist and function, for it to move others to achieve common goals and unite in a common purpose, a dynamic and yet fully unexplainable interaction must transpire between the leader and the follower. Leaders must motivate, stimulate, and inspire their followers. It is this dynamic interplay within the labyrinth of interacting variables that causes leadership to remain the enigma that it is.

LEADERSHIP PERSPECTIVES

Educational leaders need both a firm *knowledge base* (knowledge of research methods, leadership and management theory, and organizational development theory) and a command of psychological, political, and human relations skills (ability to motivate, manage conflict, and promote effective interpersonal relations) to be successful. Sergiovanni, Burlingame, Coombs, and Thurston (1992) draw a similar conclusion and describe educational administration as a "unique applied science" (p. 166). They note that the *human intensity* factor dominates the work of educational leaders who are primarily engaged "in the socializing of humans" (p. 167) and, for this reason, these leaders need an understanding of concepts and practices from various disciplines in order to be effective.

Effective principals, state Weller and Weller (1997), are innovative and "calculated" risk takers who draw on a wide array of theory, research, and practical experience to meet the daily demands of school leadership. These principals blend theory with practice and actively engage in action research projects. They garner their knowledge from various fields, such as leadership, organizational development, psychology, sociology, and political science, and this knowledge provides mental models and conceptual frameworks to test new ideas and reframe concepts. Reframing concepts provides the opportunity for principals to view existing problems or situations in different perspectives and in different contexts and allows for the "transfer of training" from theory into practice. Experience complements theory. By combining "informed intuition," which is knowledge that comes from experience and practice, with theoretical knowledge, effective principals are able to achieve high performance from their staff members. Both theory and experience are essential to leadership, but the willingness to take risks is the key to innovation and continuous improvement.

Informed intuition or reflective practice (Sergiovanni et al., 1992; Schon, 1983) is the ability to analyze and assess the effectiveness of one's own behavior. This is done by analyzing and interpreting the results of daily practice and by assessing the effectiveness of daily behaviors. Through analysis, interpretation, and discussion with colleagues, reflective practitioners improve professional performance through open-mindedness and the objective review of results. This process leads to new ideas and refined practice that, in turn, enhance the effectiveness of daily work life.

Reflective practice can be stimulated by applying Ross' reflective model (1989). Originally designed for teachers, the model is applicable to principals as well. The model presents the following three developmental levels, each at a higher level of complexity:

(1) Describe the specific reasons for the behaviors exhibited. Identify events and behaviors independently or with the help of peers. Candidly and

objectively analyze the outcomes of behavior and explore other behaviors that may have provided more effective results.

(2) Provide an objective critique of the behaviors applied in the situation from a personal point of view and exclude external influences or factors that affected the outcome.

(3) Provide an analysis of behaviors and their influence on those directly affected by the behaviors and then analyze the effect of those behaviors on those not directly affected by the behaviors. Analyze the significance of the influence the behaviors had on both populations and the length of time each population was affected.

According to Schon (1983), reflective practice is central to professional improvement for those who are confronted daily with uncertainty, complexity, and the diversity of human behavior. The results of reflective practice add to existing knowledge about motivation, decision making, and leadership.

Leadership as Persuasive Communication

Leaders function within groups or populations and do not perform their leader behaviors in isolation. Davies and Ellison (1997) maintain that leaders have a set of holistic beliefs about people and transfer their beliefs into daily actions. Communication, verbal or nonverbal, transmits ideas or concepts to subordinates to effect outcomes. English (1992) comments that leadership is effective interaction among people, and effectiveness results when the leader influences others to achieve goals or to accomplish tasks. Lunenburg and Ornstein (1996) relate that in leader-follower situations communication is the power to influence others and may stem more from one's personality or expert power than from positional power. Influence implies consent, a more-or-less state of willingness to follow another through persuasive means. Barnard (1938) relates that subordinates must first be willing to be influenced and then believe that the target objective is both reasonable and beneficial. Barnard also states "a person can and will accept a communication as authoritative only when four conditions simultaneously occur: (1) he can and does understand the communication; (2) at the time of the decision, he believes it is not inconsistent with the purpose of the organization; (3) at the time of the decision he believes it to be compatible with his personal interests; and (4) he is able mentally and physically to comply with it" (p. 165).

Influence over others increases when three salient variables are present. First, a sense of *fairness* must exist in the leader-follower relationship. When people perceive that they are treated fairly, they are more willing to consent to the request from authority. Second, people must clearly understand the direct, *personal benefit* in the presence of the influencing activity. That is, they must be able to see the direct benefit of their participation. Third, willingness to follow increases when clear *reasons* are provided for requesting subordinate involvement. Clear, concise, and honest exchange of information is essential in promoting effective leader-follower outcomes.

Cultural Context of Leadership

Leadership has been defined as influencing, persuading, and directing individuals or groups to achieve the goals of the leader and the organization. Owens (1995) comments that to understand leadership fully, one "must examine the nature and quality of the social interactions" [between leader and follower] (p. 116). Leadership is seen as being contextual in nature with the sociopolitical variables in the organization affecting the quality of the leader-follower relationship. English (1992) finds little value in exploring common behaviors or traits of leaders unless they are studied within the historical artifacts of the culture and the sociopolitical values and beliefs of that culture. Therefore, to study leadership independently of cultural variables leads to inconclusive and inaccurate findings. Successful leadership decisions and attempts to motivate and mobilize groups within the culture are made, therefore, within the context of the existing sociopolitical norms of the organization.

Culture also influences the leader's ability to bring about successful change. Weller and Weller (1997) noted that in quality-oriented schools, principals who introduced new programs that were successfully implemented, appealed first to the school's tradition of providing innovative programs and then to its ideal of being student centered. Using the existing sociopolitical infrastructure of teamwork and shared governance, new programs soon became standard operating procedures and part of the school's culture. Lunenburg and Ornstein (1996) also found that principals who appeal to the values and beliefs of the school's culture meet less resistance to changes in instructional programs and curricular content than do those who initiate change outside the context of the school's culture.

Culture, used as a metaphor, describes the internal happenings of schooling and what a school is like and stands for. Teachers behave according to the expected values and norms of the culture, and principals who are effective leaders are judged so within the context of the school's culture (Deal, 1993).

Four metaphors are used to describe leadership within a school's culture, and although they do not provide an inclusive view of leadership and culture, they do provide a representation.

(1) *Family culture:* Metaphors centered around *family, home,* and *team* capture the character of this culture. Concern for one another's well-being and respect for the "parent" or "coach" (leader) are highly evident as leader

and followers work willingly and cooperatively together to achieve the organization's goals.

(2) *Machine culture:* Metaphors for this school include *political machine, fine-tuned machine,* and *rusty machine.* Metaphors for the principal include *workaholic, the general,* and *the slug.* The school is instructionally oriented, there is a high degree of bureaucratic procedure, and the principal provides maintenance functions. Things are accomplished through structured processes and policies.

(3) *Cabaret culture:* Metaphors such as *Broadway show, circus,* and *banquet* describe this school's culture. The principal is the *master of ceremonies* or *ring master* and relationships focus on how well one performs. There are binding social events, traditions, and rituals, and teachers take pride in how they teach and in the intellectual quality of the school.

(4) *Little shop of horrors culture:* The school is unpredictable, tension exists and one never knows who will be singled out for reprimand or retaliation. The school is like a prison with the principal willing to sacrifice others to keep the position and advance in career status. The principal dominates and controls; teachers feel threatened, live isolated lives, and suffer verbal abuse; and the culture is cold and hostile (Lunenburg and Ornstein, 1996).

Leadership style has also been examined in relation to cultural characteristics by Deal and Kennedy (1982). They provide examples of the cultures that reflect leadership style and include the following:

(1) *Tough guys/macho cultures:* Leaders are individualists, take risks, want correct and immediate results, and make decisions on their own.

(2) *Work hard/play hard cultures:* Leaders are low-risk takers; work is important and emphasized, but fun and enjoyment are also emphasized.

(3) *Bet-your-company cultures:* Leaders make high-risk decisions and expect positive outcomes, but few within the school know about the decisions or expected results.

(4) *Process cultures:* Leaders emphasize bureaucratic structure and control, risk taking is avoided, employees are not involved in decision making, and employee safety comes from doing something correctly rather than doing the correct thing.

Cultural leaders *stimulate* the culture in the organization. Using less formal strategies than overtly appealing to traditions or modeling, principals can stimulate school culture by asking teachers to reexamine their values and beliefs, listening to teacher successes and disappointments, and having teachers and parents "describe" their school. They should observe the behaviors of teachers and students as they follow school policies and participate in ceremonies or rituals. From these practices, they can identify certain assumptions held by its membership and determine whether they are vision oriented or not. Sometimes assumptions become outdated or need refining as a result of external societal changes or pressures and principals can serve to stimulate those assumptions that are conducive to sustaining a strong and healthy culture. This type of leadership calls for reflective thinking on the part of principals and teachers alike (Owens, 1995).

Visionary Leadership

Effectively developing vision and mission in schools is a joint endeavor that is undertaken by teachers, parents, staff members, and administrators (Weller, Hartley, and Brown, 1994). Administrators who attempt to develop a school's vision and mission statements by themselves rarely succeed, and if successful, their success is short lived. Vision provides the organization with direction, focus, and an "agenda" for daily work. Vision is a "dream," a mental image of a possible, desirable, and attainable future. "The critical point is that a vision articulates a view of a realistic, credible, attractive future for the organization . . ." (Bennis and Nanus, 1985, p. 89).

Cunningham and Gresso (1993) examined the characteristics of visionary leaders and note that they are action oriented and think futuristically. They have strong values and beliefs and consider self-improvement and professional development as salient goals for themselves and for others. Visionary leaders know their strengths and limitations and tap the creative resources of others to augment their strengths. They promote the concept of empowerment and believe that employees *can* and *should* solve problems and make decisions affecting their work environment. Weller (1999) discusses visionary leadership and calls visionary leaders active facilitators of human energy and creativity. These leaders are catalysts, and they inspire and energize teachers and students to excel and to maximize their potential. They challenge others by asking "why not?" Owens (1995) relates that effective visionary leaders instill joint pride and ownership in the accomplishments of others and initiate new traditions and ceremonies to reinforce these accomplishments and to create new assumptions.

Visionary leaders are leaders who "think" about their decisions before they act and anticipate the responses of others. They reflect on the possible long-range outcomes and effect on both people and programs. Starratt (1995) refers to this as nonabstract, reflective, futuristic thinking. Starratt provides examples of such reflective thinking. *Problem naming* is the process used to diagnose a problem's root cause rather than its symptoms. For example, a high rate of teacher absenteeism is not viewed as a lack of responsibility, but as a morale problem. *Double-loop learning* pertains to not only looking at the immediate problem, but also viewing it as an organizational problem. For example, an inefficient teacher not only causes current problems with classroom discipline and student learning (single-loop learning) but also affects the school's reputation, the teacher's career, and parent satisfaction (double-loop learning). Decisions on how best to solve the problem are examined with these concerns in mind, which requires reflective, futuristic thinking.

Visionary thinking is also "upside-down" thinking. It requires "breaking the box" thinking or escaping the traditional mental barriers one has developed when analyzing problems. Wheatley (1994) calls this looking at the world "anew." A new consciousness must be acquired, an intuitive thinking that calls for forming mental images of the results of decisions and for anticipating their influence on other people.

Finally, visionary leadership may be likened to the metaphor "dancing with chaos." The *entropy law,* the second law of thermodynamics, states that in closed systems, randomness, disorder, and chaos prevail. There exists no meaningful purpose and disaster will eventually occur. Organized systems, if they do exist, will eventually degenerate to a chaotic state. Wheatley (1994) notes that order can result from chaos and that entropy can produce positive effects. Order or organized systems can result from chaos because of the "mirror image" effect of these two bipolar states. Order and control can result from chaos through a guiding formula or set of guiding principles that express the system's *overall* identity and allow for autonomy within the system. Vision provides the direction, order, and overall identity needed to bring order out of chaos by fusing shared values, beliefs, and goals into a unified formula for guiding conduct and providing purpose. Visionary leadership allows for individual autonomy through empowered employees who strive to achieve their vision and continuously improve their quality of performance, their work life, and their system.

Moral Leadership

Moral leadership holds that leaders and followers have a relationship based on mutual needs, aspirations, values, and beliefs (Burns, 1978). In moral leadership, leaders take responsibility for their acts and fulfill promises. "Moral leadership emerges from, and always returns to, the fundamental wants, needs, aspirations and values of the followers. It's leadership that can produce social change that will satisfy followers' authentic needs" (p. 4). Moral leadership is, therefore, a *relationship* between the leader and the subordinates, a relationship of interaction with common purpose and motivation. Central to moral leadership is moral courage. Gardner (1990) defines moral courage as the conviction to do the right thing and to pursue right and truth to the fullest. To forge this special relationship, or bond, leaders must possess self-confidence, resolution, an understanding of their constituents' needs and expectations, and the ability to embrace these needs and expectations as their own. Moral leadership views positional power as being secondary to this mutual value-based concept of moral leadership.

In a more fundamental way, leaders and followers jointly identify core values and beliefs, the meaning of work and life, and then make these values and beliefs the guiding influences by which they live and the objectives to which they strive to attain. Moral leadership gives morality to the organization and provides the standards by which the organization is judged and identified. Gardner (1990) relates that moral leadership embodies the broadly accepted values and behaviors of honesty, integrity, honor, respect, dignity, justice, and truth. Moral leaders live their values and beliefs and are committed to their membership's ideal of morality, which they integrate into their daily life's work. English (1994) cogently argues that "leadership without morality is little more than bureaucratic technique" (p. 231).

Value-Added Leadership

This leadership type maintains that moral authority is the basis for providing direction or for leading in organizations. Etzioni (1990) argues that morality and shared values are more important motivators for employees than the more traditional intrinsic motivators of achievement, recognition, responsibility, advancement, and work itself. That which means most to people, says Etzioni, is what they believe in, how they feel, and their core values. When leaders can identify with these beliefs, feelings, and values, individuals within the organization are filled with the motivation and commitment necessary to perform or excel at their expected levels. Value-added leadership, presented by Sergiovanni (1990), has moral authority which transcends the outputs of bureaucratic leadership and which is essential for maximizing teacher performance and commitment. Sergiovanni presents the following four stages of value-added leadership:

(1) *Bartering*. A bargain is agreed upon by the leader and the followers for the leader to provide something the followers desire for something desired by the leader.

(2) *Building*. A climate or environment is built by the leader and interpersonal support, which gives the followers the opportunity to meet their needs, assume responsibility, and be creative and excel, is provided.

(3) *Bonding*. A joint set of values and commitments is developed between the leader and the followers, which bonds them in their efforts to achieve common ends.

(4) *Banking.* Improvements are adopted by the leader as part of the school's accepted values, and these accepted norms are used as energizers for additional reform and improvement efforts.

Value-added leadership allows teachers to shape their own school and commit to the goals of the school through the adoption of their views of the purpose of schooling and their values. This, in turn, provides motivation, commitment, and enhanced performance.

Situational Leadership

Leader success is thought to be attributable to distinctive characteristics in the situation in which the leadership act is performed. That is, certain variables affect the leadership function, which have relevance to leader behavior and performance. Vecchio (1997) notes that several variables have been found to influence leader behavior and are considered situational determinants of leadership. These situational factors consist of the following:

(1) *Subordinate.* Personality, motivation, knowledge and skills, age and experience, responsibility, power, and tolerance for ambiguity.
(2) *Organization.* Size, line-staff hierarchical structure, and technology.
(3) *Leader role.* Position power, difficulty of task, rules and regulations, and outcome expectations.
(4) *Internal environment.* Status and the culture of the organization (teams, climate, values, beliefs, and norms).
(5) *External environment.* External social, political, and economic factors as well as the degree of stability or uncertainty.

Some research questions the importance or influence of leadership behavior in certain situations. Kerr and Jermier (1978) believe that some situational variables can substitute for leadership and that in other situations, leadership behavior is irrelevant to the outcome. Fiedler and Garcia (1987) maintain that it is possible to design a situation in which specified outcomes could be achieved without a designated leader. This substitute-for-leader model sees other variables as being more central to goal achievement than leadership behaviors.

There seems to be agreement, however, that situational variables affect the leadership function and that overemphasis or underemphasis of situational variables may not provide a complete picture of leader performance and effectiveness. What is also suggested is that situational properties combine with leadership traits to promote effective leader behaviors and that certain situational characteristics have a direct influence on leader effectiveness.

Research by Hersey and Blanchard (1992) focuses on the maturity relationship between the leader and the follower. That is, effective leadership results when the leader's style is appropriate for the maturity level of the followers. Situational leadership theory identifies two leader behaviors: (1) *task* behavior in which the leader tells and explains what, when, how, and why tasks are to be accomplished and (2) *relationship* behavior in which the leader provides socioemotional support and facilitates the completion of the job.

The maturity of the followers is central to the task and relationship behavior of leaders. Two maturity types of followers are identified: (1) *job* maturity is the individual's maturity to perform the task and includes education and experience and (2) *psychological* maturity is the individual's motivational level that includes achievement needs and the desire to accept responsibility. Those who are self-starters can work independently, need little if any direction, and have a high level of psychological maturity. The maturity of followers is job specific, and the two types of maturity are combined to form four levels of maturity with each calling for a different style of leader behavior. These four leadership styles consist of behaviors associated with the *task* and *relationship* behaviors.

Leadership effectiveness results when leadership style matches the situation. The four leadership styles are as follows:

(1) *Directing.* This is effective when individuals have low ability (job maturity) and low motivation (psychological maturity). High-task and low-relationship leadership behavior are required, and close supervision is necessary.

(2) *Coaching.* This is effective when individuals have high levels of motivation but low ability. High-task and high-relationship behavior are required. Tasks should be well explained, but suggestions should be solicited and included when appropriate for the task and the individual.

(3) *Supporting.* This is effective when individuals have low motivation and high ability. Low-task and high-relationship behavior are required. This may call for joint decision making and is appropriate for creative but reluctant self-starters.

(4) *Delegating.* This is effective when individuals have high ability and high motivation. Low-task and low-relationship behavior are required. This leadership style is for those who enjoy independence, are highly competent and trustworthy, and who follow through on difficult tasks.

Contingency leadership is an area of research that investigates leadership traits, leader-follower conditions, and leader behaviors resulting in effective action or behavior. The basic assumption is that leadership traits and characteristics of the situation interact to precipitate leader behaviors and effective outcomes.

Studies using the leader behavior description questionnaire (LBDQ) measure two basic dimensions of leader behavior: (1) *initiating structure* (task in situational terms) and (2) *consideration* (relationship in situational terms) (Stogdill and Coons, 1957). Initiating structure includes leader behaviors that involve communication, methods for achieving tasks, and other variables that delineate the relationship between the leader and the follower. Consideration includes leader behaviors such as friendship, trust, honesty, warmth, and respect in the leader–follower relationship. In the early studies of leader behavior using the LBDQ, school administrators were found most effective when they scored high on both consideration and initiating structure. Consideration is related to follower satisfaction with work and the leader. Consideration has positive effects on satisfaction for subordinates working in structured environments or in dissatisfying jobs. Initiating structure affects performance of individuals whose jobs or tasks are not well defined. When leaders are low on initiating structure, the overall outcomes of the organization may become less efficient. Low consideration also decreases follower work satisfaction. Matching consideration with initiating structure to gain optimal results is a difficult process at best (Hoy and Miskel, 1996).

Other studies indicate that leader behavior must be relevant to the individual in the leader-follower relationship. Concern for subordinates and for achieving the goals of the organization are not sufficient to explain effective leader behavior, and Yukl (1994) provides other leader behaviors related to consideration, initiating structure, or both. These behaviors include mentoring, team building, planning, problem solving, recognizing, rewarding, informing, and listening.

The path-goal theory, another situational or contingency theory, examines leader effectiveness and subordinate satisfaction within the context of situation, task characteristics, and follower characteristics. House and Mitchell (1974) provide four leader behaviors that promote effective leadership:

(1) *Supportive* leadership emphasizes consideration for followers' needs and welfare and creates a warm and friendly work environment.

(2) *Directive* leadership emphasizes the giving of clear and concise directions, making sure followers understand the specifics of the task and expected performance outcomes, providing guidance, and scheduling and coordinating work.

(3) *Participative* leadership emphasizes consulting with and incorporating follower suggestions into assigned work functions.

(4) *Achievement-oriented* leadership emphasizes setting challenging goals, setting high standards for performance, emphasizing excellence, and demonstrating confidence and support.

Supportive leadership seems to be most effective when jobs are stressful or boring. This leadership style promotes follower satisfaction by increasing self-confidence and finding means to reduce the unpleasantness of the job. When the job is interesting or satisfying and followers are confident and capable, supportive leadership behaviors seem to have little effect. Directive leadership is appropriate when jobs are complex, when followers have little experience, or when the job lacks structure. However, when jobs are structured and followers are highly competent, directive leadership seems to have a marginal effect. Close supervision may be perceived as an effort to exert control and may affect job satisfaction negatively (Yukl, 1994). The effects of participative leadership seem to promote follower effort in achieving the goals of the job and job satisfaction when the job is unstructured, but it has little effect on structured jobs. Participatory leadership also increases satisfaction for those who need autonomy and seek achievement. Achievement-oriented leadership seems to increase effort and job satisfaction when jobs are complex and/or unstructured. Setting goals and expectations increase self-confidence and the likelihood of successful outcomes (Yukl, 1994).

LEADERSHIP AND POWER

The word 'Power' is derived from the Latin word *posse,* which means *to be able.* Power is neither good nor bad—it just is. Power, therefore, is amoral. However, power may be used for good or bad purposes, and its use is judged by those who use it and by those who are subject to its use. Power's use and the outcomes of its use are relative and perceptual. That is, when power is used to reward one and punish another, the outcomes are judged as either good or bad by others (Brewer, Ainsworth, and Wynne, 1984). Every organization has a two-power structure, both a formal and an informal structure. Someone sets the rules, defines the limits, and rewards and punishes. Power, therefore, shapes organizational behavior and its outcomes. People respond to power in different ways and power is used by authority in different ways to achieve different outcomes. "Power is a key element in successful leadership" (Brewer, Ainsworth, and Wynne, 1984, p. vii).

What sets great leaders apart from others are certain understandings they possess about people, the practice of leadership, and the nature and use of power as it applies to others. Barber (1985) examined the leadership characteristics of American presidents and found the following "demarcations" that distinguished them as leaders:

- *Character*—one's view of life and how one views human nature
- *Style*—one's manner in performing duties and responsibilities
- *Power situation*—one's ability to identify situations in which one has the

power to act and the political support to use power to achieve desired outcome(s)

* *Climate of expectations*— one's ability to "know" the needs of constituents, to meet those needs, to demonstrate action, to achieve accomplishments and success, and to use power to the best advantage.

Barber (1985) states that *character* is formed early in life through family experiences and peer interactions. By adolescence, *style* begins to develop as a result of education and childhood experiences. In adulthood, character and style are tempered with professional and personal growth experiences and significant life events. The use of power and the ability to perceive and meet the needs of followers is a function of one's character and style and, taken together, comprise the "personality" of the leader, how the leader views others and their office, and how much satisfaction is derived from performing the duties of the office.

The leader-follower relationship is a dynamic dyad involving a constant interplay of give and take. English (1994) encourages the examination of an inverse relationship in the effective leader-follower phenomena. Leaders can learn much by practicing the principles of followership. That is, good followers are dedicated, self-motivated, optimistic, and encourage their peers to excel. Followers take pride in their work, have concern for others, and strive for consensus and teamwork. They are bonded by common goals, values, and beliefs, and truly care for the well-being of their colleagues. Followers openly and freely communicate with others, know their strengths and weaknesses, and seek advice and help when confronted with problem situations. Finally, followers apply power judiciously. Power comes in many forms, but it is most effective through the more subtle activities of showing disapproval or displeasure through behavior. Transmitting feelings that "you let me down" or "I never expected that of you" is psychological peer pressure to conform to standards and expectations. The use of nonthreatening persuasion techniques provides more effective results than the use of coercive techniques. Expressions of displeasure trigger feelings of shame, guilt, and the fear of nonacceptance from "the group." The fear of isolation from others can be a powerful influencing tool in seeking conformity. Leaders, therefore, can learn much about leadership by observing and then by adopting the principles of good followership.

Power and the Manager versus Leader Distinction

Distinctions have been made between a *manager* and a *leader.* Actually, leadership in effective schools requires principals to play the roles of both a manager (carrying out policy, competency in fiscal accounting and allocation, and dealing with daily requirements and problems) and a leader (planning strategically, delegating, motivating, coordinating, influencing, and persuading). Power is an inextricable part of the management and leadership functions, but how power is viewed and used within these functions is different. The term *manager* has a stronger relationship with the concept of power than does the term *leader.* Managers provide a more functionary role and rely on their title or positional authority to attain their goals or to fulfill obligations. Managers receive their power from the line-staff organizational chart, with vested power becoming "a form of raw energy that enables a person to carry out his own will despite the protestations of others" (Knezevich, 1975, p. 45). Here, power is used to gain involuntary compliance through threats of physical, social, or economic force. Power accrues from having access to resources desired by others, and power controls the behavior of others by delivering these resources as a means of motivating, manipulating, and rewarding desired behaviors.

Managers barter to accomplish their tasks. They make verbal contracts or agreements with subordinates to exchange resources for performance. Bennis and Nanus (1985) do not find these acts to be trivial because they involve job, security, and money. "The result, at best, is compliance; at worst, you get a spiteful obedience" (p. 218). Managers are manipulative. They appeal to the good nature of others to accomplish their goals and may soon forget those who helped achieve these ends. They manipulate by using their knowledge of the needs and expectations of subordinates and by making "artificial promises" or by creating "false hopes" for favors or job performance. Managers are primarily concerned with executing policy and making sure others adhere to the spirit and letter of rules and regulations while simultaneously reserving latitude for themselves. Managers are bureaucrats who govern others by rules and regulations for job performance and daily conduct. They are loyal to these rules and regulations, the most visible source of organizational power, and not to people. Further, they make policy enforcement their reason for being and flaunt it through their scepter of vested authority.

Leaders, by contrast, focus on developing human potential, on delegating responsibility, and on sharing power. Leaders seek to form bonds and relationships with subordinates and rely on influence and persuasion to accomplish organizational goals (Drucker, 1993). Power is also vested in leaders through the organization's line-staff chart, but this power is latent and called upon as a last resort. When called upon, leaders view the use of vested power as a failure to achieve their desired outcomes through the application of the leadership skills of influence and persuasion.

Leaders also view themselves as members of a group or team who strive for consensus and voluntary commitment, and work in the best interest of their followers. Leaders find they can get more with honey than they can with a stick. Leaders are fair, trustworthy, honest, and have predictable behavior. Gardner

(1990) says leaders have "mature wisdom" and provide clear direction and purpose for others. Leaders know the concerns, needs, and expectations of others and seek to form a social compact with their followers. Followers willingly entrust their future dispositions to their leader who, in turn, willingly entrusts the goals of the organization into their followers' keeping.

Informal Power

Power in an organization does not reside only with those having title or position on the organization's line-staff chart. The power of influence and persuasion are key sources of power for informal leaders. Informal leaders practice leadership by consent, the voluntary compliance of others to the informal leader's will or inclinations. This power is "unofficial" and can reside within individuals or groups within the organization itself. The informal, peer leader may lead through charisma (personal qualities or characteristics) or through the qualities of trust, honesty, or other shared values of their followers. They may attract a following by virtue of their wisdom, expertise, standing in the community, or other attributes with which followers can identify. Regardless of the "magnetic force," these leaders have power over their peers and are "power agents" who can and do wield sociopolitical power either through direct intervention or through indirect pressure such as group influence.

Informal groups exist within organizations and have their own set of rules, values, norms, rewards, and sanctions. Informal groups emerge to fulfill social needs and to provide social interaction not provided within the constraints of the formal organization. Informal groups are subcultures with clearly defined codes of conduct for its members. These informal groups have both positive and negative effects on their members and on the formal organization's efficiency and effectiveness.

Informal groups also provide status and roles for their membership and are a source of daily social interaction. The power and influence some groups have can make them key players in any change initiative in schools. Scott (1987) notes the power informal groups have in molding member behavior and defines it as "irrational forces" existing within the "technical rationality" used to understand and conduct the business of formal organizations. Schools have informal groups of teachers who serve as interlocking political and communication networks. Informal groups may initially form to fulfill social and psychological needs, to influence school administration behavior or policy decisions, to promote the selection of certain curriculum materials, to protect peers from perceived injustices, or to initiate innovative programs. Regardless of the origin of their formation, these groups exist over time, seek new membership, and target certain organizational areas as their "turf." When change is indicated, these groups are the first to assess its potential influence or infringement on their "domain" or "sphere of influence" and their members may network with other groups to stall or thwart the change effort. When principals fail to include group leaders or members of informal groups in policy-making decisions or change initiatives, they open themselves to widespread teacher discontent and, in some instances, job instability.

Power by the Covenant of Influence and Persuasion

Leaders do have power invested in them through their formal positions and can apply this "raw power" when all other leadership attributes fail to achieve results. Instead of relying on positional power to command and control, effective leaders rely on leader-follower covenants, which are rooted in mutual trust and respect, shared values and beliefs, and common goals. Leadership is exercised through influencing and persuading, and the followership understands that leaders are custodians of their welfare and will act in the followers' best interests. This results in a "caring" and "empathetic" relationship between the leader and the follower. Owens (1995) states that leaders who depend on influencing and persuading have followers who *understand* that their will and interests will be fairly represented in the inevitable conflict over the goals of the organization and the followers' self-interests.

Ideas and ideals are also sources of power. They attract a following, they serve to inspire achievement, and they identify needs. Leaders generate ideas and hold high standards of excellence and achieve these outcomes by persuading others into believing that ideas and ideals are attainable and are in their own best interests. English (1992) points out that leaders who significantly affect national events take the initiative in shaping the thinking of others and then influence the preferred outcomes by actively persuading others into believing that certain goals or ideals are more preferable and more in the self-interests of their followers than are other goals.

Power used to influence and persuade has been presented as four sources of leader power by French (1993). These power sources are

(1) *Reward power:* Rewards are provided by virtue of the leader's position and influence over others. Reward power depends on the kind and amount of reward the leader can provide and the attractiveness of the reward. Examples are salary increases, promotions, good work assignments, and intrinsic rewards such as praise.

(2) *Expert power:* Power coming from special abilities or knowledge possessed by the leader and desired by the followers. Examples are education, experience, and special training.

(3) *Referent power:* Power stemming from the ability of leaders to acquire a following through their charisma. Their personality traits command

respect and naturally attract others to their presence. Referent power is also derived from a leader's association with other powerful people, and the leader influences the behavior of others through contacts or "perceived" contacts with others.

(4) *Legitimate power:* Power vested in the leader by position within the organization. Legitimate power allows the leader to direct the follower to meet organizational goals. Power also comes from the follower's belief that legitimate power will be used sparingly, rationally, and in the follower's best interests.

Coercive power, a fifth power source identified by French (1993), is the opposite of reward power and the positive context in which influence and persuasion are presented. Coercive power is the use of threats and punishments to make people conform and achieve the leader's goals. Examples of the use of coercive power include demotions, threats to punish, undesirable work assignments, and lack of pay increases. French adds that legitimate, reward, and coercive powers are organizational based and are part of the administrator's job as designated by positional power. Expert and referent powers are personal powers and come from the personality of the leader. Early school administrators relied on coercive and legitimate power which coincided with classical organizational theorists such as Frederick Taylor and Henri Fayol. Contemporary educational leaders tend toward the use of reward, referent, and expert power. Coercive power's decline arises mainly from court rulings, teacher unions, and the changing social norms of the management-labor relationship.

Three of the five power sources have limitations if they are used in excess. Hoy and Miskel (1996) point out that *legitimate* power, when applied continuously, creates dissatisfaction, frustration, and resistance. However, when legitimate power is used with *expert* power, productivity and compliance with organizational goals increase. *Coercive* power leads to temporary compliance, but results in fear, alienation, revenge, and poor performance. *Reward* power influences behavior positively in the beginning, but too much reward power leads to feelings of manipulation and insincerity. *Expert* power produces feelings of trust and security and promotes commitment and motivation. *Referent* power generates enthusiasm, trust, compliance, and loyalty. Like expert power, referent power requires less supervision of employees and sustains commitment to organizational goals.

Coercive power is a source rarely, if ever, used by effective principals. It violates the concept behind teacher empowerment and shared governance. Coercive behavior leads to hostility and aggression and results in covert action, high absenteeism, and union strikes (Yukl, 1994). Knowledge of the outcomes associated with each of the power sources allows principals to be more effective leaders. Selecting the appropriate power source is situation specific and predicated on the fact that leaders have knowledge and understanding of their own strengths and weaknesses and those of their followers. Yukl (1981) relates that the use of expert and referent power is more a function of knowledge, personality, leadership style, and interpersonal skills than are other sources of power and that these power sources, used in combination, apply to most leader-follower situations.

Power Coalitions

Power in organizations is derived from three power sources: resources, technical skills, and knowledge. Within any organization, people have power in proportion to the power they have over these three power sources (Mintzberg, 1983). For example, principals who possess technical skills, knowledge, and resources in areas most beneficial to teachers (in areas of curriculum and instruction) have greater power and influence than those principals who lack one or more of these power sources. Knowledge and technical skills, forms of expert power, are highly prized in learning organizations and in knowledge management and are, therefore, roots of individual or group power (Wilson and Asay, 1999). When groups of teachers within schools possess various combination of these power sources, coalitions of power are formed and become informal power groups that may or may not challenge the formal authority of the principal.

Coalitions, power, and politics cannot be separated. Coalitions are interconnected by communication networks that are political in nature but lack the legitimate recognition of formal authority. Coalitions also comprise individual power players who may or may not play political games, and who may or may not work to benefit the organization or support formal authority. Often, coalitions seek a sharing of general power or shared power over their "sphere of influence." Coalitions have a greater capability to amass power when they possess high degrees of power in one or more of the three sources of power or have individuals with these power sources. When formal authority fails to recognize coalitions and share power, dissatisfaction, alienation, resentment, and the playing of power games result.

Coalitions increase their power by fulfilling the needs of individual group members. Members use coalitions to further their own interests and those of their coalition. Coalitions have strength in numbers, and their pooled knowledge and technical skills become powerful informal entities within the formal organization. Bolman and Deal (1991) note that major "interest groups" or "coalitions" in organizations have their own cultural attributes (shared values, beliefs, assumptions, norms, goals, and aspirations) that solidify, entrench, and cause stability. When left unrecognized they can challenge formal authority and thwart change efforts that are designed to enhance the organization but that are viewed as infringements on their sphere(s) of influence.

Internal coalitions are more likely to develop in organizations that are highly structured and bureaucratic with an emphasis on strict enforcement of rules and regulations. Sergiovanni et al. (1992) notes that schools with shared governance structures, a culture and vision, which are jointly developed and shared, and teachers who are actively engaged in the decision-making process are less likely to evidence the rise of coalitions. Mintzberg (1983) relates that organizations with authoritarian leadership that are tightly controlled through policy and administrative directives open themselves to coalitions, which serve to fulfill the social needs of its members and give rise to the intrigue of political games. When coalitions are omitted from "the loop" in the change process, tension and conflict increase and change efforts meet unnecessary resistance.

Political Games

Played in all types of organizations, political games are power struggles among and between coalitions, interest groups, individuals, and the administration. Hirschman (1970) identifies three choices members have when they join the organization's workforce:

(1) Remain and be loyal
(2) Remain and voice opinion, try to change existing conditions, or work to modify conditions to achieve tolerable conditions
(3) Exit the organization

Those who choose to remain and voice their opinion engage in power games and are willing to behave in ways deemed necessary to achieve their goals. Survival and success depend on their skills in planning strategy and in executing their power plays. Power plays are often clandestine and designed to benefit the individual or a group at the expense of the leader or organization (Mintzberg, 1983). Other power games focus on organizing others to help modify conditions or develop new policies that are more favorable to the ends of the power players. Some games provide positive results and fulfill the needs that are not provided by the organization. These results include providing a forum for airing grievances, gaining a voice in policy-making decisions, and forcing authority figures to confront problems affecting the welfare or work environment of the group.

Some who have engaged in power games may choose to exit the organization. Those who engage in power politics and fail in their attempts, for example, either self-select out of the organization or are pressured to exit. Failed attempts at reform and the exit of power players often result in a more stringent enforcement of policy or administrators who are less sympathetic to reform measures.

Some political games are more "informal" and are played by individuals as opposed to groups. Vecchio (1988) describes informal games as *tactics* and identifies four commonly used tactics to achieve personal goals:

(1) *Networking* refers to the forming of relationships with those who have power or influence.

(2) *Ingratiation* entails doing favors for others. Over time, obligations accrue and a "norm of reciprocity" leads to administrators viewing such activity as devotion to the job, initiative, or other positive, desirable traits.

(3) *Information management* involves releasing or withholding information at critical times. Knowledge is power, and gaining information through networking allows people to enhance their position among peers and administrators. Information giving establishes one as being "in the know" and makes them valuable as a political actor.

(4) *Impression management* is the visible appearance one displays to create a favorable image. Impression management includes dressing appropriately; making one's achievements known; and creating the image of being knowledgeable, reliable, and objective.

Many political games are complex and have their own set of rules with specific ways to achieve desired outcomes. Rules are crucial to political games because they define how the game is played, what behavior is acceptable, and how power positions are achieved within the organization by its members. Mintzberg (1983) describes five political games played in organizations.

(1) *Insurgency games* are those games designed to resist formal authority through sabotage, mutiny, or circumvention of the intent of policy or regulation. Administrators often confront such resistance with authority and punish those who engage in these games. Administrators who address only the symptoms and not the cause of the problem will spend an inordinate amount of time bargaining with game leaders whose agenda is still being developed.

(2) *Power-building games* focus on building a power base through amassing information or gaining trust from authority figures. When confidence is gained, favors are sought. Authority figures are manipulated into advancing or "sponsoring" individuals and the promoted individual is looked upon as a power player who, in turn, advances other group members. Sponsors demand respect, loyalty, and obedience, and expect favors in return.

(3) *Alliance-building games* are played among peers. Usually, one peer seeks the alliance of others who then form a group to address a personal concern

or to effect change in the organization. The group becomes a "special interest" group with a singular mission whose members may or may not disband when the objective is achieved. Special interest groups may band together, form coalitions, and create strong power blocks to the administration.

(4) *Empire-building games* exist when individuals seek to enhance their position in the organization and seek the assistance of others to advance their cause. Amassing resources, primarily fiscal, is a common route to empire building. Resource availability attracts others and the controller of these resources uses those who are attracted to influence, gain support, attract others, and accrue more personal power.

(5) *Expertise games* are played by those having highly valued knowledge and skills. These players let others know their value to the organization, keep their expertise current, and claim uniqueness. Found mainly in professional organizations, expert knowledge players use their skills to attract sponsors or attract a following to achieve their own ends. They act in ways that promote their high value and strive to create the image that they are indispensable to the organization.

Games can cause the downfall of legitimate authority figures or effect significant change in the organization. Administrators who seek to achieve the goals of the organization and retain support and loyalty must be knowledgeable of these political games and, when they are found to exist, seek council and support lest the erosion or overthrow of formal authority takes place.

Authority

Authority, in the organizational sense, comes from line-staff charts defining organizational structure. It also implies a chain-of-command, from top to bottom, with lower positions controlled by higher ones through superordinate–subordinate relationships. There are, however, several types of authority.

- *Traditional* authority implies voluntary adherence to those in control or to those who make decisions. The authority comes from history, custom, or tradition.
- *Legal* authority is based on law and defines how people must behave or comply with those in formal office who enforce the law.
- *Charismatic* authority resides in the personal qualities of an individual who has an emotional or nonrational appeal to others.
- *Formal* authority is vested in an organization through legally sanctioned rules, regulations, and policies. People joining organizations voluntarily agree to abide by a code of conduct and to accept directives from those placed in positions of authority. Central to formal authority is the principle that there exists a legally established and enforceable agreement

between the organization and its members to work toward common goals under the direction of organizational authority.
*   *Functional* authority pertains to individual competence and may not always reside in a position of authority. Competence or expertise can be a source of legitimate control with others following the will or directives of functional authority figures through voluntary submission.
*   *Informal* authority comes from personal behavior, expertise, or charisma that attracts a following of supporters. Informal authority comes from group allegiance and the general acceptance of following the leader's will (Hoy and Miskel, 1996).

In schools, authority is the basis of control. It is legally recognized and is exercised through a chain-of-command. Authority resides in the position and not the person performing the duties. Subordinates agree to obey the directives of the authority figure to receive certain contractual benefits from the school. Blau and Scott (1962) and Kotter (1985) report that legal authority cannot command others to perform at their best nor does it ensure efficient operation within the organization. It can elicit minimal compliance and expectations. Authority can be coercive and rely on discipline, but such actions do not lead to employees' taking initiative, assuming responsibility, or being highly effective at their jobs. For principals, formal authority can be used to enforce policy and regulations necessary for safety and order, and to ensure minimal compliance in areas of legal responsibility and sanctioned policy. Principals who rely on authority are little more than functional bureaucrats who manage rather than lead.

Using leadership skills to supplement the execution of formal authority is a more effective means of achieving organizational goals. Blau and Scott (1962) and Hoffman, Sabo, and Bliss (1994) maintain that informal groups also provide avenues for principals to enhance their influence and to broaden their power base. Exercising referent power and expert power to supplement the use of formal authority also promotes loyalty and trust.

Loyalty and trust are key ingredients to promoting informal authority and successful leadership. Hoffman, Sabo, and Bliss (1994) and Henderson and Hoy (1983) found that authoritarian principals are not successful in developing loyalty and trust whereas those showing support and empathy acquire informal authority and loyalty. Loyalty and trust are also awarded to principals who accept responsibility for their own behavior, remain calm during crisis situations, and are ethical and professional in their work.

Perhaps the best way to build trust is to examine how one grows to trust another. Trust is based on consistent, dependable action over time. When one acts consistently over a period of time, regardless of the situation, others can count on that behavior or verbal commitment as being reliable and dependable. Principals can best develop trust by behaving consistently and by honoring their verbal commitments.

QUALITY LEADERSHIP

Quality is a term and concept that is beginning to replace *effectiveness* in discussions and investigations of organizational outcomes and leadership (Weller and Hartley,1994; Weller, 1999; Murgatroyd and Morgan, 1993; Hoy and Miskel, 1996). The work of Deming (1986, 1993) on quality management has been popularly termed total quality management (TQM) and contains fourteen principles for transforming organizations and improving leadership. Deming's theory of management is not new knowledge on change and leadership, but "the weaving together into a coherent tapestry the threads of many ideas that have been discussed and advocated by a few students of organization, but strongly ignored or resisted by administrators, legislators, intellectual reformers, and school board members for decades" (Owens, 1995, p. 238). Deming's fourteen principles (1986) provide direction and guidance for quality leadership and outcomes by focusing attention on empowerment, organizational vision and mission, shared governance and continuous improvement, a culture dedicated to cooperation, and quality products and services to meet the needs *and* expectations of the customer. Weller (1993) notes that TQM focuses on *total* organizational involvement. In simplistic terms, he adds, "total quality management is comprised of a three-step process. This process involves *people* (assessing the needs, wants, and expectations of the customers), *processes* (implementing the principles of TQM), and *things* (providing a quality product that provides total customer satisfaction)" (p. 3).

TQM calls for transformational leadership to implement a new culture into an organization. Burns (1978) describes a transformational leader as a ". . . leader who looks for potential motives in followers, seeks to satisfy higher needs, and engages the full person of the follower. The result of transforming leadership is a relationship of mutual stimulation and elevation that converts followers into leaders and may convert leaders into moral agents" (p. 4). Principals in TQM schools bond with their faculty through a sharing of mutual needs, values, and aspirations. Cultural change in the context of TQM is changing the "inner core," the philosophy, norms, and practices of the school's population. That is, there is a change in the fundamental way people behave, act, and value others and their work (Weller, 1999).

Leaders in TQM organizations, relates Weller (1999), are facilitators of human potential. They provide the time, support, and resources necessary for people to excel in their tasks as their social and psychological needs are met. These leaders actively search for obstacles that prevent quality performance and work life and continuously listen to and act upon employee recommendations. Quality-focused leaders believe in Deming's statement (1993) that ninety percent of the problems in any given organization are process or systems problems, and that only ten percent of the organization's problems are caused by people. Failure is viewed as a learning experience and progress stems from trial and error. The focus on continuous improvement, high expectations, and teamwork are central to the leadership function in TQM organizations.

Leadership and School Restructuring

School reform movements of the previous three decades have called for innovation (1960s), accountability (1970s), and excellence (1980s). Each had their own jargon, usually vague and lacking in precise meaning, and each called for immediate action as panaceas for the ills of education. Many of these efforts have yielded varying degrees of success, but none has consistently sustained student achievement or satisfied public demands for quality education (Murgatroyd and Morgan, 1993; Weller, 1995). The primary reasons for this lack of success were the incremental approach these movements employed to revitalize education and their top-down mandates for change (Weller, 1999).

School reform and restructuring, the theme for the 1990s, has required a paradigm shift and a workable template to guide the holistic transformation of the school. Previous reform efforts were cosmetic changes that focused on symptoms rather than on the root causes of problems. Conley (1993) found that these reform efforts lacked the necessary internal desire and momentum to effect reform because they were mandated by external forces, such as legislative or policy-making agencies, with their prescriptions based on personal assumptions and expectations about education. Fullan (1992) notes that failure of this type of reform initiative is rooted in its highly regulatory nature and in its lack of representation from educators. Successful school restructuring requires a grassroots change in school governance practices and a cultural transformation. Conley (1993) states that school leaders are the catalysts for change and that change must include a different type of relationship between the leader and the followers. This relationship is one of shared vision, values, beliefs, attitudes, and assumptions about the process and outcomes of schooling.

The use of TQM as a school restructuring paradigm has yielded varying degrees of success. Schmoker and Wilson (1993) note that the theory behind Deming's quality management principles (1986) "provides a template, an overreaching body of principles that . . . promote intelligent action toward improving schools" (p. xi). They report TQM's success in promoting student achievement and self-esteem and increasing teacher morale, job satisfaction, and self-confidence. Murgatoyd and Morgan (1993) noted that teacher job commitment and morale are higher in TQM schools because of empowered teams and transformational leaders. Weller and Hartley (1994) also relate that teacher morale and self-esteem increase with TQM and shared governance. Bonstingl (1992) found TQM to be a holistic approach to schooling and describes it as an important "new conceptual framework" that yields positive results in student learning and teacher-leader cooperation. TQM is a new synthesis of knowledge about leadership and psychology that allows educators to incorporate the research-proven practices of previous reform movements (e.g., effective schools) and leadership theory (human relations movement) into Deming's principles of quality management (1986). English (1994) relates that Deming's theory on leadership is research based and emerges from the work on organizational development and the theories of behavioral science. Finally, Weller and Hartley (1994) found leaders of TQM schools to be "human engineers" who design pathways for the success of others, remove barriers to job efficiency, and provide ongoing moral and fiscal support to develop the human potential within schools. Within this concept, "everyone is a leader" and everyone is free to be innovative and creative, to develop their talents, and to set their own performance goals and objectives. Consensus management, through group decision making and shared vision, are central in promoting student achievement and teacher job satisfaction.

Creating Vision

Vision statements in quality schools differ in terms, but the objective remains constant. Vision emphasizes "people first" and focuses on the development of human talent and potential. Vision unites the leader and the followers to achieve common, agreed-upon ends, and provides the strong sense of commitment, purpose, and direction necessary to achieve quality outcomes. Vision, says Weller, Hartley, and Brown (1994), gives each school its distinct "personality" by redefining its purpose and its shared core values, beliefs, and assumptions. Principals who want to achieve quality and implement TQM in their schools find developing a shared vision to be the essential first step.

Creating vision requires proactive leadership, an optimistic view of the future, and a determination that a better future is possible *and* attainable. To move teachers along the visionary continuum from abstract concepts, to a shared vision, to the transformation of that vision into action, requires "professional artistry." Schon (1987) describes professional artistry as the application of leadership attributes through the practice of core values and beliefs. Leaders first inspire and then attract others by modeling their vision as they carry out their daily routines and complex activities.

Model for Vision Building

Vision has been looked upon as a mystical and elusive concept, but it is essential for transforming any organization into a quality-producing entity. Vision serves as a guiding philosophy, presents a tangible image, and is the compelling force of the organization (Weller, Hartley, and Brown, 1994).

Vision must be shared, and it is built upon commonly agreed-upon values, beliefs, and ideals. Shared vision is owned by all, and all are committed to it. It is built on participation in order to achieve vested interest. Vision building begins with the involvement of all teachers and representatives from support personnel and parents. Participants first must be sensitized to key characteristics of successful school visions before they develop a vision for themselves. Whitely (1991) states that vision statements should be

- clearly stated in universally understandable terms;
- memorable, short in length, and catchy;
- challenging, but not out of reach;
- empowering so as to involve all people;
- value laden to reflect the values of the organization and the people involved in product production.

A vision-building model developed by Weller, Hartley, and Brown (1994) is presented as follows:

Step 1: Representation. The process begins with the formation of three groups. One group comprises all teachers and representatives from noncertified personnel. All teachers must be included because they are the ones who will make the vision a reality. Another group comprises parent representatives, and a third group comprises community and business members.

Step 2: Vision-building orientation. Vision building begins with the principal introducing the collective membership to the purpose of their mission and what vision is all about. Providing a standard definition of *vision* as a working index launches discussion. The principal emphasizes the importance of making provisions for the future, having foresight, and meeting future demands. Often business people work in organizations having vision and can share their organization's vision with the group, clarify questions, and serve as testimonials to vision's importance.

Next, the principal provides a clear and accurate picture of where the school is at present in relation to its competition and offers a summary of stakeholders' dissatisfaction with current conditions. The principal then presents a *dream* picture of what the school would look like in the future. The picture of the current versus the future status sets the tone for vision building. The groups will then work toward identification of the three components of a vision: (1) values, (2) mission, and (3) goals.

Step 3: Identifying core values. The principal discusses how core values are the moral fabric from which mission and goals are developed and points out that core values include honesty, trust, respect for learning, the pursuit of excellence, and the belief that people should be treated with dignity and respect. These values are time honored and guide moral and ethical behavior. Senge (1990) states that when common values are discussed, the discussion leads to a sharing of the motivating forces within people. It is through the sharing of this internal force that the true core values of people can be identified. This is essential to creating an attainable and devoted vision.

The principal directs each small group to discuss core values for the school and to reach consensus on four or five values that group members deem most salient. Each group presents their results, and a large group discussion follows, with the large group reaching a consensus on the four or five core values most important to the school.

Step 4: Writing the mission statement. The principal explains that mission, part of vision and guided by core values, provides an image of the future. Mission statements address the basic question: "What do we aspire to be in the future?" A mission statement is developed when single sentences are written from each of the agreed-upon core values and are then fused together into a statement that will provide future direction for the school. Small groups now develop their own mission statements and, after the presentation of these statements to the large group, the large group reaches a consensus on a mission statement that encompasses the core values.

Step 5: Writing goals. The principal explains that goals are the third component of a vision and that they specifically state what the school hopes to accomplish. Goals are long range in nature and are the basis for strategic planning. Goals are action statements and flow naturally from the identified values and mission statements. Goals must be realistic, attainable, and few in number. Too many goals lead to fragmentation of effort, a feeling of being overpowered with achievement demands, and confusion as to which goals are most important. Therefore, three to five goals are ideal.

Each group develops its goals by discussing goals in general and then by reaching a consensus on three to five goals for the school. Goal statements are then written that are short, realistic, and specific enough to provide indices to measure the school's progress.

A large group discussion then follows and focuses on the goal statements presented by small group leaders. Goals are now prioritized and goal statements are agreed upon through consensus.

Step 6: Writing the vision statement. The principal explains that the vision statement combines the school's values, fundamental mission, and goals into one statement and serves as a futuristic road map for students, parents, teachers and community members. Vision communicates a challenge to all who are involved in the educational process. Each small group now discusses vision and then develops a vision statement for the school. (Vision statements do not have to be complete sentences.) The large group then listens to each group's vision statement and decides whether or not the agreed upon values, mission, and goals are captured within each of the vision statements. The large group must now arrive at a consensus as to the school's vision statement.

An example of one school's identified core values, mission, goals, and vision is presented below:

The core values are as follow:

(1) we believe in dignity and respect for all people;
(2) we believe that people should work to capacity and have pride in their work;
(3) we believe that students have the right to quality learning in a safe and orderly environment;
(4) we believe that schools should educate for tomorrow's challenges.

The mission statement is as follows:

Our school will provide our students with the essential skills and knowledge to compete successfully in a changing world of work through a disciplined environment in which students and teachers work to their fullest capacity, take pride in their work, and foster the idea of dignity and respect for all people.

The goals are as follow:

(1) To produce quality learning through a quality education process that is dedicated to a safe and orderly environment and that fosters intellectual inquiry, promotes student achievement and instills the dignity and worth of each person.
(2) To graduate students who have the knowledge and skills necessary to achieve in today's and tomorrow's world and who are a credit to our community as responsible and dutiful citizens.
(3) To improve continuously our educational process as well as student achievement by providing the best teachers, instructional materials, and technology available.

The vision statement is as follows:

Quality Learning: Our Job, Our Commitment, Our Future

This group effort provides a vision that is a unifying force for the school and those associated with it. The vision expresses purpose, provides a picture of the future, and generates commitment. The benefits of vision lie not in catchy phrases, but in the process used to reach the point where such a phrase embodies the purpose, meaning, and the overall desired end state of the school; and it comes from the varying perspectives of all the school's customers.

EVOLUTION OF HUMAN RESOURCE LEADERSHIP THEORY

The search to find the "one best way to lead an organization" is ongoing. Theories abound to explain the leadership phenomena and these can be used to guide practice. It is also useful to be familiar with the research that has led us to our current understanding of leadership. To this end, a short summary of theory and research follows.

Origins and Pathways to Leadership

During the early 1900s, the volume *Scientific Principles of Management,* Frederick Taylor's classic work on management science, initiated the systematic scientific inquiry as to the "one best way" for employees to perform their work to increase productivity. Taylor's goal was to eradicate wasted time and motion and to determine how workers could best be selected, trained, paid, and supervised. Often called the father of *scientific management,* Taylor introduced time and motion studies, employee performance standards, and job training methods. The leadership that resulted has been described as authoritarian and insensitive to human needs.

Another management theorist, Henri Fayol, focused attention on the entire organization instead of individual employees and believed successful management resulted from the application of a common set of principles rather than personal management traits. Common functions for maximizing employee productivity were *planning* (defining goals and outcomes), *organizing* (structuring of authority and the division of labor), *commanding* (supervising subordinates), *coordinating* (implementing measures to ensure effective interaction between resources and employees), and *controlling* (ensuring outcomes are consistent with plans). These five management principles are cyclical and are repeated for each job function. Today, Fayol's principles of planning and organizing remain, but the others have been replaced by terms such as *staffing, leading, coaching,* and *teaming.*

Promoting organizational effectiveness was the concern of Max Weber, whose ideal organization was a bureaucracy. Based on rational guidelines similar to those of Taylor and Fayol, Weber laid the foundation for current organizational theory. The classical bureaucratic model provided structure for relationships to guide activities within a complex organization. This structure was to provide fair, impartial, and predictable outcomes and treatment and to yield more effective and efficient products and services. The five basic components of a bureaucracy are (1) a hierarchical structure with well-defined authority boundaries, (2) a division of labor based on the ability to perform specialized tasks, (3) a set of rules to govern behavior and to promote conformity among all employees, (4) a system of hiring based on qualifications for the job with promotions coming from job performance, and (5) a managerial system that is free from strong personal and emotional relationships among employees.

A bureaucracy is a monolithic concept that is concerned with maximizing internal efficiency. Knezevich (1975) relates that the results of adopting the ideal bureaucratic model are impartial and unbiased treatment; minimum confusion, conflict, and friction between management and labor; promotion based on competency and job performance; and security for employees based on skill and knowledge. Critics of the model note the de-emphasis of the importance of human relations and informal groups, the rigid rules and regulations, the impersonal and authoritarian nature of management, and the inability to react quickly to pressures for change.

Human Relations Approach to Leadership

Human relations theories began with the work of Elton Mayo in the early 1930s with the findings of the Hawthorne experiments. These experiments provided significant knowledge about the influence of human relations on productivity in an organization. Results show that productivity is a function of informal social organizations in the work place. That is, informal groups emerge in organizations; they exert peer pressure, have their own code of conduct, and supply certain social needs not provided by the formal organization. This social element affects production more than demands from management or the physical environment of the workplace.

Social philosopher Mary Parker Follett described administration as an art, a science, and an ethical practice. Knezevich (1975) says her management theory opposed the work of Taylor and Fayol because she was the first to emphasize the importance of the human aspect in the work place in that *organizations are people*. To maximize performance, Follett maintained that managers must motivate, provide job satisfaction, and enhance the quality of work life.

The psychologist Kurt Lewin researched group dynamics and identified "democratic" and "authoritarian" group processes. His work concluded that democratic groups are more task oriented and more productive than are authoritarian group processes. He found that a democratic leadership style has a direct effect on organizational life and provides higher morale, greater cooperation, and higher work quality. Authoritarian leadership, stated Lewin, results in higher levels of productivity, but lower levels of morale and cooperation. Laissez-faire leadership yields poor work quality, low production levels and high employee dissatisfaction. Moreover, lack of organizational structure results in low levels of control, worker frustration, and job dissatisfaction.

The human relations movement provided insight into the complexities of organizational life and the realization that employees had multiple needs that had to be addressed if harmony and production were to be maximized. Management had the following responsibilities: (1) to provide rewards, security, and motivation; (2) to practice democratic leadership over authoritarian control; and (3) to cooperate with employees in meeting their psychological and socioeconomic needs.

Behavioral Science Approach to Leadership

The behavioral scientists contributed to the rise of human resources management by fusing the theories of scientific management with those of the human relations movement. Behavioral scientists sought a more complete picture of organizational life, focused on the individual's reaction to organizational structure and leadership style, and investigated the relationship between employee motivation and production outcomes.

Chester Barnard, a student of sociology and organizational psychology, developed a "cooperative approach" to management that stressed open, direct conversation with employees and allowed employees the freedom to be creative in achieving organizational goals. Managers must also meet the goals of the individual and work to unify the goals of the organization with those of the employees. This unification of goals brings about equilibrium in the work place and maximizes productivity.

Chris Argyris' research showed that employees and organizations have different goals and that conflict results from the dominating, formal structure of the organization and the independent nature of the individual. The hierarchy represses needs fulfillment and expectations of its employees, which leads to employee discontent and conflict. These negative factors trigger apathy toward organizational goals, the de-emphasis of work's importance, and severance from the organization. Management can decrease discontent by developing organizational policies that are employee centered, delegating more authority to employees, and involving employees in making decisions that affect their job and job performance (Argyris, 1976).

Joseph Getzels and Egon Guba provide a theory of administrative behavior as a social systems process, with the organizational and individual dimensions being both independent and interactive. Organizations have roles and role expectations whereas individuals have different personalities and need dispositions. Behavior in an organization is a function of the interaction between the expectations (goals) of the organization and the needs of the individual. When the two dimensions coincide, efficiency and effectiveness result. Managers are responsible for promoting compatible interaction by meeting the needs of employees, delegating authority, and showing concern for employees by reconciling differences between the goals of the organization and the needs of individuals (Knezevich, 1975).

Frederick Herzberg maintained that people hold positive and negative attitudes toward work and that the work environment promotes these positive or negative attitudes. Factors that motivate people in the work place are *job satisfiers* and include personal achievement, recognition, work itself, responsibility and advancement, and personal development. *Hygienes,* job dissatisfers, are the work environment, organizational policies and management practices, supervisory practices, relationships with peers, status, and salary.

Abraham Maslow investigated why people join organizations and remain in organizations. He concluded that individuals do so to meet a hierarchy of needs and that needs must be satisfied at each level before other needs appear and can be satisfied. People work hard to maintain job security and achieve higher quality psychological satisfiers. Maslow's theory suggests that the manager's job is to provide ways for people to meet their needs and the goals of the organization simultaneously. Needs are motivators and the more individual needs are met, the more satisfied employees become, and the more effective they are in their work.

Douglas McGregor's Theory X and Theory Y management present two contrasting views of employees and management strategies. These strategies serve to promote or decrease employee motivation and are based on assumptions managers have about subordinates. Theory X managers view employees as lacking in ambition, initiative, and intelligence, and as opposing change. People need to be controlled, directed, and threatened, and the average person prefers direction by authority over other supervisory practices. Theory Y managers believe that people are self-directed, seek and accept responsibility, and are intelligent, creative, and have initiative. People receive enjoyment from work and seek to fulfill the goals of the organization, and management's task is to provide avenues for individuals to maximize the assumptions of Theory Y. Managers serve to motivate and to unify the goals of the organization with those of the individual.

Contingency Theories of Leadership

Contingency theories focus on the complexities of leadership and gained prominence "after efforts to discover the one best set of leader traits and the one best set of leader behaviors in *all situations* failed" (Lunenburg and Ornstein, 1996, p. 130). Contingency theorists believe that effective leadership is contingent on the interaction of the personal traits of the leader, the situation in which leader behavior is called for, and the leadership behavior that is chosen to react to situational variables.

Fred Fiedler's contingency theory maintains that leader effectiveness is a result of matching leadership style with the leader-follower situation and the individual(s) involved. Two leadership styles promote effective results: (1) "task-motivated," which is effective when structure is needed and efficiency in performance is required and (2) "relationship motivated," which is effective when building positive interpersonal relationships with employees is required. Three factors determine leadership style to promote effective outcomes: (1) the degree to which the leader is accepted by the follower; (2) the degree to which the task is understood; and (3) the degree to which the leader has control over rewards and punishments. Effectiveness results when employees are included in planning and decision making and when they are rewarded and recognized for their efforts.

Path-goal theory, developed by Martin Evans and Robert House, attempts to explain the importance of leader behavior on employee motivation, job satisfaction, effort, and performance within the context of the work place. *Directive* leadership is effective when tasks are vague and unstructured, and *supportive* leadership is effective for increasing motivation when tasks are stressful or dissatisfying. *Participative* leadership and *achievement-oriented* leadership (setting high and challenging goals) have a positive influence on motivation and job satisfaction. The theory maintains that situational variables, personal traits, and work environment factors influence work performance and the quality of relationship between the leader and the follower. Personal traits include needs and expectations, talents and abilities, and locus of control—one's ability to influence conditions that affect personal and professional development. Work place variables include jobs performed, work groups and their performance levels, and a formal system of authority—the degree to which policies are enforced and the methods used to enforce them.

Contingency theories indicate that effective leaders display behaviors beyond the authority provided by the organization that personally influence follower behavior. To motivate employees and to promote job satisfaction, leaders must develop a climate in which followers have trust and confidence in the leader and can identify with the goals the leader attempts to achieve. How the leader relates to the follower in given situations becomes the important factor that determines outcomes. Therefore, there is no single, "best" leadership style for all situations.

REFERENCES

Argyris, C. 1976. *Increasing Leadership Effectiveness.* New York: Wiley.

Barber, J. D. 1985. *The Presidential Character.* Englewood Cliffs, NJ: Prentice-Hall.

Barnard, C. I. 1938. *The Functions of the Executive.* Cambridge, MA: Harvard University Press.

Bennis, W. and B. Nanus. 1985. *Leaders: The Strategies for Taking Charge.* New York: Harper and Row.

Berman, L. 1982. *Planning a Tragedy.* New York: W. W. Norton & Company.

Blau, P. M. and W. R. Scott. 1962. *Formal Organizations: A Comparative Approach.* San Francisco: Chandler.

Bolman, L. G. and T. E. Deal. 1991. *Reforming Organizations: Artistry, Choice, and Leadership.* San Francisco, CA: Jossey-Bass.

Bonner, S. F. 1977. *Education in Ancient Rome.* Berkeley, CA: University of California Press.

Bonstingl, J. J. 1992. "The total quality classroom." *Educational Leadership,* 50(6):66–70.

Brewer, J. H., J. M. Ainsworth, and G. E. Wynne. 1984. *Power Management: A Three Step Program for Successful Leadership.* Englewood Cliffs, NJ: Prentice-Hall.

Brussell, E. E., (ed.) 1988. *Directory of Quotable Definitions.* Englewood Cliffs, N.J.: Prentice-Hall.

Burns, J. M. 1978. *Leadership.* New York: Harper and Row.

Conley, D. T. 1993. *Roadmap to Restructuring: Policies, Practices and the Emerging Visions of Schooling.* Eugene, OR: ERIC Clearinghouse on Educational Management.

Cunningham, W. G. and D. W. Gresso. 1993. *Cultural Leadership.* Boston: Allyn and Bacon.

Davies, B. and L. Ellison. 1997. *School Leadership for the 21st Century.* New York: Routledge.

Deal, T. E. 1993. "The culture of schools," in M. Sashkin and H. J. Wolberg eds., *Educational Leadership and School Culture.* Berkeley, CA: McCutchan.

Deal, T. E. and A. A. Kennedy. 1982. *Corporate cultures.* Reading, MA: Addison-Wesley.

Deming, W. E. 1986. *Out of the Crisis.* Cambridge, MA: MIT Press.

Deming, W. E. 1993. *The New Economics for Industry, Government, Education.* Cambridge, MA: MIT Press.

Drucker, P. F. 1993. *The Effective Executive.* New York: Harper Collins.

English, F. W. 1992. *Educational Administration: The Human Science.* New York: Harper Collins.

English, F. W. 1994. *Theory in Educational Administration.* New York: Harper Collins.

Etzioni, A. 1990. *The Moral Dimension.* New York: Macmillan.

Fiedler, F. E. and Garcia, J. E. 1987. *New Approaches to Effective Leadership: Cognitive Resources and Organizational Performance.* New York: Wiley.

French, J. R. 1993. *A Formal Theory of Social Power.* New York: Irvington.

Fullan, M. G. 1992. *The New Meaning of Educational Change.* New York: Teachers College Press.

Gardner, J. 1990. *On Leadership.* New York: The Free Press.

Henderson, J. E. and W. K. Hoy. 1983. "Leader Authenticity: The Development and Test of an Operational Measure." *Educational and Psychological Research,* 2:123–130.

Hersey, P. and K. Blanchard. 1992. *Management of Organizational Behavior.* Sixth edition. Englewood Cliffs, NJ: Prentice-Hall.

Hirschman, A. O. 1970. *Exit, Voice, and Loyalty: Responses to the Decline in Firms, Organizations, and States.* Cambridge, MA: Harvard University Press.

Hoffman, J. D., D. Sabo, and J. Bliss. 1994. "Building a Culture of Trust." *Journal of School Leadership,* 3:17–23.

Hogan, R., G. J. Curphy, and J. Hogan. 1994. "What we Know about Leadership: Effectiveness and Personality." *American Psychologist,* 492–493.

House, R. J. and T. R. Mitchell. 1974. "Path–Goal Theory of Leadership." *Contemporary Business,* 3:81–98.

Hoy, W. K. and C. G. Miskel. 1996. *Educational Administration: Theory, Research, Practice.* Fifth edition. New York: McGraw-Hill.

Keegan, J. 1987. *The Mask of Command.* New York: Wiley.

Kerr, S. and J. M. Jermier. 1978. "Substitutes for Leadership: Their Meaning and Measurement." *Organizational Behavior and Human Performance,* 22:375–403.

Knezevich, S. J. 1975. *Administration of Public Education.* Third edition. New York: Harper and Row.

Kotter, J. P. 1985. *Power and Influence: Beyond Formal Authority.* New York: Free Press.

Lunenburg, F. C. and A. C. Ornstein. 1996. *Educational Administration: Concepts and Practices.* Second edition. Belmont, C.A.: Wadsworth Publishing.

Mintzberg, H. 1983. *Power in and Around Organizations.* Englewood Cliffs, NJ: Prentice-Hall.

Murgatroyd, S. and C. Morgan. 1993. *Total Quality Management and the School.* Philadelphia, P.A.: Open University Press.

Owens, R. G. 1995. *Organizational Behavior in Education.* Boston: Allyn and Bacon.

Ross, D. D. 1989. "First Steps in Developing a Reflective Approach." *Journal of Teacher Education,* 40:22–30.

Schmoker, M. J. and R. B. Wilson. 1993. *Total Quality Management Education: Profiles of Schools that Demonstrate the Power of Deming's Management Principles.* Bloomington, IN: Phi Delta Kappa.

Schon, D. A. 1987. *Educating the Reflective Practitioner.* San Francisco: Jossey-Bass.

Schon, D. A. 1983. *The Reflective Practitioner: How Professionals Think in Action.* New York: Basic Books.

Scott, W. R. 1987. *Organizations: Rational, Natural, and Open System.* Second edition. Englewood Cliffs, NJ: Prentice-Hall.

Senge, P. M. 1990. *The Fifth Discipline: The Art and Practice of the Learning Organization.* New York: Doubleday/Currency.

Sergiovanni, T. J. 1990. *Value-Added Leadership: How to Get Extraordinary Performance in Schools.* New York: Harcourt Brace Jovanovich.

Sergiovanni, T. J., M. Burlingame, F. S. Coombs, and P. W. Thurston. 1992. *Educational Governance and Administration.* Boston: Allyn and Bacon.

Starratt, R. J. 1995. *Leaders with Vision: The Quest for School Renewal.* Thousand Oaks, CA: Corwin Press.

Stogdill, R. M. and Coons, A. eds. *Leader Behavior: Its Description and Measurement,*

Research Monograph No. 88. Columbus: Bureau of Business Research, Ohio State University.

Vecchio, R. P. 1988. *Organizational Behavior.* Chicago: Dryden Press.

Vecchio, R. P. 1997. *Leadership: Understanding the Dynamics of Power and Influence in Organizations.* Notre Dame, IN: University of Notre Dame Press.

Weller, L. D. 1993. *Total Quality Management: A Conceptual Overview and Applications for Education.* Athens, GA: College of Education, University of Georgia.

Weller, L. D. 1995. "School Restructuring and Downsizing: Using TQM to Promote Cost Effectiveness." *The TQM Magazine,* 7(6):11–16.

Weller, L. D. 1999. *Quality Middle School Leadership: Eleven Central Skill Areas.* Lancaster, PA: Technomic Publishing.

Weller, L. D. and S. H. Hartley. 1994. "Why are Educators Stonewalling Total Quality Management?" *Quality Assurance in Education,* 2(2):18–25.

Weller, L. D. and S. J. Weller. 1997. "Quality Learning Organizations and Continuous Improvement: Implementing the Concept." *National Association of Secondary School Principals Bulletin,* 81(591):62–70.

Weller, L. D., S. H. Hartley, and C. L. Brown. 1994. "Principals and TQM: Developing Vision." *The Clearing House,* 67(5):298–301.

Wheatley, M. J. 1994. *Leadership and the New Science: Learning About Organization from an Orderly Universe.* San Francisco, CA: Berrett-Koehler Publishing.

Whitely, R. C. 1991. *The Customer Driven Company—Moving from Talk to Action.* New York: Addison-Wesley.

Wilson, L. T. and D. Asay. 1999. "Putting Quality in Knowledge Management." *Quality Progress,* 32(1):25–31.

Yukl, G. A. 1981. *Leadership in Organizations.* Englewood Cliffs, NJ: Prentice-Hall.

Yukl, G. A. 1994. *Leadership in Organizations.* Third edition. Englewood Cliffs, NJ: Prentice-Hall.

METHODS USED BY PRINCIPALS TO TRANSFORM THE CULTURES OF THEIR SCHOOLS

CHAPTER 3

Communications and Human Relations for Effective Education

This chapter stresses the importance of principals' having good communication and human relation skills to bring people together, to sustain the school's culture, and to build strong, positive working relationships, all of which are essential for effective educational outcomes. Effective principals lead through persuasion and influence, and must have an ability to communicate accurately and concisely for achieving quality outcomes. Good human relations skills are central to motivating people, attaining their cooperation, and sustaining their unity and commitment. Principals have to build strong communication networks among their staff to minimize misunderstanding and conflict and to maximize trust and credibility.

THE COMMUNICATION PROCESS

Principals are required to have good communication skills for promoting effective human relations, achieving quality educational outcomes, bringing people together, facilitating problem solving, minimizing conflict and misunderstanding, promoting unity, and fostering morale and commitment. Communication, both verbal and nonverbal, can attract or repel and make a difference between successful and unsuccessful school programs. Good communication skills promote successful interactions among teachers, students, parents, and community members. Open and honest communication helps schools achieve their vision, promotes credibility, reduces conflict and alienation, and promotes confidence in leadership.

Communication entails a mutual sharing of ideas and feelings among people. Communication comes from the Latin word *communicate* which means "to share" or "to make common" (Kindred, Bagin, and Gallagher, 1990). Principals

63

depend on oral and written communication to bring about understanding and to gain support for their ideas. Communication entails sending and receiving information, and it is a cooperative process, not a singular endeavor. In essence, communication is the substance that determines the quality of human relationships and the foundation for successful school outcomes.

The way in which communication takes place affects teacher morale and motivation. Clearly communicating to teachers the goals and expectations of their jobs, and how their teaching performance will be evaluated, has a positive correlation with job satisfaction (Hoy and Miskel, 1996). Myers and Myers (1982) relate that educators earn their living by communicating and that the successful achievement of the school's goals depends on how successfully the principal communicates these goals to teachers. Barnard (1938) addressed the importance of communication as a leadership function when he noted that the communication process underlies all organizational and administrative action and is the most salient component for attaining successful administrative outcomes.

A Case Study: Communication

Given the importance of effective communication skills, it would seem that principals would take steps to establish an effective communication structure and to improve interpersonal skills. However, many principals do not. They continue to place the blame for the negative results of poor communication on things such as politics, lack of support from the superintendent, or the poor interpersonal skills of others.

Effective communication is achieved by hard work, takes time, and requires dedicated effort. Some principals think they have neither the time nor the energy to dedicate to improving communication in their schools. Many do not realize their mistake until the results of poor communication culminate in their own job dissatisfaction, or that of others. If they had taken the time initially to improve communication, they would have eliminated early on many of the problems on which they now spend the majority of their time. Consider, for example, the following case study:

> After four years at a rural high school with approximately 100 certified staff members, a high school principal finds that the results of a survey the superintendent administers every two years to gauge morale at individual schools indicate serious problems in a variety of areas. The consensus on the part of teachers is that they do not feel comfortable approaching the principal with their problems, that decisions are made by the principal without their input and expertise, and that they do not feel the school is making significant progress in addressing their concerns about low standardized test scores, poor student attendance, and overcrowded conditions.

The superintendent asks the principal to devise a professional improvement plan for the upcoming year that will address and alleviate the teachers' concerns. When the principal offers his standard repertoire of excuses for the current problems—that there are 1,500 students in a facility designed for 900; that there is a core of teachers that he has had to "call on the carpet" because of complaints from students and parents, and the teachers resent this; and that he has had to make some difficult decisions concerning school policy, including student management, which some of the teachers disagree with and want to question him on—the superintendent remains firm. The principal has two choices: (1) he can continue to blame the problems in his school on factors that exonerate him or (2) he can try to get to the root of the problems and resolve them. Fortunately, the principal is one who sincerely wants to do a good job, and he chooses the latter option.

The principal does some reading of the research conducted in the areas of leadership effectiveness and begins to connect many of the problems to a single source—communication. What would you do as principal to correct these problems? The communication objectives that the principal developed will appear at the end of this chapter.

An Overview of the Components of Communication

Communication, composed of words and symbols, conveys meaning and describes objects, ideas, and feelings. Fused together, words and symbols become discourse, which is verbal interaction among people designed to shape perception, create concepts and images, and influence and persuade. Discourse can be both descriptive and prescriptive because it conveys independent realities, "what is" and what "ought to be," within the cultural environment and through cultural metaphor (English, 1994). Discourse can be complex or simple, deceptive or real. Katz and Kahn (1978) relate that discourse in schools can hide or suppress problems that teachers, parents, and students wish to ignore. Discourse can also trigger positive and creative action to solve problems or promote change. However, good communication cannot be a substitute for inadequate leadership, poor judgment, or faulty practice.

Principals in effective schools use their communication skills to lead others by influencing, persuading, and building consensus rather than by relying on positional authority and policy (Kawalski and Reitzug, 1993). Zaleznik (1989) observed that managers rely more on symbolic messages and directives, which are less personal, whereas leaders use a more personal approach when interacting with subordinates. Weller (1996) and Fullan (1991) report that good communication skills are essential for a school's transformation. When communication from principals is not clear, reliable, nor continuous, sociopolitical tension increases and results in teacher frustration and dissatisfaction with school-reform efforts. Miles (1993) relates that sharing information, seeking feedback, listening, and resolving conflict are essential communication skills for a school's restructuring success.

Effective Communication Skills

Effective communication requires planning, and the method of communication has to be carefully selected to reach the target audience. To communicate successfully is to bring about change in behavior through understanding, acceptance, and support (Kindred, Bagin, and Gallagher, 1990). Communication is a sharing process, a cooperative enterprise to exchange ideas and information to establish effective human relations and outcomes.

Communication theory supports a five-step process when sending and receiving information. Figure 3.1 presents a generic communication model depicting the five-step communication process.

Messages or ideas are the source of the communication process and convey a need or feeling to be transmitted to another. Effective communication begins with careful planning regarding the selection of words or expressions and of the medium of transmittal. Central to the planning process are the target audience and the circumstance(s) surrounding the message. Dolan (1996) relates that the method of encoding the message is essential for gaining the "active attention" of the receiver and that the method should depend on the intended receiver of the message. Encoding may be oral, written, or nonverbal depending on the time, circumstance, and preferred communication mode. Previous experience largely dictates the type of encoding the sender will use for targeted receivers. Harris (1993) stresses that the effective encoding process

GENERIC COMMUNICATION MODEL

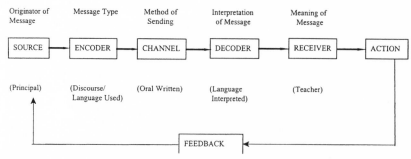

FIGURE 3.1. A generic communication model for sending and receiving information.

begins with the sender having a clear idea of what is to be transmitted and then using correct, easily interpreted words or symbols. The message must also be important to the receiver to prompt his or her immediate attention.

The channel is the device that carries the message—oral, written, or non-verbal. Decoding the message accurately depends on the receiver's ability to understand the message. When unfamiliar words or symbols are used, the receiver may lose the intent of the message. Receiving the message and understanding its true meaning depend on the successful completion of the preceding steps. Feedback, the receiver's action, provides evidence of communication. Unsuccessful messages require the process to be repeated.

One-Way Communication

One-way communication refers to speaking or lecturing with no intention of feedback from the receiver. Clampitt (1991) states that although this communication type may save time, its success depends on the sender's use of language which must be clear, specific, and understandable. Unless time is allotted later for feedback, shared understanding is not likely to exist and desired outcomes may not be achieved. One-way communication is often regulatory in nature and causes selective compliance and fragmented implementation of policy. Lewis (1987) suggests that management-by-walking-around is more effective than a constant flow of memos that are thrown away unread. Frequent interaction with subordinates provides opportunities to solve problems and to answer questions in a more personal way that promotes understanding and task completion. Principals can also provide time during faculty meetings for an "open forum" to address questions and respond to concerns resulting from one-way communication. The downward flow of information, regardless of the correct usage of words, symbols, or cues, will not guarantee effective communication.

Two-Way Communication

Two-way communication is a cooperative, reciprocal process in which the sharing of ideas takes place through exchanges between the sender and the receiver. Messages are exchanged until the receiver accurately understands the sender's message. Burbules (1993) notes that dialogue, the mutual sharing of information, is central to informed decision making, allows for greater understanding of problems, and is essential in the implementation of shared governance and teacher empowerment.

Two-way communication facilitates commitment from both the sender and the receiver. Commitment develops when communication is mutually beneficial. Tolerance of and respect for the expression of opinion is essential in situations where topics are controversial, where personality conflicts exist, or both. This allows the focus to be placed on the importance and accuracy of the message instead of on personalities, and facilitates open dialogue between conflicting parties. This type of communication allows leaders to receive constructive criticism that is essential for successful change and for promoting high teacher morale, motivation, and the flow of creative ideas (Burbules, 1993).

In the absence of open and honest communication, "filtering" takes place. Middlemist and Hitt (1988) define filtering as the elimination of important information on the part of the receiver. This occurs for a variety of reasons. For example, when receivers are not receptive to constructive criticism, selective listening takes place. Filtering is also employed to screen administrative edicts when subordinates feel threatened, or to support career advancement. Filtering contributes to the start of rumors and speculation.

Rumor

Rumor, according to Allport and Postman (1954), is a message or action devoid of fact and transmitted with great speed. Rumor is perhaps the most rapid form of communication and depends largely on wishful thinking and inaccurate listening. Speculation refers to wild guessing or advanced information built on little or no fact. Speculation usually does not convey the negative aspects often associated with rumor. Bass (1965) states that rumors are rife when (1) people feel threatened or insecure and (2) there are inadequate facts, inaccurate information, or clandestine activity. Moreover, "when formal communications in an organization are infrequent, slow to be transmitted, or given less than complete credibility, rumors are transmitted instead" (Bass, p. 311).

According to Allport and Postman (1954), three characteristics of rumors exist.

(1) As a rumor spreads, fewer details are provided, which makes it easier to repeat.

(2) A rumor tends to focus on a specific detail. People will emphasize or embellish on different aspects of the rumor.

(3) Different people "choose" to listen to different things in a rumor and choice is largely a function of interest and bias. The rumor is also repeated in the context of personal bias or interest.

Principals must combat rumors immediately with facts. Ignoring a rumor tends to add credence to the story. Culbertson, Jacobson, and Reller (1960) make the following recommendations to school administrators on how to confront rumors:

(1) When rumors arise, provide accurate facts immediately to demonstrate the inaccuracy of the rumor.

(2) Develop skills in assessing rumors. Often, rumors are symptoms of group tension, fear, hostility, and anxiety or aspirations. Determine the cause and address the needs that caused the rumor.

(3) Develop a formal and comprehensive communication system that allows teachers, parents, students, and community members to be informed continuously of the school's projects, programs, and activities. A communication program is essential when change of any kind takes place in the school. By involving those affected by the change process, rumors and speculation can be eliminated.

COMMUNICATION FOR PERSUASION AND INFLUENCE

Communication is power, and the idea that communication is neutral or apolitical is naive. Language is used to sway opinion and users of language have objectives to accomplish. Language also reflects the culture in which communication is conducted and, therefore, communication becomes the practice of *exclusion*. That is, effective communication is that which is generally endorsed and supported, and is in the best interests of those affected. Perhaps Faucault (1972) says it best when he states "that we are not free to say just anything, that we cannot simply speak of anything, when we like or where we like; not just anyone, finally, may speak of just anything" (p. 216). The situation in which communication is conducted greatly influences language, tone, and nonverbal behavior. English (1994) notes that both language and knowledge are power. The effective use of language or nonverbal behavior sets knowledge into practice and allows administrators to achieve their ends without using their formal or positional power. English discusses the "law of situation" which dictates that authority is not determined by administrative hierarchy alone, but by the situation and the person who can exercise competence and leadership in the situation. Effective leaders have theory, a body of knowledge, and competency in language, and they rely more on communication to influence others than they do on their authority to accomplish objectives. Authority, says English, intimidates, threatens, and makes subordinates resentful. The use of power arouses negative feelings toward superiors regardless of how appropriate the use of authority may be. "Getting others to do what they don't want to do and like it" (attributed to Harry S. Truman) and "getting others to accomplish tasks for the leader because they believe in that leader" (attributed to Dwight D. Eisenhower) focus more on the use of influence and persuasion than on the use of power or authority.

The idea that in a democracy one has freedom to express one's opinions is, of course, not always true. Teachers are often placed in situations that compromise the benefits of telling the truth or of expressing candid opinions. The idea that one can say anything at anytime in their work environment simply does not hold. The following are excerpts from interviews with teachers on the question of whether they feel free to say anything at any time in their work environment.

"Staff meetings are video taped and people feel intimidated, threatened, and remain quiet on important issues. Teachers remain silent on issues that impact our morale and work climate. The principal actually goes back and spends time viewing these tapes."

"The assistant principal does not handle discipline referrals well. I'm being kind here. Yet, she evaluates me and others and we all know better than to discuss the problem with her or the principal. We just suffer in silence."

"A parent was yelling and cursing at me about a policy that even I did not agree with. But I can't yell or curse back. First, the principal would call me unprofessional and second, a letter of reprimand would be put in my file. Forget telling the principal, he won't argue with parents. I think they run the school."

"My interdisciplinary team works hard. We stay late, come in early, use our planning periods, call parents, and have frequent parent conferences. Our test scores are real high and our kids are motivated, too. But the other team, well, they are older, two are ready to retire, they have low test scores, never call parents, never plan together, and never stay after school. The principal keeps tabs on us, but never on them because one is a relative of a board member and the other can give you fits if you say anything at all. So our team just plows ahead because we know that saying anything at all to the principal is like talking to deaf ears."

Unfortunately, some teachers feel threatened or sense that speaking candidly about issues that negatively affect morale, job satisfaction, and student learning is not in their own best personal or professional interests. When principals are unwilling to create a culture that values honest opinion and fact-based information, it is not surprising that teachers become dissatisfied with teaching. Unfortunately, many of these principals try to achieve high educational outcomes but fall short of their goals, and they remain clueless as to the root causes of their problems.

Persuasion and influence are best accomplished through face-to-face meetings and in surroundings that are nonintimidating. Lionberger (1960) presents a five-stage persuasion model for shaping attitudes and behaviors. The five stages are as follows:

(1) *Awareness:* a new idea or behavior is introduced.
(2) *Interest:* information is provided to trigger interest, which causes the listener to explore and question the merits of the idea.

(3) *Evaluation:* after further exploring the merits of the idea, the listener evaluates the goodness or personal benefits of the idea. If the change is deemed good or beneficial, the listener tries the idea.

(4) *Trial:* the idea is adopted and tried for a short period of time during which feedback and support are essential.

(5) *Adoption:* the idea or behavior is adopted because the change is deemed good or personally beneficial.

Change requires one to see a *personal* benefit. Interest has to be sufficiently aroused to make the change personally desirable and rewarding. When personal benefit is realized and the change is positively reinforced, change becomes a matter of practice, and reinforcement is best achieved through two-way communication on a face-to-face basis.

Credibility

Change in behavior and attitude increases with the degree of credibility the leader has in the eyes of the subordinates. Adler and Rodman (1991) relate that credibility influences the effectiveness of the message and that credibility is based on expertise and trustworthiness. The listener is more likely to be receptive to a message, which is less likely to be filtered, when the receiver has trust and confidence in the sender. Bowers (1976) observed that the identity and the reputation of the sender have an effect, regardless of whether the message is filtered or ignored. When perceived as being untrustworthy or incompetent, administrators lose credibility and the power of persuasion and influence, thereby lessening their effectiveness as leaders.

Cognitive Styles of Communication

Carl Jung's work on cognitive style has direct implications for principals to increase the effectiveness of communication. Isabel B. Myers and Katherine Briggs developed an instrument, based on Jung's theory of psychological type, known as the *Myers–Briggs Type Indicator.* This instrument is rooted in empirical research and is used in a wide variety of fields including leadership and management development. The *Myers–Briggs Type Indicator* and psychological type theory provide a method for understanding individual differences among people. This understanding has unlimited practical applications. Psychological type theory is mentioned in this chapter on communication because its practical applications in this area can be useful to a principal in understanding how individual differences among people affect their preferences for receiving and sending information. However, its usefulness in all areas of dealing with people cannot be stressed enough. In fact, the study of

Jung's psychological type theory and the use of this theory can do more to help principals understand differences in human behavior and to respond to those differences in ways that will raise leadership effectiveness than any course, workshop, or book on the topic of leadership could possibly effect. A note of caution, however: This is not a theory or instrument that can be mastered in a short period of time, although practical applications will be immediately evident to principals who set out to add this theory to their understanding of human beings and to apply it in the area of leadership.

An example of how a principal can use type theory for improving communication is offered in the following example. Nasca (1994) points out that there are two dimensions and four cognitive styles based on Jung's theory that can be used to promote effective communication. The two dimensions are (1) perception or the way one views the world, and (2) decision making or the way one processes information through *thinking* and *feeling*.

Four cognitive styles exist within each person, and each person has a preference for using one of the two cognitive styles categorized under each of the two dimensions. The four cognitive styles are sensor, intuitor, thinker, and feeler. These preferences interact to form four different combinations or four different cognitive styles.

(1) The Sensor–thinker has a preference for detail, fact, and sequential order in giving and receiving information. As a sender, information is provided mainly through facts, practical examples, and concrete terms.

(2) The Sensor–feeler has a preference for communication that displays feelings of warmth and empathy. Communication to others has the personal touch and includes specific, humanistic examples.

(3) The Intuitor–thinker has a preference for theoretical, logical, and rational information, but is not highly detail oriented. Communication is mainly accomplished through rational and general examples.

(4) The Intuitor–feeler has a preference for warmth and empathy in communication and emphasizes and is attuned to the personal touch in the message. Intuitive-feelers can detect subtle words or symbols in communication. Intuitive-feelers prefer communication of creative expression, personal experience, and personal challenge.

The principal who uses this knowledge of the different preferences people have concerning communication based on individual psychological type differences will do so by tailoring information and messages to fit the needs and preferences of the faculty. As the faculty will be made up of all types of people (no one psychological type enters the teaching profession at the exclusion of all other types), the principal knows that *all* communication will take these differences into account.

This may raise the question of whether the principal must administer the instrument to all faculty members to identify specific psychological types. This is not necessary, although the principal who learns more about psychological type theory may eventually decide that this information would be helpful in aiding the understanding of individual staff members. A general understanding of type theory, however, makes classification of individual staff members unnecessary for the following two reasons:

(1) All psychological types exist in the general population, to greater and lesser degrees, and the principal, as stated before, may safely assume that any communication which is directed to the entire faculty should take into account differences in psychological type.

(2) On acquiring an understanding of psychological type, the principal will be able to identify aspects of type in individuals based on clues and cues coming from those individuals and will be able to use this information to facilitate communication on an individual level. Even without an understanding of psychological type, principals already use such cues and clues that reveal "human nature" to decide that one staff member needs a response of warmth and empathy rather than, for example, a detailed logical explanation in a certain situation. The study of psychological type will broaden the principal's understanding of these aspects of human differences. Such understanding can also be used to see *ourselves* more clearly. This understanding of the self leads to an awareness that just because *we* may need a detailed logical explanation in a particular situation does not mean that communication tailored in such a way will be most effective for another individual in a similar situation. In other words, knowledge of psychological type leads to an understanding of the "bigger picture" that principals can use to their advantage.

For the principal who wishes to explore the benefits of using psychological type theory please see Myers and McCaulley (1985), Myers (1980), Kersey and Bates (1978), Lawrence (1993), and Fitzgerald and Kirby (1997).

Nonverbal Communication

Nonverbal communication is as important as verbal communication. A basic tenet of psychotherapy is that if you want to understand what a person is trying to communicate to you, then you should examine how his behavior makes you feel. Nonverbal communication is generally defined as interaction with others that does not include words or symbolic messages. Harris (1993) provides examples of nonverbal *kinesis* communication such as raised eyebrows, firm handshake, silence, and the shifting of posture. Heintzman et al. (1993) found that behaviors communicating a sense of warmth, interest, and enthusiasm were smiling, touching, head nods, leaning forward, and eye behavior. These positive movements strengthen rapport between two or more people. Harris notes that facial expressions are the most common form of nonverbal communication, and most people can easily "read" the emotions of others through this medium. Eye-to-eye contact is direct and powerful. Prolonged eye contact indicates honesty, credibility, and sincerity; conveys attention to the message; and helps ensure content understanding. However, prolonged eye contact can be threatening or indicate that a more detailed response is needed.

Luthans (1989) discusses the importance of paralanguage or voice qualities that are not strictly oral but add emphasis to a nonverbal message. These include grunts, sighs, laughter, yawning, and noninfluences such as "ah" and "um."

Proxemis or physical environment is also a form of nonverbal communication. Hall (1980) and McCaskey (1979) discuss the importance of space in communicating messages. Hall observed that there are four personal "space zones" that people use to communicate certain messages:

(1) *Intimate zone:* Two feet or closer implies an intimate relationship or one is socially domineering.

(2) *Personal zone:* Two to four feet indicates that close association exists, that one is well acquainted with another, or that a friendship bond exists.

(3) *Social zone:* Four to twelve feet indicates minimal acquaintance and that a definite reason exists for communication. Most business behavior is conducted in this zone.

(4) *Public zone:* Twelve or more feet represents detached interest, with little business being conducted.

Time also represents nonverbal communication. Vecchio (1991) discusses the use of *chronemics* to translate messages. Being tardy to meetings indicates power or having a busy schedule. Being late for meetings sends several messages including forgetfulness, lack of interest, lack of involvement, or the reaffirmation of the high status of a person to subordinates. Effective use of time indicates efficiency, preparation, commitment, and organization.

The Grapevine

Grapevines are part of the informal organizational structure. They develop through necessity and fill a void created by insufficient communication. Groups, teams, or cliques are sources of information that fill a social need, and they gather and transmit information rapidly. Grapevines also provide a channel for circumventing formal policy or procedure (Robbins, 1991). Peters and Waterman (1982) note that grapevines are used constructively by administrators in quality organizations to disseminate and receive information, to implement new ideas, and to solicit opinions. As information networks, grapevines acquire information that, according to Newstrom and Davis (1992), is over seventy-five percent correct.

Correct information flows freely among colleagues and is easily accessible when trust and openness exist. Deal and Kennedy (1984) relate that teacher teams and teacher social contacts outside the school promote accurate grapevine information. Positive aspects of grapevine information include (1) updating subordinates on organizational developments that affect their work, (2) providing subordinates a safety valve to release emotional tension, and (3) building employee morale by providing timely and positive information, support, and encouragement.

Benefits of grapevines also exist for school administrators. Deal and Kennedy (1984) note that effective principals rely on certain teachers to provide feedback about the morale and attitudes of other teachers and to assess teachers' reactions to new policy or planned change without making formal inquiries. Licata and Hack (1980) found grapevine sources to differ among principals in elementary and secondary schools. Principals in elementary schools have closer relationships with teachers and rely less on grapevine information than do secondary school principals who have a more formal communication structure with teachers. Grapevines in secondary schools are more common, and principals use them primarily for assessing teacher attitudes on current issues and areas of policy dissatisfaction.

Negative aspects of grapevines also exist and consist of rumors and speculation. Rumor and speculation spread quickly and because much information cannot be verified, facts become distorted and different parts of the rumor or speculation are emphasized or embellished by different people. Rumor control can be achieved by providing fact-based information through formal and informal channels of communication. Rumors are best rebutted with facts that should be provided quickly and through credible sources.

Informal Networks

Informal networks exist in all types of organizations and have similar patterns of information flow. The importance and reliability of networks depend on information accuracy, speed, and the credibility of the source (Griffin, 1993). Informal communication flows upward, downward, and horizontally and is accomplished primarily through grapevines. Principals need to know the informal network structure(s) in their school to assess the accuracy and credibility of information. Networks can provide assistance in promoting change and combating rumor; serve as a source of direct, reliable information to teachers to increase morale; and be used to detect inclinations toward change. Research on communication has provided many reliable methods to assess the components of informal network communication patterns. In schools, Deal and Kennedy (1984) relate that teacher team meetings, shared planning periods, extra curricular or sports events, and membership in civic or social organizations provide information on their network patterns. Principals who observe these networking patterns can use this information to enhance their leadership effectiveness.

Sharing and Receiving Information

Surveys can provide sociometric data that are useful in identifying inter- and intragroup communication patterns in organizations. Sociometric data can be collected through interviews, observations, or questionnaires. and can then be used to develop charts to plot patterns of information flow. Table 3.1 presents a survey instrument to assess formal and informal network patterns in schools.

In Table 3.1, information is gathered to assess the quality and kinds of information flow from the principal. Principals can observe interactions among teachers over time to validate survey results.

Members in groups, teams, or networks perform certain functions within the membership that affect information flow. The *gatekeeper* has the ability to control information flow among the members. The *liaison* is a member of the group and may have membership in other groups within the organization. Liaisons connect these groups and serve as an informational source and a harmonizing force. An *isolate* is one who has few, if any, network connections and depends

TABLE 3.1. Communication survey.

	Strongly disagree				Strongly agree	
1. Administration practices (circle the most appropriate numeral).						
1. The principal shares accurate information.	1	2	3	4	5	6
2. The principal provides important information in a timely manner.	1	2	3	4	5	6
3. The principal provides information on a regular basis.	1	2	3	4	5	6
4. The principal is receptive to listening to my ideas.	1	2	3	4	5	6
5. The principal solicits my ideas or opinions frequently.	1	2	3	4	5	6
6. The principal is easily accessible for sharing information.	1	2	3	4	5	6
7. The principal has a formal communication process to inform the faculty about important events.	1	2	3	4	5	6
8. The principal uses informal communication channels.	1	2	3	4	5	6
9. The principal is honest in sharing important information.	1	2	3	4	5	6
10. The principal is selective with whom important information is shared.	1	2	3	4	5	6

on formal communication channels. An isolate may be a source of disruption or dissatisfaction and may promote dysfunctional activities within the school or school system. Principals seeking to establish good communications within the school should identify and work closely with gatekeepers and liaisons and establish an interpersonal rapport with isolates (Rogers and Rogers, 1976).

Principals who strive to increase their leadership effectiveness adhere to a few basic communication principles. Hoy and Miskel (1996) relate that increasing effective information flow can be accomplished by (1) letting teachers know the formal communication channels and the medium of delivery, (2) including all teachers, parents, support personnel, and community members in the formal information flow, and (3) providing complete, accurate, and timely information.

Principals' everyday behaviors are statements of their leadership styles. Bozik (1989) and Cooke (1994) view leader behavior as communication, and the perceptions of this behavior by subordinates are as important as all other types of communication. Communication through behavior is a form of modeling, and this modeling sends messages to subordinates regarding expected behavior. For example, if the principal has good listening skills, provides timely and appropriate responses, and adapts to the communication style of others to promote the effective flow of communication, faculty members will recognize the importance of these skills. Some effective principals conduct inservice programs on the development of communication and listening skills for teachers and support personnel.

Written Communications

Effective communication is also written communication, and many of the same rules that apply to spoken communication also apply to written communication. Written communication can be both formal and informal. Writing style should remain simple, emphasizing clarity and conciseness. Kindred, Bagin, and Gallagher (1990) relate that effective written messages have definite objectives, each of which is clearly stated and presented so that the reader knows what action or response is expected. If the message is for information purposes, then only relevant, fact-based information should be provided. Written communication that requires a response should state the type of response desired, the medium for conveying the response, and when the response is due.

A standard rule of thumb for written communication to teachers is the "5 × 3 method." That is, if a message takes longer than five minutes to write or three minutes to read, it will probably be circular filed. Written messages should contain standard vocabulary, relate how the message directly affects the reader, be free of writer bias, and contain both the pros and the cons of the issue so that readers can draw their own conclusions (Dolan, 1996).

The message should be carefully edited for grammar, spelling, and content by a third party skilled in these areas. Neatness and professional presentation are essential because the messages represent an impression statement from the principal. Personal notes that thank teachers for assistance or acknowledge achievement serve to increase teacher morale and maintain positive interpersonal relations (Kindred, Bagin, and Gallagher, 1990). Memos, although less formal than letters, should still be on the school's letterhead, be free of jargon, and be concise. Negative statements or "threat words" should be avoided because written messages have an emotional effect that cannot be clarified by immediate feedback or by body language. Threats include phrases such as "lack of caring," "again I must call your attention," and "this behavior must stop."

Listening Skills

Studies on school administrators "have consistently shown that about seventy-five percent of the contacts an administrator has in a school day are one-on-one meetings" (Dolan, p. 113). Skill in listening is essential to effective leadership, with daily demands coming from teachers, students, parents, and community members. Dainow and Bailey (1988) relate that listening involves all parties, but the receiver of the message must convey to the sender signs of listening and understanding. These signs include eye contact, facial expressions, head nods, body gestures, and tone of voice.

Barriers to effective listening are many, but the greatest barrier is ourselves. Most people prefer to talk rather than to listen because talking is more self-centered (Kawalski and Reitzug, 1993). The following barriers to good listening can be learned and are reported by Golen (1990):

(1) Listening for facts or details and not content

(2) Being distracted by noises during the conversation

(3) Daydreaming

(4) Being occupied with another topic or remembering an important task that must be accomplished

(5) Having little or no interest in the topic

(6) Focusing on the sender's physical appearance or mannerisms

(7) Thinking about the length of time the sender takes in communicating the message

(8) Concluding what the sender says before the message is concluded

(9) Getting emotional over the message

(10) Pretending to be interested in the message

(11) Being bored with the complexity or difficulty of the message

(12) Allowing personal bias or prejudice to interfere with the sender's message

(13) Avoiding eye contact and refusing to provide feedback

(14) Neglecting to clarify or seek clarification in the message

Poor listening costs the organization in terms of time, effort, and resources. Poor listeners often have to redo work, spend time in seeking clarification or redirection, and waste resources in doing so. They are often the object of jokes and can be omitted from important assignments or meetings that could enhance their careers, and they are often characterized as being forgetful or inefficient.

Listening skills can be improved; however, this takes time and effort and may require professional training. Many people can improve their listening skills by making a personal commitment to become better listeners. O'Hair and Friedrich (1992) provide ways to improve one's listening:

(1) Develop a positive attitude toward the sender and the sender's message.

(2) Screen out noise—disregard environmental and personal distractions that interfere with concentration on the message's content.

(3) Maintain eye contact and be alert for facial expressions or nonverbal cues.

(4) Remind yourself that the message is important and that you must hear it regardless of the topic or bias toward the sender. Look for hidden meanings and seek clarification.

(5) Do not draw conclusions while the sender is speaking.

(6) Concentrate on what is said *and* on how it is said. Difficult messages are sometimes conveyed in paralanguage.

(7) Provide periodic feedback, either nonverbal or verbal, to the sender.

(8) Paraphrase the content of the message with your own interpretations and seek feedback from the sender.

Applying the skills of good listening prevents principals from experiencing the negative effects of the saying "I hear what you say, but I do not understand what you mean." Acting on incomplete or misunderstood information is costly in terms of time, resources, and image.

Group Meetings

Administrators can assist others in becoming effective listeners in group meetings by following a basic format. Communicating to groups of people is more difficult than communicating to one or two people. Observing the following procedures in group meetings will stimulate active listening.

(1) Circulate an agenda well in advance of the meeting. Include copies of documents to be discussed and expect attendees to have read the documents before the meeting.
(2) Expect prompt attendance, start the meeting on time, and follow the agenda.
(3) Establish the objectives of the meeting and specify the allotted time for each topic if applicable.
(4) Cover each topic using visual aides, if appropriate, to stimulate listening and memory.
(5) Refer to the documents disseminated before the meeting when the topic is discussed.

A COMMUNICATION IMPROVEMENT PLAN

Effective communication requires dedicated work and an awareness of formal and informal communication processes. The objectives for the improvement plan for the principal mentioned in the case study at the beginning of the chapter follow.

Objectives for Establishing More Effective Communication

The following objectives are designed to achieve more effective communication:

(1) Administering a Communication Survey to assess formal and informal communication patterns within the school, and using results to target specific areas for improvement.
(2) Setting up a formal communication network that includes the following:
   a. Establishing a leadership team made up of department heads, administrators, and at-large faculty members chosen by the faculty; this will be a formal decision-making body within the school. Establish a monthly meeting schedule and provide agendas to members well in advance of meetings. Advise members on methods for placing items on the agenda. Use consensus building to reach decisions.
   b. Having a weekly meeting schedule for building administrators where planning and information sharing will take place.
   c. Appointing a member of the administrative team to attend all departmental meetings to answer questions, clarify information, and share information with department members.
   d. Setting a schedule for monthly faculty meetings that all faculty members must attend.

e. Using a variety of communication methods.

(3) Establishing a more effective informal communication network that includes the following:

a. Introducing an open-door policy for faculty members to approach administrators.

b. Seeking input from informal leaders on an individual basis when initiating change.

c. Combating rumors with facts.

d. Assessing informal communication networks among faculty members and using these networks to send and receive information.

e. Providing in-service programs on communication and listening skills for faculty members.

(4) Improving communication skills on a personal basis to include the following:

a. Improving listening skills.

b. Establishing interpersonal relationships with "isolates" on the faculty.

c. Improving understanding of differences among people, as reflected in psychological type. This includes reading books on the topic and attending a workshop on psychological type offered through the Center for Applications of Psychological Type (2815 NW 13th Street, Suite 401, Gainesville, FL 32609; Phone, 800-777-2278).

REFERENCES

Adler, R. B. and G. Rodman. 1991. *Understanding Human Communication.* Fort Worth, TX: Holt, Rinehart, and Winstons.

Allport, G. and L. Postman 1954. "The Basic Psychology of Rumor. The Process and Effects of Mass Communication," in W. Schramm, ed., Urbana, IL: University of Illinois Press.

Barnard, C. I. 1938. *Functions of an Executive.* Cambridge, MA: Harvard University Press.

Bass B. M. 1965. *Organizational Psychology.* Boston: Allyn and Bacon.

Bowers, D. G. 1976. *Systems of Organizations: Management of the Human Resource.* Ann Arbor: University of Michigan Press.

Bozik, M. 1989. "Ten Ways that Principals Can Promote Effective Communication." *Principal,* 69:34–36.

Burbules, N. C. 1993. *Dialogue in Teaching: Theory and Practice.* New York: Teachers College Press.

Clampitt, P. G. 1991. *Communicating for Managerial Effectiveness.* Newbury Park, CA: Sage.

Cooke, G. J. 1994. "Communication Tips for School Leaders." *High School Magazine,* 1:12–14.

Culbertson, J. A., P. B. Jacobson, and T. L. Reller. 1960. *Administrative Relationships: A Casebook.* Englewood Cliffs, NJ: Prentice-Hall.

Dainow, S. and C. Bailey. 1988. *Developing Skills with People.* New York: Wiley.

Deal, T. and A. Kennedy. 1984. *Corporate Culture.* Reading, MA: Addison-Wesley.

Dolan, G. K. 1996. *Communication: A Practical Guide to School and Community Relations.* Belmont, CA: Wadsworth Publishing.

English, F. W. 1994. *Theory in Educational Administration.* New York: Harper Collins.

Faucault, M. 1972. *The Archeology of Knowledge.* New York: Pantheon Books.

Fitzgerald, C. and L. K. Kirby, eds. 1997. *Developing Leaders.* Palo Alto, CA: Davies-Black Publishing.

Fullan, M. G. 1991. *The New Meaning of Educational Change.* New York: Teachers College Press.

Golen, S. 1990. "A Factor Analysis of Barriers to Effective Listening." *Journal of Business Communication,* 27:25–36.

Griffin, E. 1993. *A First Look at Communication Theory.* Second edition. New York: McGraw-Hill.

Hall, E. T. 1980. *The Silent Language.* Westport, CT: Greenwood.

Harris, T. E. 1993. *Applied Organizational Communication.* Hillsdale, NJ: Erlbaum.

Heintzman, M., D. G. Leathers, R. L. Parrot, and A. B. Cairns. (1993). "Non-Verbal Rapport-Building Behavior's Effects on Perceptions of a Supervisor." *Management Communication Quarterly,* 7(2):181–208.

Hoy, W. K. and C. G. Miskel. 1996. *Educational Administration: Theory, Research, and Practice.* Fifth edition. New York: McGraw-Hill.

Katz, D. and R. L. Kahn. 1978. *The Social Psychology of Organizations.* Second edition. New York: Wiley.

Kawalski, T. J. 1996. *Public relations in educational organizations: Practice in an age of information and reform.* Englewood Cliffs, NJ: Prentice Hall.

Kawalski, T. J. and U. C. Reitzug 1993. *Contemporary School Administration.* New York: Longman.

Kersey, D. and M. Bates. 1978. *Please Understand Me: Character and Temperament Types.* Third edition. Del Mar, CA: Promethean Nemesis Books.

Kindred, L. W., D. Bagin, and D. R. Gallagher. 1990. *The School and Community Relations.* Fourth edition. Englewood Cliffs, NJ: Prentice Hall.

Lawrence, G. 1993. *People Types and Tiger Stripes.* Third ediiton. Gainesville, FL: Center for Applications of Psychological Type.

Lewis, P. L. 1987. *Organizational Communication: The Essence of Effective Management.* New York: Wiley.

Licata, J. W. and W. G. Hack. 1980. "School Administrator Grapevine Structure." *Educational Administration Quarterly,* 16:82–99.

Lionberger, H. F. 1960. *Adoption of New Ideas and Practice.* Ames, I.A.: Iowa State University Press.

Luthans, F. 1989. *Organizational Behavior.* Fifth edition. New York: McGraw-Hill.

McCaskey, M. B. 1979. "The Hidden Messages Managers Send." *Harvard Business Review,* 57:135–148.

Middlemist, R. D. and M. A. Hitt. 1988. *Organizational Behavior: Managerial Strategies for Performance.* St. Paul: West.

Miles, M. B. 1993. "Forty Years of Change in School: Some Personal Reflections." *Educational Administration Quarterly,* 29(2), 213–248.

Myers, M. T. and G. E. Myers. 1982. *Managing by Communication: An Organizational Approach.* New York: McGraw-Hill.

Myers, I. B. and M. H. McCaulley. 1985. *Manual: A Guide to the Development and Use of the Myers–Briggs Type Indicator.* Palo Alto, CA: Consulting Psychologists Press.

Myers, I. B. 1980. *Introduction to Type.* Palo Alto, CA: Consulting Psychologists Press.

Nasca, D. 1994. "The Impact of Cognitive Style on Communication." National Association of Secondary School Principals.

Newstrom, J. W. and K. Davis. 1992. *Human Behavior at Work: Organizational Behavior.* Ninth edition. New York: McGraw-Hill.

O'Hair, D. and H. G. Friedrich. 1992. *Strategic Communication in Business and the Professions.* Boston: Houghton Mifflin.

Peters, T. J. and R. H. Waterman Jr. 1982. *In Search of Excellence.* New York: Harper and Row.

Robbins, S. P. 1991. *Organizational Behavior: Concepts, Controversies, and Applications.* Fifth edition. Englewood Cliffs, NJ: Prentice Hall.

Rogers, E. M.. and R. A. Rogers. 1976. *Communication in Organizations.* New York: Free Press.

Vecchio, R. P. 1991. *Organizational Behavior.* Second edition. New York: Dryden.

Weller, L. D. 1996. "The Next Generation of School Reform." *Quality Progress,* 29(10):65–70.

Zaleznik, A. A. 1989. *The Managerial Mystique: Restoring Leadership in Business.* New York: Harper & Row.

CHAPTER 4

Maximizing Human Resource Potential Through Team Building and Teamwork

Educational theorists have stated that the 1990s has been the decade of teacher empowerment. The redesign of the infrastructure of schooling through the involvement of teachers in problem solving and decision making is a significant step toward maximizing human potential. Empowerment is directly related to the goals of human resource administration: (a) maximizing human talents and skills to achieve organizational goals, (b) maximizing personal and professional career development, and (c) reconciling individual and organizational objectives.

Teams in quality-producing and service-oriented schools have the following characteristics: a principal who is highly supportive and dedicated to the team concept; a clear vision with high expectations and clearly defined goals; a results-driven organizational structure; a unified commitment to quality performance and outcomes; a collaborative culture that emphasizes continuous improvement; and a rewards and recognition system that emphasizes teamwork within a community of purpose.

EMPOWERMENT AND POWER

Empowerment is a term that is loosely defined in the literature. Generally, empowerment is defined as a liberating force for subordinates through a system of shared power and responsibility. The phrase "empowerment of teachers" means allowing teachers to make decisions and to solve problems that affect their personal and professional work and well-being (Schermerhorn, Hunt, and Osborn, 1994). Empowered decision making has yielded highly positive results in site-based managed schools and in those schools applying the quality management theory of Deming (1986). In these schools, teamwork is central in promoting teacher morale, student self-concept, and increased student achievement on standardized tests (Weller, 1996; Weller and Weller, 1997; Weller and Hartley, 1994; Schenkat, 1993; Schmoker and Wilson, 1993; West-Burnham, 1993). Team decision making has become a major element in the school reform and restructuring movement of the 1990s. English (1994) notes the recent efforts of progressive school administrators who have finally heeded the research from human relations theory by initiating teamwork and shared governance models to promote quality educational outcomes. Sohol and Morrison (1995) found a link between TQM's (total quality management's) quality teams that implement continuous improvement and student achievement. They noted that, for teachers, teamwork improved morale, job satisfaction, and interpersonal relationships. Teamwork is central to Senge's description of a learning organization (1992) where "people continually expand their capacity to create desired results, where new patterns of thinking are nurtured, and where people are continuously learning how to learn together" (p. 41).

Empowerment requires a new kind of school leader, a leader who is willing to collaborate, share power, and free teachers to take initiatives for promoting excellence in the classroom (Conley, 1993). Education has become too complex for principals to remain experts in all areas of instruction. Knowledge on effective teaching and learning and advances in technology have also made quality instruction too complex for individual teachers to remain isolated specialists. "Conley states that the future lies down the road of mutual interdependence, of teamwork among adults and children, of human capital development, of enhanced interpersonal skills, of inclusive leadership approaches and styles, and of organizations that resemble living organic, more than inert, structures" (p. 280). Teamwork and collaborative management in schools must be a part of the school's culture and the commitment of the principal in initiating these reform elements is crucial for effective education. Sagor (1992) relates that successful principals have a clear vision, a dedication to the idea of continuous improvement, and a commitment to the participatory style of management. They view teachers as capable and competent professionals—they view teachers as leaders.

Teacher teams do more than enhance instruction. Teacher teams help develop and sustain school culture, serve as informal communication networks, and spearhead change and innovation (English, 1992). Weller and Weller (1997) noted that teacher team decision making fosters positive teacher self-concept and vested interest in school reform programs. West-Burnham (1993) relates that teamwork has a distinct advantage for principals who value the expertise of others in solving problems. The following case study illustrates how some principals use the power of teams to work in their schools.

The Georgia School Public Relations Association (GSPRA) presents an annual award designated as the Outstanding Leadership in School/Community

Relations Award. The purpose of the award is to recognize individuals, other than those responsible for a public relations program, who have proved themselves to be leaders in building support for public education in their communities. These individuals may come from any occupation; in fact, the 1998 nominees included a school superintendent, a teacher, a parapro, a firefighter, a business owner, and a middle school principal, among others.

The 1998 winner of the Outstanding Leadership in School/Community Relations Award was the middle school principal from a rural school system in Georgia, who used teams of teachers and community members to solve problems and to build support for public education. These teams included a local school advisory council composed of teachers, parents, and community members whose purpose is to help the school in its quest for continuous improvement; a People United Promoting School (PUPS) program, the first formal parent volunteer program at the school; and a parent Outreach Program (POP), that utilizes teacher teams in holding parent meetings in the community outside the school setting.

Empowerment, therefore, refers to releasing the potential in others to improve and to be autonomous. Principals who delegate power allow others to maximize their potential and, in turn, receive greater benefits and rewards. Tracy's power pyramid (1990) depicts the principle of power as flowing upward and as synomous with love—the more you give, the more you get in return. The following shows that one gives power away by

(1) clearly delineating responsibilities and expectations;

(2) giving authority to accomplish the task;

(3) maintaining high standards of performance;

(4) providing complete information, training, and resources to be successful;

(5) providing continuous feedback and recognition for achievements;

(6) treating people with dignity and respect;

(7) giving permission to fail without fear of retribution.

Empowering teachers translates the rhetoric of trust into action, provides tangible results by allowing others to be free to be creative and independent, and promotes job satisfaction through improved self-esteem and professional development. Empowerment of teachers is essential, therefore, in maximizing human potential and promoting principal effectiveness.

Teacher satisfaction through teamwork is well documented. West-Burnham (1993) reports that in TQM schools, self-satisfaction is high among teachers. According to Csikentmihalyi (1990), people have a feeling of self-satisfaction when they feel challenged, use their skills and creativity at work, and gain satisfaction and fulfillment by helping others achieve their work-related goals. Teamwork provides this kind of on-the-job satisfaction. Csikentmihalyi also notes that teamwork allows people to become a part of larger, more challenging experiences, which provide added purpose and meaning to their work. This collective conscious pursuit for achievement is psychologically healthy and allows individuals to achieve greater outcomes than they can achieve as individuals. Empowered teams, says Glasser (1990), is a collective concept that allows teachers to move from "I" to "We" in thinking and doing. Teams promote cooperation over competition and provide schools with a sense of "community." Cooperation and community are essential to Covey's (1992) call for interdependence over independence, an idea that promotes solidarity and self-efficacy in schools. Kohn (1986) notes that studies consistently show that when competition is reduced or eliminated, and cooperative effort is substituted, excellence is more likely to be achieved. Sagor and Barnett (1994) observed that TQM schools empower teachers to solve problems and to make decisions, and they have principals who practice "people-first" leadership, which emphasizes personal growth and development. Weller (1996) notes that only when school principals take care of their teachers first, will teachers take care of their students *and* the organization.

ROLE OF THE PRINCIPAL IN EFFECTIVE TEAM BUILDING

Principals provide the critical mass necessary for high-performing teams. Principals set the tone for teamwork by adopting the "we" and "what do you think we should do?" philosophy. Principals model expected behavior by consulting with teachers, parents, and community members before making decisions and by appointing ad hoc committees to solve problems. Teams create democracy in the workplace; call for self-control, autonomy of team members, and cooperation; and thwart complacency and stagnation among employees. Swift, Ross, and Omachonu (1998) noted that as a way to maximize human resource potential in the workplace, teamwork is perhaps the best process a leader can infuse into the organization. Effective principals use teacher teams to solve curricular and instructional problems, to design school-based policy, to solve parent and student problems, and to allocate budget resources.

Principals also model their commitment to teamwork by participating in team meetings. Attending team meetings, participating in team discussions, and volunteering for or accepting team assignments demonstrate commitment and send the message that "we're in this together." Varney (1991) notes that the leader's presence and participation help energize teams and endorse the importance of the work.

Principals frequently want to know which team configurations are most productive and how best to select team membership. Creating teams and selecting team membership depend on the purpose or goals to be accomplished. Some teams are created for a short term, specific purpose, and are disbanded when the goal is achieved. Others are long-range or ongoing teams with ongoing goals and objectives. Weller (1995) presents examples of the types of teams found in quality-oriented schools:

- *Multi-functional teams:* Teams that have specific goals and a designated purpose and often function as the school's management team or as the school council. They include teachers from all grade levels or subject areas, have specified meeting times, and are empowered to develop the school's policy and budget.
- *Cross-functional teams:* Teams of teachers representing specific grade levels or subject areas working on specific goals or problems that directly affect their connecting areas of work. These teams are temporary, may be voluntary, and are achievement oriented. Cross-functional teams are ideal for conducting action research projects.
- *Self-directed teams:* Teams of teachers who work together on a daily basis and are responsible for the instructional program in their areas of expertise. Interdisciplinary teacher teams are self-directed teams that plan and implement instruction with a specific number of students for a set period of time. Middle school interdisciplinary teams are examples of self-directed teams.

Regardless of the team type, empowerment is the essential ingredient. Empowered teams serve as the link between administrators and students and facilitate the achievement of school goals. Team membership can result from peer or self-nomination or selection by the principal. However, the election process promotes morale, whereas selection can provide a "rubber stamp" impression.

The principal's leadership style has to complement empowerment. Leaders who believe in liberating human potential, value initiative and creativity, and believe work should be satisfying find that empowered teams complement the leadership role (Handy, 1990).

Team Vision

Vision for teams is as essential as vision for quality schools, and principals provide leadership in developing team vision. Weller, Hartley, and Brown (1994) describe the purpose and the essential components required to set up empowered teams. Vision is the overarching purpose and compelling force that drives the team. Vision provides the guiding philosophy and presents a tangible image of what the team has to achieve. Vision is the ideal for which all aspire, and it triggers inspiration and motivation to excel and achieve through joint ownership and commitment.

Principals promote vision in teams by modeling the vision's expected behaviors and through *kaisha hoshin,* Japanese for providing the "basic challenge," to excel. As principals interact with teachers, they point to the images of the future and stress individual and team excellence. High-achieving teams have the following commonalities: clearly stated goals and clearly defined expectations, a time frame for goal achievement, delineated constraints under which the team must perform, a system of formative and summative evaluations of team progress, and knowledge and skills in group dynamics and conflict resolution. Principals provide the necessary resources and moral support required for teams to achieve their goals.

Team member involvement and commitment are essential to goal completion. Schmuck and Runkel (1994) relate three factors enhancing team members' involvement: (1) goals must be realistic and attainable; (2) the task must be professionally and personally rewarding; and (3) team members must have the necessary problem-solving and conflict-resolution skills to work as an effective team. Factors enhancing commitment are as follows: (1) members must clearly see the personal benefit in the task and the benefit to the target population to deem the team effort worthwhile; (2) the task must be interesting and challenging to the individual and to the team; and (3) the individual must know that the task is personally important to the leader and the organization.

Motivating and Rewarding Teams

Motivation is first and foremost an individual element. Schmuck and Runkel (1994) relate that seeking personal satisfaction in work is a major concern and that personal reward comes through personal satisfaction on the job. Satisfaction stems from achievement, from the autonomy and freedom to take the initiative and be creative, and from being successful in the task. Social support is also essential to motivate individuals and teams. Satisfying working relationships with peers and working in safe and pleasant surroundings promote positive attitudes toward work and authority. The culture of the school must value teamwork and team membership, and teamwork must be recognized and rewarded on both peer and leader levels.

Teams, like individuals, respond to extrinsic and intrinsic rewards. Teams need incentives to encourage them to perform, and these may include money, praise, achievement, social affiliation, professional challenge, or an outlet for creativity. Incentives serve as motivators that improve performance by making the task attractive, interesting, and rewarding (Hoy and Miskel, 1996). Motivation through incentives, however, largely depends on matching types of incentives with the individual's needs, values, and expectations. Mitchell, Ortiz, and Mitchell (1987) pointed out that incentive type is a major factor in motivating teachers to perform their responsibilities. Vroom (1964) and

Lawler (1973) relate that people work hardest on tasks for which they receive the greatest rewards. The reward system must be congruent with the culture and the overall management style of the leader. When principals really "know their teachers," (i.e., know what excites them both personally and profession-ally), they have the essential bridge that links incentives to needs and produces motivation. This "knowing" of teachers comes from daily communication and working with teachers in teams or through the process of providing individual assistance.

Intrinsic rewards are greater motivators than are extrinsic rewards. Intrinsic rewards strengthen confidence, enhance self-esteem, and promote morale. Sallis (1993) notes that intrinsic rewards include nonverbal behavior express-ing satisfaction or encouragement, letters or awards of recognition, peer recog-nition, and responsibility. Cohn and Kottkamp (1993) reported that student achievement was an intrinsic reward for teachers, whereas Wright (1985) found working in curriculum-related areas to be job satisfiers. Other intrinsic rewards include chairing team meetings or ad hoc committees, presenting reports to central office personnel or the board of education, and being recog-nized by the media or community organizations. Allowing teachers to assume more and different leadership roles in the school and the school system is an intrinsic reward that is currently gaining favor.

Extrinsic rewards, such as money, promotion, job assignments, committee appointments, and advancement, are important motivators for teachers. Money is a major factor for attracting and retaining teachers in school systems (Firestone and Bader, 1992) and is a dominant concern to teachers when salaries are low (Bok, 1993). Bok also noted that higher salaries contribute to teacher job longevity, job satisfaction, and morale when the opportunity for increased earnings exists. Johnson (1986) makes it clear that, although intrin-sic satisfiers are important, money does matter and salary structures in school systems should provide adequate extrinsic satisfaction. Johnson also observed that money motivates teachers to volunteer for responsibility, accept heavier work assignments, and accept more difficult tasks. Firestone and Bader (1992) and Weller (1996) note that teacher respect is higher for principals who pro-vide adequate compensation for extra duties and for those who do not "hide" behind the standard contract clause that requires teachers "to perform other assigned duties and responsibilities deemed necessary" by the principal.

Providing compensation time to teachers is not a new idea but is one that seems to be practiced rarely by school administrators. After interviewing over 200 teachers, the interviewers were provided with only a few examples of how principals awarded compensation time for engaged time outside the class-room, despite teachers' responses that compensation time would and did increase their morale and foster principal loyalty. Presented next are excerpts from principal interviews that asked the question, "How do you provide compensation time to teachers for work outside normal classroom instruction?" Methods for those principals providing compensation time varied; however, many principals did not award compensation time and these reasons are best reflected by the following comments:

> There is no way, in this school system, to award comp time. Period! It's not allowed by the board.

> Teachers sign a contract, they are professionals, and are expected to attend all outside events. If they have to stay late, come in early, so be it! It's their job.

> One principal focused on teacher morale in the context of providing compensation time. His reason was "I give no compensation time or money for rewards. Compensation time is counterproductive and lowers morale. I've seen it at the central office and it doesn't work."

Those principals who provide compensation time believe that the activity promotes teacher morale and they have different methods for rewarding teachers for time engaged outside classroom instruction. A sample of those methods used to award compensation time to teachers follows:

> "Mental health days" are provided for attending PTA meetings, working on committee assignments or chaperoning social or athletic events. Teachers record their time, submit the hours accrued to the principal, and can accumulate up to three days of leave.

> "Bank of hours" is a method whereby teachers submit the number of hours spent attending PTA meetings or other extracurricular events to the principal's secretary. Coupons are issued in fifty-minute modules and teachers can "draw" from their account for days off. Compensation time is also provided for teachers who have won local, state, or national awards and honors.

> Many principals allow teachers to come to school late or to leave early. Times range from thirty minutes to one hour. One principal allowed a maximum of ten early and ten late leaves, whereas other principals allowed five early and five late leaves for time spent attending after-school events or committee work.

> One principal allows teachers to work at their homes when working on committee assignments or writing grants and allows up to two days off for chaperoning social or athletic events and holding evening parent conferences. Another principal allows teachers two half-day personal leaves a year, taken separately, and ten early leaves from school. Some principals allow teachers to work during the summer to accrue time that can then be taken off during the academic year, whereas other principals allow teachers to plan at home during teacher planning days.

> Not all principals, however, interpret compensation time the same way. One principal related that if teachers wanted to leave early to attend graduate classes

during the academic year, they had to estimate the time they would be absent from school and "log-in that time during the summer." And one principal noted that "if teachers really need comp time, they can take their personal leave days." Finally, one principal who does not believe in awarding compensation time to teachers only does so as an "emergency exception." A community organized event, for example, scheduled five speakers in one evening at the school. Preregistration indicated very low attendance numbers in one of the sessions. Teachers who attended the session were awarded sixty minutes compensation time during the current grading period only.

Despite the positive effects of awarding teachers compensation time, many principals choose to place the "good" of the organization over the "good" of their teachers. These principals are good managers, enforcers of policy, and have yet to realize the benefits of donning the mantle of leadership.

Other extrinsic motivators include plaques, trips, gift certificates, recognition banquets, and paid attendance at conventions or workshops. These rewards must be personally valued and satisfying enough to motivate staff members to achieve the desired outcome. Principals should not provide extrinsic rewards that *they* value or find satisfying and assume that their teachers place equal value on the same rewards. Extrinsic rewards can be more beneficial as motivators when teachers have several choices within a reward system.

Pay for performance and merit pay are alternative pay arrangements that can be used for increased motivation and performance. The private sector has a history of using alternative compensation methods to increase performance and commitment through bonuses, profit sharing, and group and individual incentive plans. Elam, Rose, and Gallup (1991) noted that pay for performance was favored by the public, whereas the National Education Association believes the practice to be inappropriate.

Merit pay, a form of compensation, is money paid for quality performance outcomes. Pay can be added to the base salary or given as a bonus and is based on performance ratings by principals or supervisors. Malen, Murphy, and Hart (1988) argue for merit pay for team performance and teamwork and base some of their argument on goal and expectancy theories of motivation. Goal theory states that incentives motivate employees to set goals with defined expectations, and expectancy theory maintains that people are motivated to achieve personally desired incentives. In the final analysis, the old adage, "you get what you pay for," may be true.

Team rewards should not be an end objective but should be valued by individual members as a motivator. Lawler (1973) believes teams should determine their own rewards within a reward system developed by employees. Teachers who develop a reward system know their needs, values, and priorities better than principals, who are usually confined by traditional thinking or organizational priorities.

Managing Effective Meetings

Effective team performance is related to how well team meetings are planned and conducted. Team leaders are responsible for planning and conducting team meetings and for implementing the outcomes of the meeting. Efficient and productive meetings are well planned, have specific goals and set agendas, and have input from all team members regarding the goals of the meeting and agenda items to be addressed.

Reaching a common agreement on how meetings should be conducted promotes team productivity and reduces team member conflict. Consensus must be reached on team meeting procedures to increase the likelihood of commitment to task, goal achievement, and personal satisfaction. Common agreement should be reached on the following items to promote effective meetings:

(1) Placing a high priority on attendance and promptness. Well-planned and action-oriented meetings foster good attendance and promptness.

(2) Beginning and ending meetings on time. Do not reward lateness and punish promptness, and be considerate of others' schedules.

(3) Deciding on the frequency, time, and place of the meetings, and whether meetings should be open to others.

(4) Deciding how to handle issues concerning confidentiality and how to handle a breach in confidentiality.

(5) Deciding who should perform maintenance tasks. This includes naming a recorder, timekeeper, synthesizer, and team leader. Opinions vary, but when team leaders are appointed by the principal, some view this as an extension of the principal's presence, and they are hesitant to express opinions. Rotating leadership among committee members mitigates these concerns.

(6) Deciding how unresolved agenda items will be handled. Some teams assign these items to specific individuals, whereas others appoint ad hoc committees.

(7) Deciding whether total participation should be required. Each team member's views are important, and their perspectives are to be respected. After an initial response to each topic, however, members may choose to "pass" in the discussion.

(8) Deciding how absences will be handled. Absences often signify lack of commitment or interest. Absenteeism is contagious and may lead to the demise of the group.

(9) Deciding whether preparation for all meetings is expected. Each team member should be responsible for reading materials or completing assignments before the meeting. Lack of preparation indicates disinterest

and a lack of consideration for others and causes frustration and stress within the group.

(10) Identifying the goals of the team. Clearly stated goals provide focus and serve as an index for team progress and efficient use of time.

Planning for Effective Meetings

Planning for effective team meetings takes time and requires preparation, and the purpose of each meeting should be developed with input from team members. The following questions provide the basis for a well-planned meeting:

(1) Why should this meeting be conducted? The question focuses on the specific purpose for the meeting that should be of great interest to team members. An example of a focused purpose is, "How can we increase student test scores in reading and mathematics by the end of school?"

(2) What is the best way to communicate the purpose of the meeting? The purpose should be clearly stated in concise, simple language, and a team member can act as a sounding board for the purpose statement. How the purpose is introduced to the team is also important. Because purpose should serve as a motivator, introduction of the topic should create immediate interest. Using an overhead, videos, or other visual aides arouses quick interest.

(3) What are the desired outcomes of the meeting? Team members need to know, up front, what is expected of them when the meeting concludes. The results and purpose of the meeting are often intertwined, but the intended results of the meeting must be clearly stated.

DEVELOPING A MEETING AGENDA

Structured agendas set the tone for meetings. Prepared and distributed well in advance of each meeting, the agenda is an advanced organizer for productive and efficiently conducted meetings. Agendas should be short and logically sequenced, and the topics included for discussion should fit the allocated meeting time. An agenda model is presented in Figure 4.1.

As seen in Figure 4.1, the agenda presents the meeting topic, place, date, and time. The purpose of the meeting should be clear and presented to stimulate interest. Next, agenda items should be reviewed and time limits noted, if desirable. Old business and committee progress reports should be conducted before discussing agenda items. Decisions should be made by team members on how topics should be discussed (small groups, for example) and when meeting breaks should occur. Adequate time should be allowed for closure,

I.   Meeting topic
    a.   Meeting Place
    b.   Date
    c.   Time

II.   Purpose and expected results (introduce purpose in a way to stimulate member interest)

III.   Review agenda and note time limits for each topic

IV.   Old business (if applicable)

V.   Progress reports from team members (if applicable)

VI.   Agenda items (shorter items may be chosen first due to time constraints)
    a.   Decide on what group procedures to use to accomplish the purpose of the meeting
    b.   Decide when to take breaks and the length of the breaks

VII.   Closure
    a.   Team assignments
    b.   Summation
    c.   Dates, locations, and times of future meetings

FIGURE 4.1. Model of agenda for team meetings.

which includes team assignments; summary of accomplishments; and dates, times, and locations of subsequent meetings.

PROBLEM SOLVING AND DECISION MAKING

Problem Solving

Problems have historical antecedents and first need to be identified through facts. Causes of problems are often based on previous events and occur in the context of the existing environment and aura of their times. Katzenbach and Smith (1993) note that effective managers use *vertical loading,* teams of employees to solve problems. Frequently, team members are aware of the root causes of problems and can identify them quickly. This approach allows those closest to the problem to solve the problem. *Horizontal loading,* management-dominated problem solving, is more expeditious but less apt to identify root causes. Osburn, et al. (1990) identify three problem types. *Analytical problems* call for data, facts, and logical thinking; *problems that need creative solutions* call for brainstorming, imagination, and data to stimulate thought; and *judgmental problems* require intuition and policy in dealing with issues of morality, right or wrong, good or bad. Deciding which type problem exists helps team members focus more clearly on the issue and provides structure to the problem-solving process.

Problems represent a gap between an unsatisfactory current situation and a desired future state. Problem solving is a process used to proceed from the unsatisfactory to the desirable (Schmuck and Runkel, 1994). The "law of delineating factors" provides four questions to address when problems exist. These are "Where are we?", "Where do we want to be?", "How best can we get there?", and "How do we know when we get there?" Knowing where "we" are is knowing the facts of the current situation and requires objective agreement on the state of existing conditions. It requires open and honest discussion regarding the root causes of the problem. Determining where "we" want to be calls for team members to identify and agree on the ideal state to be achieved. This calls for brainstorming, imagination, and long-range vision. How "we" get to the ideal state is through the determination of the process necessary to proceed from the unsatisfactory current state to the desired future state. Schmuck and Runkel suggest generating alternative paths or plans to achieve the desired end state. Force field analysis, which calls for a listing of driving and restraining forces can help identify factors working for and against the desired state. Other quality problem-solving tools identified by Deming (1986) are brainstorming and the use of the affinity diagram and the fish bone or cause-and-effect diagram. These tools help identify root causes of the problem and the precise steps needed to reach the desired end state. When teams agree on the causes, they can identify the needed resources and personnel to achieve their goal. This translates into an *action* process whereby time schedules and workloads are assigned. (See Chapter 5, Figure 5.2 for a sample action plan format that can be used by teams when they reach this point in the problem-solving process.)

The end state, knowing when "we" get there, is determined through an evaluation and monitoring process. The plan and results matrix allows team members to look at the two-dimensional outcomes of their problem-solving efforts. That is, was the problem-solving plan accomplished? Was the end state achieved? By identifying the causes, the personnel responsible for tasks and the solution steps needed to reach the end state, a three-way matrix is developed to monitor and evaluate the team's progress. (A complete list of the quality tools can be found in Nancy R. Tague's, *The Quality Toolbox.*)

An overarching model for team problem solving that incorporates the steps presented above is Deming's Plan, Do, Check, Act cycle. The model calls for *planning* how to solve a problem, *doing* or carrying out the problem-solving process, *checking* or monitoring the activities through data sources, and *acting* or deciding whether the goal was or was not attained. If the end state was not attained, the cyclical model allows for incorporating the results from the past into a newly developed plan. Figure 4.2 presents the Plan, Do, Check, Act cycle.

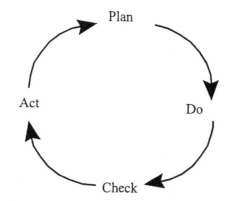

FIGURE 4.2. Plan, Do, Check, Act cycle for problem solving.

Decision Making

Effective decision making is essential to the success of an organization. Decision making has been called the "heart" of executive activity and the one "generic" expectation of an administrator (Duncan, 1989). School reform places emphasis on shared governance, with teacher teams having a major say in formulating school policy. Duncan notes that those inexperienced at making decisions rely on intuition and personal experiences to reach conclusions. Effective decisions come from analytical thought and logic and dominate the intuition and experience factors.

Early decision-making models emphasized top-down decisions by administrators and the use of logical, sequential steps to arrive at solutions. This *rational* or *nominative* prescriptive model reinforced the scientific management and bueaucratic theories emphasizing hierarchical control (Kepner and Tregore, 1976). *Participatory* or *site-based* decision-making models are more contemporary and reflect the democratic process. Shared decision making emphasizes choosing rationally through collective agreement based on the common values and beliefs of the decision makers. Firestone and Wilson (1985) relate that participatory decision making may have negative effects for principals. First, the administrator has limited control over the educational outcomes of the school. Second, decisions may be influenced by personalities, values, and personal experiences rather than by intellect or reason. Principals are also likely to view problems as cultural rather than as administrative. Hoy and Miskel (1996) relate that the benefits of shared decision making are not highly touted by all in the research literature, but that shared decision making has high potential for effecting lasting reform in educational practice.

Strategic decision making, a third model, is nested within the competing interests for resources, power, or authority. Decisions made by administrators in this model are based on an analysis of internal and external pressures and demands (Wirt and Kirst, 1982). Many nonrational decisions are made because competing interests and influences affect the decision-making process. This *differentiated* decision-making model holds that decisions result from unexpected variables (such as events, ethical considerations, and behavior) that cause chaos and limit decision choices (Peters, 1987). The model also implies that the organizational environment is replete with ambiguity and uncertainty and that decisions made to move the organization toward effectiveness will reflect this.

The *step model* for decision making is presented in Figure 4.3. Whether decisions are made by administrators or by empowered teams is determined by the generic steps involved in decision making. This eight-step decision-making process promotes more effective outcomes, more efficient use of time, and greater subordinate satisfaction

This decision-making model begins with the need for action, the need to

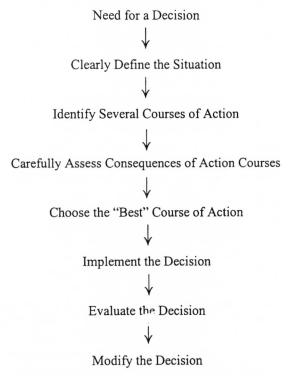

FIGURE 4.3. Generic eight-step decision-making model.

make a decision. Clearly defining the situation through facts and data allows for problem analysis and objective focus on the situation. Understanding the problem fully is essential to effective decision making. Identifying alternative courses of action is the third step, and several (three or more) possible courses of action should be generated. A careful assessment of the consequences of selected courses of action is essential. However, the action that is taken is based on assumptions made at the time of the decision, and unanticipated environmental influences cannot be taken into account. Assumptions made must be realistic and logical and based on known or projected data. Anticipating the result of the decision is based on feasibility and the resulting impact on those affected by the decision. Choosing the "best" course of action is the fifth step and should be done without personal bias and with adequate resources and authority to carry the decision to conclusion. The effect on the target population is another factor to consider. Does the population have the knowledge or skills necessary to implement the decision? Will the decision be satisfactory or unsatisfactory to those who are affected? Unpopular decisions will lack support and commitment and cause environmental stress and tension among employees. Team decision making provides a good index on how target populations will react to the decision and team members can generate ideas for increasing its popularity. There is no course of action that is ideal or will meet with complete acceptance and satisfaction. Sometimes selecting "the path of least resistance" is the best decision choice.

Implementing the decision is the next step, and this is easier when those affected have been consulted first. The perception of whether the person(s) who makes the decision has the authority and the power to do so also influences whether or not the decision will be accepted. Perceptions of affected individuals will vary on the principal's or team's "right" to make decisions regarding certain topics. When the decision is sufficiently unpopular with the targeted population, decision modification can take place, the administrator can attempt to change perceptions, or the principal can enforce the decision, regardless of its popularity. Evaluating the decision will determine how well the desired or anticipated outcomes of the decisions were achieved. Formative and summative evaluation techniques should then be used to assess the effect, both positive and negative, of the decision.

Finally, modifying a decision is an option and should be undertaken when enough negative attitudes trigger stress and tension among employees. Decision dissatisfaction may result from a belief that the decision was poor, that the decision reflected personal bias, that the decision was premature or based on incorrect information, or that the decision caused greater harm than good. When faced with sufficient dissatisfaction, principals should attempt to get at the root cause of the discontentment through open and honest dialogue with those expressing dissatisfaction. Several reasons may develop for teacher discontentment, and if these causes cannot be overcome, modifying or withdrawing the decision may be the best course of action.

Weller and Hartley (1994) note that effective teams in TQM schools make higher quality decisions (more efficient use of time and greater teacher satisfaction) when principals provide training to teachers in three essential skills before initiating shared governance. These skills are conflict resolution, group dynamics, and the TQM tools and techniques for solving problems and making decisions. Expecting teachers to produce quality outcomes without training is analogous to expecting students to work well in cooperative groups without instruction from the teacher on how to do so. Conflict management will be presented in Chapter 9. The remainder of this chapter deals with group dynamics and the use of problem-solving and decision-making tools and techniques.

GROUP DYNAMICS: DECISION MAKING THROUGH CONSENSUS

Consensus can be defined as "a collective opinion arrived at by a group of individuals working together under conditions that permit communication to be sufficiently open—and the group climate to be sufficiently supportive—for everyone in the group to feel that he has had his fair chance to influence the decision" (Johnson and Johnson, 1982, p. 106). Decision making through consensus is the method used to achieve unified commitment and joint ownership. "Decision by majority vote" is a common method for making decisions, but such a method does not ensure group commitment and ownership. "Decision by experts" lacks unified agreement as to what qualifications fulfill the criteria to be an expert. "Decision by authority" is also open to criticism. Most often organization-centered decision by authority brings about individual compliance, but not voluntary commitment, through fear of retribution.

Consensus is a unified, jointly agreed upon outcome that all can support and "live with." Consensus does not signify total agreement, nor does it suggest the conclusion of an "ideal" arrangement. An ideal solution suggests that each group member's solution is incorporated into the final, agreed-upon outcome. Consensus is, however, the next best thing—the best solution to which all members can commit to *at the time.*

For teams to reach consensus, the following conditions must exist among team members:

(1) Trust and honesty among members to speak openly and freely, with directness and candor and no hidden agenda. Apathy and fear will negate reaching consensus.

(2) Respect for the opinions of others and the appreciation for divergent points of view. Tolerance of diversity and creativity in thought are essential.

(3) Freedom to reach solutions that may go against the opinions and wishes of the leader or administration. Solutions that are made to appease the leader indicate fear and lack of trust and honesty in the group.

Leaders or team facilitators have specific roles to play in fostering consensus building.

(1) Making sure each individual has the opportunity to express opinions frequently, free from the criticism of others.
(2) Encouraging all members to listen actively to one another's point of view without bias and looking for the *positive* points presented in the proposal. Focusing on negative points only leads to criticism, delay, and frustration and may negate the reaching of consensus.
(3) Discussing the underlying assumption of opinions and exploring alternative courses of action.
(4) Encouraging logical, data-based opinions that are free from emotional appeals.
(5) Resolving conflict and not resorting to majority rule in making decisions over impasses in order to arrive at a quick solution. Disagreement is healthy and improves the perspective of team members and the quality of the solution.
(6) Avoiding quick solutions. Members of teams often seek quick solutions to disband or to provide immediate relief after lengthy discussion. Emotional excitement often results in hastily developed solutions that address symptoms and not causes.

Knowledge of group development theory is essential to building consensus among team members. All teams progress through similar stages of development to make decisions and achieve goals. Tuckman's (1965) model describes group development resulting from *forming, storming, norming,* and *performing,* a process that takes the group from immature to mature status. Tuckman's four stage model follows:

Stage 1: Forming. Cautious affiliation to the team exists. Members explore and test relationships, whereas some seek disaffiliation. Some question the mission of the team and the ability of its membership to achieve team goals. Many assess others' abilities and attitudes to see how they fit in with the group and its goals. Roles are assessed and tentative partnerships are formed as members seek alliances and look for potential conflict. Those seeking leadership roles seek alliances to provide direction and purpose. Productivity is minimal as relationships are tentative and guarded and members are cautious about sharing their ideas and feelings.

Stage 2: Storming. Competitive and tenuous relationships exist. Conflict with others surface with blame, defensiveness, and disagreements over team goals and the commitment of others. Leaders of sub-groups enter into confrontation to test their following and influence. Alliances begin to switch as ideas and feelings are more easily expressed. Members think in the "I" mode and relate personal experiences, beliefs, and needs. Wasting time is a concern, goals begin to be clarified, and the task becomes more difficult than originally perceived. Performance expectations develop, the group begins to think in terms of "we," and a leader emerges through conflict and consensus. Leaders emerge through alliances formed from knowledge, skills, and other personal attributes the membership finds as essential qualifications to achieve team goals.

Stage 3: Norming. Cohesiveness and harmony solidify. Major conflicts are resolved and members begin to focus on team goals by setting aside personal bias. Roles are identified within the group and respect develops for individual rights and differences. Trust is strengthened and opinions are more freely expressed. The idea of a team develops with "We" being emphasized over "I." Cooperation is emphasized, and areas that trigger interpersonal conflict are avoided as much as possible. Work progresses more rapidly as friendships develop, and a more tranquil atmosphere comes into being.

Stage 4: Performing. Committed teamwork exists. Work dominates team activities as members function as a committed, cohesive, goal-oriented team. Tasks are assigned, resources are allocated, and time becomes an important factor. Members speak freely about their concerns, divergent opinions are welcomed, and the goals of the team are continuously stressed. Leadership is acquired by others as they volunteer for assignments or work independently. Members take pride in their work, are motivated by peer recognition, and receive personal satisfaction from their accomplishments.

Mature teams are high-performing teams wherein group members pride themselves on joint ownership of their achievements. Varney (1991) notes that the performing stage is where real collaboration arises through a cooperative and productive team climate. Communication is open, relevant, and businesslike, and productivity is mainly a part of understanding others' strengths and weaknesses which calls for others to rally in support.

QUALITY TOOLS FOR SOLVING PROBLEMS AND MAKING DECISIONS

The use of TQM tools to solve team problems and to make decisions leads to more effective outcomes and efficient use of time, resources, and personnel (Weller, 1995, 1996; Weller and Hartley, 1994; West-Burnham, 1993). A discussion of the more common and effective TQM tools follows.

Benchmarking is an investigative process whereby team members make on-site visits to other similar organizations to observe and discuss problems regarding "best-in-class" programs. This process negates "reinventing the wheel" and leads to quality products and services more quickly and efficiently (Juran, 1979). Benchmarking allows team members to observe the gap between where they are and where they want to be. This comparative analysis approach to quality improvement can allow teams to enter the norming and performing stages of team conflict without going through much of the indecision and confusion associated with these stages.

The following steps are necessary for effective benchmarking outcomes:

(1) Carefully reviewing the problem or determining the desired process needed for improvement and basing this analysis on data—a review of the literature and careful analysis of one's own situation
(2) Identifying "best-in-class"
(3) Making on-site assessments of their mistakes and successes in their improvement process
(4) Analyzing their process carefully while asking, "Can we adopt this process to fit our situation?"
(5) Planning for and then implementing the process
(6) Continuously evaluating the outcomes and then modifying the process based on the specific outcomes

Teachers and principals investigating school restructuring models find benchmarking an invaluable tool. Weller and Hartley (1994) note that many educators using TQM to restructure their schools begin with benchmarking. The strongest persuasive information, they maintain, comes from teacher-to-teacher and principal-to-principal conversations. Nothing, they add, has more credence than open and honest discussion among professional peers.

Brainstorming is another TQM tool and is used to generate creative ideas. Brainstorming can be used to identify and solve problems and calls for divergent and creative thinking. Practical people, seeking only practical solutions, can inhibit creativity within the team and the desired outcomes of brainstorming. Those who seek the "right answer" often wish to follow logic and avoid ambiguity, or they fear bending the rules. This also inhibits creative thinking.

Several types of brainstorming models exist; however, three models are the most popular. *Random brainstorming* calls for rapid-fire ideas from any group member, with no set order for participation. *Formal or structured brainstorming* calls for written or verbal responses, with each member having several turns to share their ideas. *Reverse brainstorming* can be random or structured, with participants focusing on reasons as to why something may or will go wrong—this is most beneficial once a solution is agreed upon. In any brainstorming session, leaders must emphasize that no idea is too far out and that criticism of any kind—verbal or facial expression—will not be tolerated. The structured brainstorming process has the following rules:

(1) All members verbally express their ideas, one at a time, until no more ideas are generated (write ideas down on a flip chart, eliminate duplicate ideas, and stress quantity of ideas).
(2) Do not explain the idea or try to sell it (this comes later).
(3) Each person proposes an idea now and explains the idea, free from criticism, for clarification (no comments are allowed from participants).
(4) When all ideas are presented, participants individually rank order the ideas on paper.
(5) The group now discusses the ideas with comments and criticisms.
(6) Members again individually rank order the top three ideas on paper and provide their reasons for supporting each idea.
(7) Members discuss the ideas openly until a *consensus* is reached.
(8) Members identify one idea that will be used to solve the problem and another as the alternative solution.

Force field analysis is a perception and a data-oriented technique developed by Kurt Lewin (1951), which identifies forces that promote or restrict change or problem solving. Change, the outcome of a struggle between change forces and current forces, is an attempt to upset the status quo. When driving forces are stronger than resisting forces, change will occur. When resisting forces are equal to or stronger than driving forces, no movement will occur. Leaders can conduct a force field analysis by doing the following:

(1) Circulate copies of a force field diagram and post a large copy of the diagram on a wall overhead.
(2) Ask team members to individually write driving and restraining forces (rank order is not important) related to the proposed change or problem.
(3) Ask team members to share their driving and restraining forces on wall charts or overhead (duplicates are discarded).
(4) Use brainstorming to refine driving and restraining forces.

(5) Prioritize driving and restraining forces through consensus, and place them on a master diagram.

(6) Develp action plans to reduce resisting forces through the application of Deming's Plan, Do, Check, Act cycle (1986).

Figure 4.4 presents an example of a force field diagram. The diagram lists driving and restraining forces for effective and efficient team productivity.

Cause-and-effect or fish bone diagrams (sometimes called an Ishikowa diagram) help teams identify relationships between causes and effects within problem areas. The problem is the *effect* or "head" of the fish, with the *causes* of the problem being frustration, goal ambiguity, or root causes of problems. Fish bone diagrams present the various causes affecting the process by identifying the relating causes. Each diagram usually has four major categories that are referred to as the 4P's: *people, procedures, policies,* and *practices.* However, any major category can be used to stimulate thinking to get at the causes. The following procedures are used to generate root causes for an effect:

(1) Members agree on the problem and clearly state the problem on a wall chart or overhead within a box.

(2) Members agree on the categories to be used and place the categories in boxes, above and below the "spine" of the fish, and then extend branching lines from the spine to each category. The spine ends at the "head" of the fish, which contains the investigative topic.

(3) Members brainstorm causes for the problem, with the leader asking questions such as "What causes this?", "Why does this condition exist?", and "Why does this happen?" "Why" questions are asked until the group reaches consensus on the root causes of the problem.

EFFECTIVE AND EFFICIENT WORK TEAMS

DRIVING/FACILITATING FORCES	GOAL/PROBLEM	RESTRAINING FORCES
1. Clear goals/mission →		← Vague goals, no mission
2. Open, honest communication →		← Attack personalities, distrust others
3. Active participation →		← Avoid discussion, withdraw psychologically, close-minded
4. Listening to understand →		← Dominate discussions, engage in sub-conversations
5. Cooperative, committed, optimistic →		← Manipulative, sarcastic, negative
6. Clearly defined roles →		← Unclear roles, question competence of others
7. Work distributed evenly →		← Unequal distribution of work load

FIGURE 4.4. Force field diagram to promote effective and efficient teamwork.

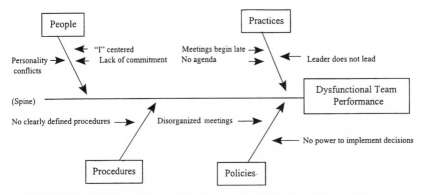

FIGURE 4.5. Fish bone diagram of root causes for dysfunctional team performance.

(4) The team develops plans of action to solve the problem.

Figure 4.5 presents a fish bone diagram relating major causes for dysfunctional team performance.

The affinity diagram is best used when there are many complex facts or thoughts or when problems call for high levels of creativity. The affinity diagram is helpful after a brainstorming exercise to allow the team to become more focused in their thinking about the problem. Affinity diagrams allow for silent and personal reflection and more privacy than brainstorming. The following process is to be followed:

(1) Have team members silently record each idea on a 3 × 5 note card.

(2) Collect all cards and randomly spread cards on a large table for all to see.

(3) Each person, in turn and silently, looks for ideas that are related in some way and groups the idea cards together.

(4) When each person has had a chance, the process is repeated. "Loner" cards will exist and should be saved. If an idea card belongs to two groups, make another card. When idea cards are grouped for the second time, team members can make comments on the ideas and how they should be arranged and suggest broad headings for idea card groupings.

(5) Loner cards are discussed and either discarded or placed in a group.

(6) Action plans are developed through consensus.

EVALUATING TEAM PERFORMANCE

Warning Signals of Team Trouble

Effective teams make effective decisions by working cooperatively together with shared commitment, mutual trust, open and honest communication, and dedication to team goals. Parker (1990) provides early warning signals of team problems.

(1) Members have difficulty defining the goals of the team.

(2) Meetings become increasingly formal and tense.

(3) Minimal accomplishments exist.

(4) There is much nonproductive talk and little communication among team members.

(5) Disagreements are aired privately after meetings.

(6) The formal leader begins to make all the decisions.

(7) Members are confused as to what their roles and work assignments are.

(8) Members are frequently late or tardy for meetings, and dissatisfaction is expressed with meeting times and/or agenda topics.

(9) Members do not assess their progress toward goal achievement.

Low performing or nonproductive teams develop gradually over time and have early indicators of trouble that are not readily detected through observation. A team effectiveness inventory is presented in Figure 4.6 that can be used to determine team maturity and cohesiveness. The inventory can be used to assess both individual and group performance indicators. The assessment

TEAM EFFECTIVENESS INVENTORY

Almost Never			Almost Always				Almost Never			Almost Always		
1	2	3	4	5	6		1	2	3	4	5	6
SELF			**COMMUNICATION**									**TEAM**
___ 1.		I/We use open and honest communications.										___
___ 2.		I/We actively listen to each other.										___
___ 3.		I/We hesitate to share our feelings.										___
___ 4.		I/We feel comfortable in giving feedback to each other.										___
___ 5.		I/We are willing to interpret and clarify for others.										___
___ 6.		I/We feel uncomfortable in expressing what we think for fear of criticism or reprisals.										___
___ 7.		I/We feel uncomfortable in supporting decisions based on intuition and/or personal experiences.										___
___ 8.		I/We feel certain topics cannot be discussed because they cause resentment or inhibit dialogue.										___
___ 9.		I/We feel some members dominate team conversations.										___
___ 10.		I/We feel comfortable in presenting different perspectives.										___

FIGURE 4.6. Team effectiveness inventory.

SELF	CONFLICT	TEAM
_____ 1.	I/We pretend conflict does not exist.	_____
_____ 2.	I/We try to stop conflict before it surfaces.	_____
_____ 3.	I/We let others have their own way to avoid conflict.	_____
_____ 4.	I/We do not recognize the early signs of conflict.	_____
_____ 5.	I/We feel that our attempts to solve conflict are unsuccessful.	_____
_____ 6.	I/We feel that conflict is resolved in timely and productive ways.	_____

SELF	INDIVIDUAL ABILITIES	TEAM
_____ 1.	I/We do all the work.	_____
_____ 2.	I/We feel some team members are selected to do more work than others.	_____
_____ 3.	I/We feel the leader plays favorites among team members.	_____
_____ 4.	I/We feel our personal strengths are best used in team assignments.	_____
_____ 5.	I/We feel that more leadership should be shared among team members.	_____
_____ 6.	I/We feel the leader provides time to express opinions and ideas.	_____
_____ 7.	I/We feel the leader recognizes members for their effort and accomplishments.	_____

SELF	COMMITMENT TO GOALS	TEAM
_____ 1.	I/We feel addressing personal interests comes before addressing team goals.	_____
_____ 2.	I/We feel a personal commitment to achieving team goals.	_____
_____ 3.	I/We feel motivated in achieving team goals.	_____
_____ 4.	I/We understand the goals of the team.	_____
_____ 5.	I/We feel team members support each other in achieving team goals.	_____

SELF	TEAM MEETINGS	TEAM
_____ 1.	I/We feel meetings start and end on time.	_____
_____ 2.	I/We feel meetings are organized.	_____
_____ 3.	I/We feel meetings have specific goals or objectives to achieve.	_____
_____ 4.	I/We feel meetings are productive and personally satisfying.	_____
_____ 5.	I/We feel the leader conducts meetings in an orderly and efficient manner.	_____
_____ 6.	I/We feel the leader manages conflict effectively.	_____
_____ 7.	I/We feel the agenda is followed and items are fully discussed.	_____
_____ 8.	I/We feel the leader monitors unacceptable behavior and addresses these behaviors in an appropriate and timely manner.	_____

FIGURE 4.6. (continued) Team effectiveness inventory.

inventory should be circulated when the leader senses or detects signals of team trouble and at the conclusion of a team project. Stem items are placed in the middle of the inventory with self- and team-assessment scales on either side of each stem item. Using an even-number response scale "forces" respondents to choose a position on the scale other than a midpoint, such as three on a one to five scale, which can be interpreted as a "safe" response and which provides ambiguous data for interpretation.

The team effectiveness inventory can be scored by either the leader or the team members. Results should be shared and openly discussed to develop immediate solutions for areas causing dissatisfaction. The open discussion of the team scores will do much to bring problems into the open where they can be dealt with by the team.

ADULT LEARNING AND TEAMS

Adult learners are more self-directed and less dependent than children and are challenged by planning and coordinating their own learning activities (Levinson, 1978; Sheehy, 1976). Adult learners enjoy taking responsibility for shaping their own learning experiences, and they enjoy the risk taking that is often involved in gaining new knowledge and skills. Adults also have previous knowledge and experiences and draw on this background to increase self-confidence and self-worth. Learning is more self-motivated when it is deemed personally important to their social or professional lives. Immediate and direct application is essential to sustain motivation and interest. Learning that helps adults perform their job functions better is deemed important and satisfying.

Learning environments for adults need to be informal and action oriented. Adults learn quickly, and rapid pacing stimulates interest and attention. Lectures and long periods of noninvolvement often create a lack of interest, whereas demonstrations and case studies trigger interest and attention. Direct and immediate feedback regarding learning mastery is essential, and any remediation in learning should be done quickly through activities that are different from the original stimulus.

Adult development stages also influence adult learning. Cross (1981) notes that those who are eighteen to twenty-two years of age focus on adventure, and autonomy is a major concern. Adults between twenty-two and twenty-eight years old look for new friendships, are more mature, begin to contemplate marriage, and begin to explore different careers or contemplate career goals. From twenty-nine through thirty-four years of age, job stability is desired, mentors are sought for guidance, singles often marry, separation and divorce occur, and long-range security becomes important. Here, being successful takes on major importance, and teachers may experience conflict between leaving the profession and job security. Between thirty-nine and forty-two years of age, promotions become very important and mortality confronts them. Dependent ties with the boss and spouse are reduced as reassessment of personal priorities, values, and marriage takes place. The time to change is "running out." Between ages forty-three and fifty-five careers peak, and they serve as mentors to others. Community involvement is high as children leave home. New hobbies and interests emerge and self-satisfaction and lifestyle enjoyment begins. This is the age for greatest job productivity for teachers and administrators remaining in their career field. From ages fifty-six to sixty-three, retirement preparation is a major concern. Health problems surface and goals to be fulfilled consume effort and planning. Spouses and friendships become important as do sharing joys and sorrows.

Designing Adult Learning Experiences

Designing effective learning experiences for teachers requires the application of how adults learn best and the characteristics of adult life stages. Teachers need autonomy to plan and design their own learning experiences and the type of learning activities desirable for learning. Teachers of all ages need challenges and a sense of autonomy over their own professional lives. Empowered teams, says Castello (1992), provide autonomy and challenge for teachers and allow teachers the freedom to exercise creativity and initiative while reaping personal and professional satisfaction. Planning for self-learning or for school staff development provides career teachers with the benefits sought by adult learners.

Career teachers, those over age forty, have their time and priorities well planned. They do not want to waste time in meetings, are not highly receptive to new ideas or innovations, view nurturing positively, and seek satisfaction from professional achievements. They may feel that working with younger teachers is satisfying, but that achieving personal and professional goals are more important (Krupp, 1983).

A summary of the findings of Dalellew and Montinez (1988) regarding characteristics about adult learners is presented in the following:

(1) *Motivation.* Internal, not external motivators, promote adult learning. Forcing training may cause animosity.

(2) *Self-learner.* Adults are self-directed learners and gain satisfaction from choosing how and what they learn. Learning for learning's sake is secondary to job enrichment learning.

(3) *Immediate gratification.* Adults want to apply new knowledge and skills immediately and enjoy success in their own work environment.

(4) *Experience.* Adults have many life experiences and their perceptions, val-

ues, and beliefs are rigid. Change is slow and must represent "something better" that coincides with their own views of reality.

REFERENCES

Bok, D. 1993. *The Cost of Talent.* New York: The Free Press.

Castello, R. T. 1992. *School Personnel Administrator: A Practitioner's Guide.* Boston: Allyn and Bacon.

Cohn, M. M. and R. B. Kottkamp. 1993. *Teachers: The Missing Voice in Education.* Albany, N.Y.: State University of New York Press.

Conley, D. T. 1993. *Road Map to Restructuring: Policies, Practices, and the Emerging Visions of Schooling.* Eugene, OR: ERIC Clearinghouse on Educational Management.

Covey, S. R. 1992. *Principle-Centered Leadership.* New York: Fireside.

Csikentmihalyi, M. 1990. *Flow: The Psychology of Optimal Experience.* New York: Harper & Row.

Cross, P. 1981. *Adults as Learners.* San Francisco: Jossey-Bass.

Dalellew, T. and Y. Montinez. 1988. "A Search for the Meaning of Staff Development," *Journal of Staff Development,* 9(3):28–31.

Deming, W. E. 1993. *The New Economics for Industry, Government, and Education.* Cambridge, MA: MIT Press.

Deming, W. E. 1986. *Out of the Crisis.* Cambridge, MA: MIT Press.

Duncan, W. J. 1989. *Great Ideas in Management.* San Francisco: Jossey-Bass.

Elam, S. M., L. E. Rose, and A. M. Gallup. 1991. "The 23rd Annual Gallup Poll of the Public's Attitudes Toward the Public Schools," *Phi Delta Kappan,* 73(1):41–56.

English, F. W. 1994. *Theory in Educational Administration.* New York: Harper Collins.

English, F. W. 1992. *Educational Administration: The Human Science.* New York: Harper Collins.

Firestone, W. A. and B. D. Bader. 1992. *Redesigning Teaching: Professionalism or Bureaucracy.* Albany, NY: State University of New York Press.

Firestone, W. A. and B. L. Wilson. 1985. "Using Bureaucratic and Cultural Linkages to Improve Instruction: The Principal's Contribution" *Educational Administration Quarterly,* 21:7–30.

Gardner, J. W. 1990. *On Leadership.* New York: The Free Press.

Getzels, J. W. and E. G. Guba. 1957. "Social Behavior and the Administrative Process,". *The School Review,* 65(4):423–441.

Glasser, W. 1990. *The Quality School.* New York: Harper and Row.

Handy, C. 1990. *Inside Organizations: 21 Ideas for Managers.* London, England: British Broadcasting Company Books.

Hoy, W. K. and C. G. Miskel. 1996. "Educational Administration: Theory, research, and practice." Fifth edition. New York: McGraw-Hill.

Johnson, D. W. and F. P. Johnson. 1982. *Joining Together.* Englewood Cliffs, NJ: Prentice Hall.

Johnson, S. M. 1986. "Incentives for Teachers: What Motivates, What Matters." *Educational Administration Quarterly,* 22:54–79.

Juran, J. M. 1979. *Quality Control Handbook.* New York: McGraw-Hill.

Katzenbach, J. R. and D. K. Smith. 1993. *The Wisdom of Teams: Creating the High Performance Organization.* Boston: Harvard Business School Press.

Kepner, C. H. and B. B. Tregore. 1976. *The Rational Manager.* New York: McGraw-Hill.

Kohn, A. 1986. *No contest: The Case against Competition.* Boston: Houghton Mifflin.

Krupp, J. A. 1983. "Sparking an Aging Staff through Increased Awareness of Adult Developmental Changes." *School Administrators Association of New York Journal,* 10:9–13.

Lawler, E. 1973. *Motivation in Work Organizations.* Monterey, CA: Brooks/Cole Publishers.

Lefton, R. E., V. R. Buzzotta, and M. Sherberg. 1980. *Improving Productivity through People Skills.* Cambridge, MA: Ballinger.

Levinson, D. J. 1978. *The Season's of a Man's Life.* New York: Knopf.

Lewin, K. 1951. *Field Theory in Social Sciences.* New York: Harper and Row.

Lunenburg, F. C. and A. C. Ornstein. 1996. *Educational Administration: Concepts and Practices.* Belmont, CA: Wadsworth Publishing.

Malen, B., M. J. Murphy, and A. W. Hart. 1988. "Restructuring Teacher Compensation Systems: An Analysis of Three Incentive Strategies," in K. Alexander and D. H. Monk, eds. 91–142. *Eighth Annual Yearbook of the American Educational Finance Association.* Cambridge, MA: Ballinger.

Mitchell, D. E., F. I. Ortiz, and T. K. Mitchell. 1987. *Work Orientation and Job Performance: The Cultural Bias of Teaching Rewards and Incentives.* Albany, NY: State University of New York Press.

Osburn, S. D., L. Moran, E. Musselwhite, and J. Zenger. 1990. *Self-Directed Work Teams: The New American Challenge.* Homewood, IL: Business One Irwin.

Owens, R. G. 1995. *Organizational Behavior in Education.* Fifth edition. Boston: Allyn and Bacon.

Parker, G. M. 1990. *Team Players and Teamwork.* San Francisco: Jossey-Bass.

Peters, T. 1987. *Thriving on Chaos: Handbook for a Management Revolution.* New York: Knopf.

Sagor, R. and B. G. Barnett. 1994. *The TQE principal: A Transformed Leader* (Vol. 4). Thousand Oaks, CA: Corwin Press.

Sagor, R. 1992. "Three Principals Who Make a Difference," *Educational Leadership,* 49(6):13–18.

Sallis, E. 1993. *Total Quality Management in Education.* Philadelphia, PA: Kogan Page.

Schmuck, R. A. and P. J. Runkel. 1994. *The Handbook of Organizational Development in Schools and Colleges.* Fourth edition. Prospect Heights, IL: Waveland Press.

Schenkat, R. 1993. *Quality Connections: Transforming Schools Through Total Quality Management.* Alexandria, VA: Association for Supervision and Curriculum Development.

Schermerhorn, J. R., J. G. Hunt, and R. N. Osborn. 1994. *Managing Organizational Behavior.* New York: Wiley.

Schmoker, M. J. and R. B. Wilson. 1993. *Total Quality Education: Profiles of Schools that Demonstrate the Power of Deming's Management Principles.* Bloomington, IN: Phi Delta Kappa.

Sheehy, G. 1976. *Passages: Predictable Crises of Adult Life.* New York: Dutton.

Sohol, A. and M. Morrison. 1995. "Is There a Link—Total Quality Management and Learning Organizations?" *The TQM Magazine,* 3(2):41–44.

Swift, J. A., J. E. Ross, and V. K. Omachonu 1998. *Principals of Total Quality.* Second edition. Boca Raton: St. Lucie Press.

Tracy, D. 1990. *The Power Pyramid: How to Get Power by Giving it Away.* New York: Morrow.

Varney, G. H. 1991. *Building Productive Teams: An Action Guide and Resource Book.* San Francisco, CA: Jossey-Bass.

Vroom, V. H. 1964. *Work and Motivation.* New York: Wiley.

Weller, L. D. and S. J. Weller. 1997. "Quality Learning Organizations and Continuous Improvement: Implementing the Concept," *National Association of Secondary School Principals Bulletin,* 81(591):62–70.

Weller, L. D. 1996. "The Next Generation of School Reform," *Quality Progress,* 29(10):65–70.

Weller, L. D. 1995. "Quality Teams: Problems, Causes, Solutions," *The TQM Magazine,* 7(3):45–49.

Weller, L. D., S. H. Hartley, and C. L. Brown. 1994. "Principals and TQM: Developing Vision," *The Clearing House,* 67(5):298–301.

Weller, L. D. and S. H. Hartley. 1994. "Teamwork and Cooperative Learning: An Educational Perspective for Business," *Quality Management Journal,* 1(4):30–41.

West-Burnham, J. 1993. *Managing Quality in Schools.* Harlow, Essex: Longman Group U.K., Ltd.

Wirt, F. M. and M. W. Kirst. 1982. *Schools in conflict.* Berkeley, CA: McCutchan.

Wright, R. 1985. "Motivating Teacher Involvement in Professional Growth Activities," *Canadian Administrator,* 24:1–6.

CHAPTER 5

Staff Development: Maximizing Human Potential through Continuous Improvement

Maximizing human potential, a major goal of effective learning organizations, is best accomplished by principals through structured, systematic designs targeted to develop individual skills and knowledge. This chapter addresses the importance of designing systematic, comprehensive staff development that is responsive to teacher needs. Principals in high-performing schools know that change is constant and that responding rapidly to innovations and demanding environmental pressures is essential to promoting excellence. Adopting the quality management tenet of continuous improvement provides the nucleus for effective and practical staff development programs.

PROVIDING FOR CONTINUOUS IMPROVEMENT THROUGH STAFF DEVELOPMENT

Effective principals realize that the selection and orientation stages of hiring new staff represent only the beginning of the employment phase and that these stages do not address the need for maximizing the potential of each individual teacher. It is only when human potential is maximized that educational excellence can be achieved. The cultivation of individual potential is the primary responsibility of the principal and is best accomplished through staff development programs at the school level.

Effective staff-development programs have essential components that include a professional and personal commitment from the principal to develop structured, systematic staff development programs that are centered on and designed by teachers and the allocation of resources to adequately support these programs. In these programs, teachers identify their professional needs and are responsible for helping to plan and coordinate their own professional

115

development activities. Because these programs are teacher designed, the activities are personally meaningful and professionally rewarding.

Evaluating the effectiveness of staff-development programs is essential to judging their impact and participant satisfaction. Both summative and formative evaluation methods are used to assess staff development effectiveness, and they provide the basis for the continuous improvement of teaching and the instructional process.

PROCESS MANAGEMENT: DESIGNING QUALITY PROGRAMS

Process management, a highly effective method used in business to promote efficiency and effectiveness, is being instituted in quality-conscious schools by quality-oriented principals. Process management is a systems thinking approach to leadership that calls for an improvement program that is planned, coordinated, and evaluated through the synergistic efforts of management and labor (Swift, Ross, and Omachonu, 1998).

As shown in Figure 5.1, process design begins with the leader's commitment to improving existing conditions through the synergistic model of leader or member problem-solving and decision-making teams. Improvement planning begins with conceptualizing, generating improvement ideas through quality tools such as brainstorming, force field analysis, and cause-and-effect diagrams. The design of the improvement process is a comprehensive, step-by-step plan, which specifically states goals and objectives and clearly delineates roles and responsibilities, to improve existing conditions. Coordinating the improvement process requires the leadership skills of managing and delegating. Both shared responsibility and authority are essential to program success because the magnitude of the proposed change demands more than unilateral control and progress monitoring. Formative evaluation methods are used in the coordination phase to adjust for inadequacies in the process design. It is here that the component of *flexibility,* an essential element of successful systems models, is introduced and is initiated by leader or member teams. The keystone is the quality tenet that "those closest to the problem have the authority to solve the problem."

Evaluation, the fourth phase of the process design model, provides ongoing assessment to ensure quality outcomes. Summative evaluation methods provide an overall assessment of the results of program implementation, whereas formative evaluation methods are continuously applied to the adjustments made from summative results. The infusion of formative evaluation methods eliminates the traditional practice of after-the-fact assessment, which evaluates artifacts that may or may not fulfill the original objective. These end-line evaluations often result in wasted time, resources, and effort.

Process management also replaces "volume thinking," the idea that more is

1. Conceptualizing – Ideas for improving are generated through leader and member participation.

2. Designing – Process improvement plan is developed with clearly defined goals and objectives and delineated roles and responsibilities for program attainment.

3. Coordinating – Managing and delegating responsibility and authority take place to implement and adjust the process design until program completion.

4. Evaluating – Summative and formative evaluation methods are used to assess program or product quality both during the process and at completion. Line inspection is replaced with efficient use of time, resources, and effort.

5. Quality Outcomes

FIGURE 5.1. Process management model: a systems approach to quality performance and outcomes.

better, regardless of what it is, and "randomized prescription," that anything labeled as innovative and somewhat successful must produce positive results. Volume thinking merely supplies more of the same, whereas randomized thinking negates the need for the personalized approach to solving problems. Each school differs from other schools by the nature of its faculty, staff, students, administrators, and parents and for successful outcomes to take place, the needs and expectations of each school must be addressed. Warwick (1995) found that effective principals realize the "individuality" of their schools and seek reform through "personalized" process reform methods. The personal approach to reform, which entails a full understanding of the strengths and weaknesses of the school as an organization, precludes process design and its improvement plan and activities.

PROBLEMS WITH TRADITIONAL STAFF-DEVELOPMENT PROGRAMS

Traditionally, teachers have viewed staff development as ineffective, time consuming, and time wasting (Rebore, 1982). Seyfarth (1996) reports that ineffective teacher staff development results from central office personnel deciding what programs teachers need and then prescribing the activities based on available resources. These kinds of staff-development programs, aimed at improving teacher performance are often marginal at best and often result in distancing teachers from the staff-development process. Fullan (1990) relates that poorly planned and delivered staff development programs have a negative influence on teacher morale and contribute little to enhancing teacher performance or educational outcomes in general.

Staff development has been defined differently depending on the source affixing a name to the process. Terms, such as *in-service education, human resources development,* and *professional or continuing development,* are frequently used synonyms. Each term, however, shares common goals: to change teacher behavior and to provide processes that promote more effective and efficient outcomes. Basically *reactive* in nature, staff development focuses on providing new knowledge and skills, attitudes and beliefs, or delivery systems to classrooms. Fullan (1990) defines staff development as an activity specifically designed to change or strengthen teachers' professional performance with an emphasis on improving classroom instruction and meeting the needs of students. Duke (1990) defines staff development as activities to "generally improve" school systems, schools, and teachers and to help all participants achieve their respective goals to strengthen individual task performance. Weller (1993) relates that effective schools address the personal aspects of teacher needs through staff development and reports that, in these schools, teacher teams design staff development programs that address both the professional and personal concerns of teachers. These programs are proactive in nature and holistic in scope. Proactive programs address the anticipated professional needs of teachers and their personal needs as individuals. Holistic programs are systematic comprehensive programs rather than one-shot attempts at reform. This approach to staff development has a positive influence on teacher self-image, morale, and motivation.

Remediation, often a major objective of many staff-development programs, has received both criticism and praise. Evertson (1986) notes that although programs driven by state or local mandates to upgrade outcomes may have been based on good intentions to improve schools and teachers, they tend to send a negative message. That is, that without the force of policy, schools and teachers are content with the status quo and that improvement, unless externally initiated, is unlikely to take place. Seyfarth (1996) states that externally mandated staff-development programs are designed around technological change or structural change (change in school policy and governance) and serve as a maintenance function. Mandated programs, be they oriented toward change or maintenance, are generally planned by nonteachers, focus on the *perceived* needs of schools and teachers, and are mostly theoretical in content. As adult learners, teachers are oriented toward the practical. They want relevant information with specific examples that can be easily adopted, adapted, or applied to their classrooms. Programs that fail to convince teachers that new practices are superior to existing ones will fail in their attempts to change teacher behavior.

Staff-development programs planned by principals or central office staff are often products of volume and randomized thinking. Making teachers attend regularly scheduled workshops, seminars, or in-service programs with "more of the same" content and delivery systems is grounded in the belief that more is better. These unilaterally planned programs fail to address teacher needs directly, and they regulate how and what teachers will learn. Selection is replaced by prescription with consideration neither for what teachers need or want to learn nor for the research on adult learning styles and models. Staff-development in effective schools, however, is designed around addressing teacher concerns through a personal approach to program design and an interest in maximizing human potential. Staff development is viewed as a systemic process, driven by process thinking and focusing on continuous improvement.

Schmoker and Wilson (1993) warn that, without teacher input in the planning and conducting of staff-development programs, top-down improvement mandates often cause a "deficit mentality" among teachers. Calls for personal improvement, such as change, are threatening and imply condemnation of practice or performance,which triggers defense mechanisms. Such improvement processes are viewed by teachers as "the need to improve as a deficiency, and that to even admit there is room for improvement is to write oneself off as worthless and incompetent" (Schmoker and Wilson, 1993, p. 48). Deficit mentality, they add, is one of the most common sources of resistance to continuous improvement thinking among teachers. Deficit thinking's worst manifestation is the immediate unwillingness to change, even before the advantage of improvement can be fairly and accurately presented. New and untested methods become targets as a result of doubt, suspicion, and fear.

Castetter (1996) criticizes traditional staff-development programs for their (1) poorly designed delivery systems, which are weakened by fragmentation, (2) lack of adequate resources, and (3) inadequate activities used in these programs. Evertson (1986) found staff-development programs to be mostly maintenance functions to support the status quo, whereas DuBrin (1995) states that these programs do little more than tell teachers how dissatisfied the administration is with their performance. Frequently, the message is work harder, work longer, and provide evidence of the same. Webb, Montello, and Norton (1994) found that most staff-development programs are viewed by teachers, as "regulatory" and ineffective, and they do not meet the intended purpose of staff-development—to maximize human effectiveness. Further, they note that most programs "shape" rather than "change" teacher behavior and that shaping behavior has both minimal and short-term effects.

EFFECTIVE STAFF-DEVELOPMENT PROGRAMS

Externally mandated or developed programs are viewed by teachers as obligatory hurdles that must be overcome to foster job security and to maintain good working relations with the administration. Teachers view top-down programs as infringements on their time and work autonomy. With these negative overtones, resistance to these programs remains high, whereas the probability of maximizing human potential remains low (Weller, 1996).

In high-performing schools, maximizing human potential is accomplished through process-structured, custom-designed programs (West-Burnham, 1993, Schenkat, 1993). Central to the process structure, claims West-Burnham, is a learning paradigm developed around research on effective learning. The core components are (1) employing learning strategies that are individualized or group oriented, (2) varying time requirements for learning within programs that are sequential and comprehensive, (3) employing instructional strategies that are determined by learners, rather than by ideology, (4) basing instruction on previous knowledge and skills, and (6) making formative and summative assessments designed to redirect and enrich both learning and instruction. Instructional leadership "is not a matter of prescribing the one best way, but rather identifying needs and then relating teaching and learning strategies to them" (West-Burnham, p. 37). Schenkat notes that quality learning paradigms are not built around administrative convenience but around what learners want and expect. This requires discarding tradition-bound thinking that embraces prescription, regulation, and regimentation.

One high school principal wanted to individualize the learning strategies in the school's staff development offerings as well as base the staff-development instruction on teachers' previous knowledge and skills. The following case study shows how he achieved his objectives:

> The principal had been successful in involving teams of teachers at all levels of the organization to test new ideas and knowledge using data and simple statistical tools to find out what works and to transfer that knowledge to others in the school. The first team the principal had formed was a leadership team, made up of administrators, department heads, and at-large faculty members, which dealt successfully with a wide variety of issues including rule, policy, procedural change, and issues related to student management and attendance.
>
> He wanted to combine the use of teams and staff development to improve classroom instruction. The principal knew, however, that classroom instruction is an area that many teachers, particularly at the high school level, are initially reluc-

tant to discuss with their peers and administrators. He needed a way to remove this barrier.

After some research in the area of staff development, he initiated teacher collegial groups (TCGs). The guidelines for TCGs were developed using staff development and group research data to develop a format for such groups.

The TCG was made up of a trained facilitator for the group and six teachers. At the beginning of the school year, each teacher identified a year-long goal to improve classroom instruction. The group then met regularly eight times during the year, outside the school.

The principal provided release time for these teachers through staff development funds. At each meeting, the group helped members devise strategies to help them attain their goals. Members tried the strategies in the classroom, reported to the group on their successes and failures, and jointly devised new strategies based on group input.

Peer observations and TCG member surveys were used for formative and summative evaluations and teachers received staff development units for their work in the group. (Weller and Weller, 1997)

Weller (1996), Weller and Hartley (1994), and Weller and Weller (1997) found that principals in quality-oriented, high-achieving schools revise the process for delivering staff-development programs by adopting the following tenets of Deming (1993):

- Ninety percent of organizational problems result from the management process, whereas ten percent result from people.
- Team work is more productive than individual effort.
- Systems thinking yields more effective outcomes than does fragmented efforts.
- Systems thinking and process models are more effective problem solvers than are isolated efforts.
- Sustained motivation and satisfaction comes from meeting the needs of personal growth and development and the meaningful application of new learning.

In this context, maximizing human capital comes not from control, but from liberating intelligence, from fostering pride in one's work, and from allowing people to have a vested interest in their accomplishments. Traditional organizational structures in schools work against the benefits of *distributed intelligence*—freely sharing knowledge and ideas and working cooperatively to improve continuously both individual and organizational goals. For distributive intelligence to materialize, highly integrated process and information systems are needed that encourage and reward the use of data and creativity to solve problems and make decisions.

CONTINUOUS IMPROVEMENT

Continuous improvement has been defined several times in the literature. However, Deming's definition (1986, 1993), the never-ending quest for producing quality products and services, captures the gestalt of the idea. Central to the continuous improvement process is the Plan, Do, Check, Act (PDCA) cycle that teachers apply daily during the preparation of lesson plans (Plan), the teaching of the lesson (Do), the evaluation of student learning (Check), and the reteaching or the new teaching of knowledge and skills (Act). As a process management system, the PDCA cycle promotes continuous improvement at the classroom level.

At the building level, principals find the PDCA model to be too large a task for unilateral implementation. Sagor and Barnett (1994) note the principal's "sphere of influence" to effect change is wider, more complex, and more demanding than that of the teachers. Teamwork, they maintain, is required to change building level programs and practices. Principals, as "managing partners," empower teachers to take the lead in making school reform and staff development programs more effective by instituting the PDCA cycle with adequate resources, support, and time for school improvement provided by the principal.

In a broader sense, Swift, Ross, and Omachonu (1998) note that continuous improvement's PDCA model translates to "adding value" to products and services. Here, the term "added value" refers to making use of the creative abilities, talents, and expertise of principals and teachers to change or enhance programs. Osborn and Gaebler (1992) relate that contentment with the status quo can be more quickly overcome when employees are accountable for solving their own problems and for making decisions on how best to improve their individual performance. They term this the "entrepreneurial spirit," a spirit with the purpose to excel and a commitment to improve continuously and to experiment and seek innovative ways to serve their clients better and satisfy their needs. Improvement is the result of exploring, taking risks, and seizing opportunities to change possibility into a reality. This is achieved by adopting a synergistic approach to planning and implementing staff development programs.

DEVELOPING HUMAN RESOURCES

The overarching goal of staff development is to maximize human potential. Subsets of this goal are (1) to stimulate the realization that changing current attitudes and behaviors can be personally and professionally rewarding, (2) to inculcate the understanding that satisfaction and growth comes from taking risks and being creative and proactive, and (3) to develop the attitude that learning and applying the results of learning for professional and personal development are challenging and rewarding. These goals reflect a new paradigm for maximizing human potential through staff development, which instills in teachers the personal satisfaction and motivation to improve continuously and to apply new knowledge and skills in classrooms. This paradigm for change must be the principal's major goal for improving teaching and promoting quality education.

Teachers have strengths and weaknesses. Consequently, they have personal and professional goals that must be met. Effective principals are committed to helping teachers eradicate deficiencies and develop personally and professionally through teacher-planned and teacher-coordinated staff-development programs. Staff-development programs will focus on topics that are designed by teachers for their personal and professional growth. Arends (1990) relates that effective staff development programs are long term, comprehensive in scope, and sequential in their provision of learning. Programs lasting three or more years are necessary to effect change in teacher behavior. Joyce and Showers (1982) found that teacher behavior changes when information is timely and relevant and specifically addresses their personal needs. Moreover, programs must be limited in theory, must be presented in practical terms with demonstrations, and must allow time for direct application and have provisions for immediate feedback. Peer coaching best facilitates this aspect of such programs.

Immediate feedback can also be provided through peer-support networks. These networks consist of peer teachers and consultants providing ongoing observation and assistance to teachers through classroom modeling, discussion groups, and visits to the classrooms of teachers who have successfully implemented change. Peer networks reduce the threat associated with administrator supervision or assistance and increase information credibility.

PROCESS MODELS FOR CHANGE

Improvement planning models should be selected more for their situational relevance than for their academic credibility. The Delimiting Factors Model is often selected for its simplicity and comprehensiveness in designing staff development programs. Capturing the essence of process management, the model poses a series of questions that, when addressed, promotes a structured, systematic process for change. The following questions are posed in the Delimiting Factors Model:

(1) "Where are we?" This calls for a clear and objective analysis of the existing situation based on data.

(2) "Where do we want to be?" This question is future oriented and allows for

the targeting of a future state that includes specific goals and objectives for achieving them.

(3) "What is keeping us from getting there?" This calls for the use of the TQM tools to identify the barriers to improvement and to decide how best to overcome these barriers.

(4) "How can we best get there?" This calls for clear and free choice among existing alternative routes. Many factors influence this decision, but consensus ultimately lies within existing situational variables such as fiscal resources; teacher attitudes, knowledge, and skills; and space and technology limitations.

(5) "How will we know when we get there?" This question addresses the use of evaluation methods, both formative and summative, and their application to the PDCA cycle (presented earlier) for achieving quality outcomes.

O'Brien, Heroschak, and Eadie (1990), report that effectively planned staff-development programs include (1) joint planning with clearly defined goals and objectives based on specific needs, (2) a well-designed delivery system that allows for continuity and comprehensiveness, and (3) strategies for formative and summative evaluations. Hirsh (1997) finds effective planning to be essential to effective change, and this planning is facilitated by the mental attitude that learning is a continuous and important goal for professional development. Wilmore (1993) relates that effective programs are planned to meet both individual and group needs. Each teacher's individual expectations must first be met before common areas for improvement can be addressed. Lunenburg and Ornstein (1996) note that teacher-planned programs address both individual and common concerns, with teachers deciding on staff development topics, how and when these programs are conducted, and the specific content and learning activities used to change teacher behavior. Rewards and recognition for improvement are essential for promoting change, and teachers are in the best position to develop a system of rewards and recognition that is meaningful to them.

How does a principal synthesize all the information and research on effective staff-development programs for teachers and implement a program to meet the needs of teachers in an individual school? First, the principal should consult the person in charge of the total staff-development program at the central office level to discuss future staff-development offerings at the school level.

This is especially important if previous staff-development efforts were arranged at the central office level. Armed with research and information such as that presented in the beginning of this chapter, the principal should make a case for more school autonomy in the type of staff development offered for the school, as well as the way in which the outcomes will be evaluated or assessed.

ACTION PLAN

_____SCHOOL

Objective:

Activities (Part 1)	Personnel Responsible	Time Frame		Constraints/ Enablers	Budget Needs
		Begin	End		

Evaluation Components (Part 2)	Personnel Responsible	Time Frame		Constraints/ Enablers	Budget Needs
		Begin	End		

FIGURE 5.2. Sample action plan.

It will be an unusual central office administrator who does not agree that effective staff development for teachers will need input from teachers. More likely, the staff-development coordinator will want to know how a site-based program is going to be developed without creating more work at the central office level. In response to this question, an action plan should be presented by the principal that outlines the steps in developing, implementing, and evaluating staff-development offerings, including the names and positions of the people responsible at each step, along with a time line that details the duration of each program.

The time line must take into account the responsibilities of central office staff in meeting district- or state-generated deadlines related to staff development, and, as a result, the principal may have to modify the original time line to meet these mandates (see Figure 5.2 for a sample action plan). Some mandated constraints may include deadlines for spending staff-development monies and for filing a district staff-development plan with the State Department of Education. The principal will take all external mandates into account when finalizing the school's action plan. Having an action plan prepared for the meeting will convince the coordinator that the principal has given careful thought to the staff-development process, and it will help the principal to finalize ideas on the topic before a face-to-face meeting.

The preceding step is based on the idea that the individual schools in a district have not been granted autonomy over or input in the design of the school's staff-development plan. If the school has been allowed input, the principal should adjust the objectives for a face-to-face meeting with the district staff-development coordinator to take this into account.

The remainder of this chapter provides the principal with the additional information needed for the action plan, including the assessment of teacher staff-development needs; the evaluation of staff-development offerings, including evaluation designs; and the decision-making steps that will occur as a result of these offerings.

ASSESSING TEACHER NEEDS

The needs of teachers in the area of staff development may be identified in several ways: first, through classroom observation; second, through the voluntary exchange of ideas with peers and administrators; and third, through needs-assessment inventories. The identification of needs should precede the planning phase, and effective staff-development programs focus on both *operational* and *individual* needs. Operational needs are those of work groups with specific duties and responsibilities, whereas individual needs are those specific to the individual (Dessler, 1991). Effective change in behavior requires satisfaction of needs at both levels. DuBrin (1995) found that when personal satisfaction is achieved first, teachers can then concentrate on changes essential for group improvement. Programs to meet individual and group needs may be conducted at the same time, over multiple sessions, to facilitate staff-development goals.

Some teachers are uncomfortable expressing their needs or deficiencies in an open forum and respond best to anonymous questionnaires, both as individuals and as group members. Needs-assessment inventories allow teachers to respond candidly without self-identification. Suggestions for staff-development topics can also come from individual teachers, ad hoc committees, principal observations, or other sources. Figure 5.3 presents a needs assessment for staff-development topics for both personal and professional development. Topics for inclusion should be identified through teacher conversations with the principal, with peers, and with team members; therefore, the instrument will be adapted to fit the needs of individual schools.

The Delphi Technique can also be used to identify staff-development topics. Developed by the Rand Corporation, the Delphi Technique is used to assess opinions, identify needs, or make decisions, with some groups using the technique to set goals or plan for change. The process requires the following steps:

(1) Define the problem or question in specific terms (What are the staff-development needs of our teachers for continued professional growth?).

(2) Use 3 × 5 index cards and, to ensure anonymous responses, ask each participant to print in pencil their responses to the problem or question, with one response per card (e.g., methods for enhanced student management, designing assessments and evaluations to gauge student learning).

(3) Cards are placed in a box, shuffled, and arranged on a table under headings (e.g., student discipline and management, instructional techniques). Broad interpretation is expected when arranging responses.

(4) Headings are written on a wall chart. Participants now rank their top five needs (responses) under each heading on a 3 × 5 card, and the responses are tabulated and placed on the wall chart. To tabulate the responses that will go on the chart, award points to each individual's responses. The top three needs receive three points each, the top fourth need receives two points, and the top fifth need receives one point.

(5) Results are written on a wall chart under each heading and group discussion is initiated.

Generally, the group will agree with the rankings, but consensus must be reached on the needs that should be addressed first. Next, discussion focuses on exactly how these needs are to be met with a planning committee being appointed to plan and coordinate program activities through the development of action plans.

Completing comprehensive staff-development programs can be a time-consuming process. Wade (1985) relates that the length of training should be dictated by the complexity of the topic and not by the school calendar. Sparks (1983) recommends that large-scale workshops be planned and coordinated by teachers, be conducted at a "leisurely pace," and be focused on practical application. Small-scale workshops, a series of three-hour sessions over three or more weeks, produces effective results when teacher interest is high and the need for change is evident.

Needs Assessment Inventory
For
Staff Development

Directions: Listed below are proposed topics for staff development programs to be conducted at our school. Please circle the number on the Interest Scale that corresponds to your perception of the need for staff development on each topic.

I.	**Personal needs**	**Interest Scale**			
		Very high (4)	High (3)	Moderate (2)	Low (1)
1.	Stress Management	4	3	2	1
2.	Time Management	4	3	2	1
3.	Home Budget Management	4	3	2	1
4.	Personal Loss and Grief	4	3	2	1
5.	Health and Exercise	4	3	2	1
6.	Other(s): 1._____ 2._____ 3._____				

FIGURE 5.3. Teacher needs-assessment inventory for staff development topics.

Feedback and Support

Providing prompt and accurate feedback and support is essential for obtaining effective change. Joyce and Showers (1995) found that principals who actively support the change effort have more positive outcomes than do those who have either indifferent or negative attitudes. Further, when support and feedback come directly from the principal, when they occur at frequent intervals, and when they coincide with teachers' expectations, change is more likely to result. Support by way of prompt and adequate resources and peer assistance is most beneficial in promoting behavior change. Feedback and recognition from peers, parents, and students are effective change stimuli. Principals should write personal notes and engage in personal conversations with teachers about their progress to support the change process.

Peer feedback and recognition are vital for effective change in teacher behavior. Peer coaching is effective in helping teachers learn new classroom methods. This has greater effect when peer coaches provide ongoing assis-

II.	Professional needs	Interest Scale			
		Very High (4)	High (3)	Moderate (2)	Low (1)
1.	Applying the multiple intelligences concept to classroom instruction	4	3	2	1
2.	Applying the multiple thinking concept to classroom instruction	4	3	2	1
3.	Applying the Myers–Brigg Personality-Type Indicator to classroom instruction	4	3	2	1
4.	Building validity and reliability into teacher-made tests	4	3	2	1
5.	Applying technology to the classroom	4	3	2	1
6.	Motivating marginal students	4	3	2	1
7.	Teaching gifted students	4	3	2	1
8.	Building student self-esteem	4	3	2	1
9.	Teaching students with special needs	4	3	2	1
10.	Using standardized test results to increase student classroom performance	4	3	2	1
11.	Using cooperative learning techniques in the classroom	4	3	2	1
12.	Involving parents and community members in promoting classroom learning	4	3	2	1
13.	Classroom management techniques	4	3	2	1
14.	Other(s) 1._____ 2._____ 3._____				

FIGURE 5.3. (continued) Teacher needs-assessment inventory for staff development topics.

tance through regular classroom visits and immediate conferences to critique observed behavior (Joyce and Showers, 1995). Dutweiler (1989) endorses the value of peer observation and found that developing personal improvement plans helps facilitate behavior change in teachers. Dutweiler maintains that the quantity, quality, and objectivity of the feedback and performance assistance are increased when two peers coach one teacher. Joyce and Showers also observed that coached teachers demonstrate greater gains in behavior change because they spend more time practicing new strategies than do their non-coached counterparts. Coached teachers retain new behaviors or knowledge for longer time periods and have a better understanding of the purpose and value of the behavior than do noncoached teachers. Effective coaching largely depends on the willingness of the teacher to be coached, the skills of the coaches, and the degree of trust that exists between the teacher and the coach.

However, changes in teacher behavior are greater when the change is congruent with the values and needs of the coached teacher (Sparks, 1983).

Ineffective Staff-Development Characteristics

Ineffective staff-development characteristics, according to Killion and Kaylor (1991), are (1) poor planning designs resulting in fragmented programs and activities, (2) lack of sufficient resources and administrative support, (3) lack of systematic follow-up procedures to address specific teacher concerns and to provide assistance in practicing desired behaviors, and (4) lack of a theoretical base and specific examples of practical application. Smylie and Conyers (1991) noted that teachers who understand the theoretical base for new practices and see modeled behavior understand the importance of its application to their work and practice desired behaviors for longer time periods than those teachers who do not have the benefit of both theory and modeling.

Administrative support for staff-development programs is essential to program success. In site-based schools, delegating responsibility for programs to teachers is a part of the shared-governance concept (Smylie and Conyers, 1991). Principals and teachers share leadership roles in planning professional development activities, with teachers having the primary responsibility for organizing, coordinating, and conducting the programs. Weller and Hartley (1994) note that teachers in quality-oriented schools find the leadership component challenging but need time and resources to be effective in their role. Principals can provide adequate time through salaried time (time on the job), released time (substitutes hired to free teachers), and stipend time (salary supplement). Personal time (the teachers' own) should not be used for staff-development work. Principals should provide resources to include the use of school space, the hiring of consultants, the instructional materials that are necessary to conduct program activities, the salaries for substitute teachers, and the refreshments. Joyce and Showers (1995) relates that the school's culture plays an integral part in making staff-development programs successful. The value and belief that continuous improvement is essential for quality outcomes makes staff development a high priority for teachers and administrators alike.

Ineffective results may be obtained when principals decide that *all* teachers will benefit from a particular program and require total teacher attendance. Usually planned and coordinated by the principal, such programs have little positive effect on teacher morale and behavior change (Joekel, 1994). Frequently, these programs are designed for the one-shot, quick-fix effect and have little to do with teachers' actual needs. In fact, many teachers resent infringements on their time through forced attendance in programs that have no direct personal or professional benefit, and this results in their forming negative opinions about staff development in general.

EVALUATING STAFF-DEVELOPMENT PROGRAMS

Evaluation of staff-development programs should be comprehensive in scope, structured, and multidimensional. Both formative and summative evaluation practices should be used. Good evaluation designs assess the value, quality, and effect of the treatment. Evaluation results should then be used to make decisions, based on the data, to refine or improve performance outcomes. Assessment results should also be used to make future decisions or to guide subsequent actions. The distinction between *research* and *evaluation* goals is an important one, and confusing the goals of the two can lead to the misuse of findings. In a broad sense, *research* attempts to understand a phenomena, to draw conclusions about the relationship among investigated variables, and to apply the results to larger populations. *Evaluation* investigates a particular program or variable at a particular site to ascertain the degree of effectiveness or the influence of the treatment through data (Popham, 1988). Analyzing data concerning the effectiveness of a treatment promotes better decision making and more effective outcomes.

In assessing evaluation outcomes, three assessment types are useful: (1) *process,* (2) *product,* and (3) *effect. Process assessment* focuses on determining the effectiveness of a process in achieving its intended results or goals. *Processes* in this case are the staff-development programs and methods of instruction, and their assessment entails the measurement of their effects. *Product evaluation* focuses on the value or benefit of a product such as the instructional materials used to change behavior in the staff-development process. *Impact assessment* determines the amount or degree of changed behavior as a result of a specific process or product. In staff-development settings, process assessment would involve the evaluation of the overall effectiveness or worth of the program, product assessment would be the evaluation of the value or benefit of instructional materials used to achieve the program's goals, and impact assessment would be the evaluation of the degree of changed behavior in program participants' knowledge, skills, and attitudes.

Evaluation Designs

Evaluation designs are systematic plans developed to assess treatment effectiveness through data. Evaluation designs set the conditions and prescribe the measurements necessary to determine degrees of effect and quality and to make meaningful decisions about future actions. Evaluation designs can be experimental (with *random* sampling or subject assignment) or quasi-experimental (*nonrandom* assignment). Readers are referred to Campbell and Stanley's (1963) classic work *Experimental and Quasi-Experimental Designs for Research* for a complete description of design types and their use in evaluation and research. The most common evaluation designs used to assess the effectiveness and influence of treatment variables at the school level are described next.

One-Shot Case Study Design

The one-shot case study is used to assess the effects of a treatment on a group of selected individuals. Evaluators observe or analyze the results of the treatment on the target group only once. An example of this is the evaluation of the influence of an in-service workshop on a group of teachers. Because extraneous variables were not controlled for (such as with a pretest) no quantitative decisions can be made about the treatment's influence, and no decisions should be made about adopting the program for widespread use. One-shot case studies are most appropriate for formative evaluation processes to obtain baseline data on initial cognitive or affective domain states following the treatment.

The one-shot case study design is as shown in the following:

$$X \longrightarrow 0_1$$

$$X = \text{Treatment}$$

$$O = \text{Observations or measurement one time only}$$

One Group Pretest–Posttest Design

One group pretest–posttest design entails pretesting and posttesting a group with the treatment applied between the two testings. In the absence of random assignment and a control group, results may be spurious, but in a formative evaluation context, the results are helpful in assessing the tentative effectiveness of the treatment. For summative evaluation purposes, a control or comparison group should be used to reduce threats to internal validity. Control groups are those subjects not receiving the treatment, whereas experimental groups receive the treatment. Control groups are common to *research,* whereas comparison groups are common to *evaluation.* Evaluators should attempt to have one or more comparison groups from the same population to draw conclusions about the effects of the treatment. Comparison groups allow one to conclude that differences are found between the two subject groups, but one cannot conclude that the difference arises from the treatment itself unless random assignment of subjects exists (McMillan and Schumacher, 1984).

The one group pretest–posttest design is as shown in the following:

$$0_1 \longrightarrow X \longrightarrow 0_2$$

$$0_1 \longrightarrow 0_2$$

Here, both experimental and comparison groups were pretested and posttested. However, the treatment was applied to only one group, the experimental group. Changes in the experimental groups can indicate influence of the treatment, but no direct relationship between the treatment and the change can be made. Many educators use this design in action projects to assess tentative effectiveness of a program or changes in teacher attitudes.

Random Pretest–Posttest Control Group Design

A random group design calls for random assignment of both treatment and comparison subjects to allow evaluators to have confidence in respondent results and to make sound interpretations of the data. Pretest and posttest differences can be attributed mainly to the treatment. The design looks as is shown in the following:

$$\text{Treatment group: } RO_1 \longrightarrow X \longrightarrow 0_2$$

$$\text{Control group: } RO_1 \longrightarrow 0_2$$

The random control group design can be applied in situations such as a workshop for teachers on improving student motivation in classrooms. For example, a randomly chosen experimental group of teachers views a video separately from a randomly chosen control group who receives no video presentation; however, all teachers in both groups receive the same lecture, handouts, and small-group work. The video is action oriented and provides modeled behaviors as well. After pretests and posttests are compared, data might indicate higher cognitive gains for experimental subjects on posttests over pretests. The evaluator could conclude that using the video to enhance traditional instruction was more effective than the traditional approach to teaching classroom motivation techniques.

EVALUATING PROGRAM GOALS

The goals and objectives of any program help determine the evaluation design. *Goals* are desired outcomes, whereas *objectives* are the means to achieving these outcomes. Objective-based evaluation determines the degree to which program objectives were met and, in turn, the degree to which program goals were accomplished. Put another way, "the discrepancy between the stated objectives and the outcomes is the measure of success of the practice" (McMillan and Schumacher, 1984, p. 341). *Discrepancy* as defined is the degree of variation of change in behavior on an expected-to-actual continuum.

Measurable or behavioral objectives assess change in behavior. Well-written behavioral objectives contain the following components: when, who, what, how, and why. An example of a behavioral objective is by the end of in-service activities, program participants will be able to identify at least ninety percent of the learned practices deemed necessary to enhance student morale in the classroom. This example is a performance or behavioral objective that is measurable and directly relates to program content designed to change teacher behavior.

Evaluators either develop or assess existing project objectives and select an evaluation design that is most appropriate to assess the process, product, or effect of the objective. As noted earlier, several designs exist and design selection should be based on acquiring data that provide high inference and confidence. Borg and Gall (1983) relate that randomized evaluation designs are best for objective-based evaluation but are not always feasible in school situations. Matching groups within quasi-experimental designs are more realistic, and inference and confidence in these results are acceptable (having sufficient inference and confidence) for site-based decision making. Matching can be based on things such as experience, level of education, interest, and personality variables.

Instruments and data analysis techniques used to measure program outcomes are selected after the evaluation design is chosen. Instruments may be standardized tests or self-made tests, interviews, questionnaires, rating sales, and observations with checklists. Concerns over reliability and validity are important and need to be addressed. Existing tests, both cognitive and affective, can be found in *Mental Measurements Yearbooks* with their validity and reliability coefficients reported. Self-made tests must follow the prescribed methods for assessing content validity and test reliability. Content validity can be assessed by a panel of judges who are experts in their field whereas reliability can be determined by using the Kuder–Richardson (K-R21) reliability formula. Reliability coefficients of 0.70 or greater are acceptable for most cognitive and attitudinal measurements. For a complete discussion of developing self-made instruments and means of assessing validity and reliability, readers should consult *Educational Research: An Introduction,* fourth edition, by Walter R. Borg and Meredith D. Gall.

SUMMATIVE AND FORMATIVE EVALUATION

"Formative evaluation refers to appraisals of quality focused on instructional programs that are still capable of being modified" (Popham, 1988, p. 13). *Formative evaluation,* in a more general sense, is used to assess effect, worth, or progress while the treatment is in progress. The process is proactive in nature. When evaluation results indicate a need for program modification, the evaluator makes recommendations for change and provides suggestions for program improvement. Therefore, formative evaluation serves to improve the program or process to maximize its effectiveness as it moves toward completion.

Summative evaluation is the appraisal of quality at the end of program or project activities and is retroactive in nature. Decisions pertaining to the overall worth or effectiveness are made based on the results of summative evaluation, and it is these decisions that influence current and future practices. Stufflebeam (1974) looks at summative evaluation as a means of providing accountability to the public by objectively presenting the results of program activities and making decisions regarding the quality and effectiveness of the program. Summative evaluation results also serve as the basis for goals or objectives for future program planning and improvement.

MEASUREMENTS FOR DECISION MAKING

Assessing change in behavior in the cognitive and affective domains calls for different types of evaluation instruments. In the cognitive domain, rating scales are commonly used to assess knowledge or skill change or the perception of one's own change in behavior. Rating scales are often referred to as surveys, questionnaires, or assessment instruments and often use Likert-type response scales with numerals one through five or six. Debate exists over the use of odd- or even-numbered scales. An even-numbered scale, one through four or six, lacks a mid-point on the scale and forces the respondent to choose either toward the top or bottom end of the scale. Odd numbered scales, one through five or seven, has a "safe" or noncommittal midpoint. Too many midpoint responses work counter to the evaluator's mission of ascertaining the degree of effectiveness of a treatment. An example of an odd-numbered rating sale is as follows:

<u>5</u>	<u>4</u>	<u>3</u>	<u>2</u>	<u>1</u>
strongly agree	agree	undecided	disagree	strongly disagree

People really do have inclinations one way or another, and evaluators should refrain from using odd-numbered scales to "force" respondents to share these inclinations. Also, only one concept or construct should appear on the stem item or question. That is, do not assess the respondent's perception of their "ability to *prepare* and *apply* student motivational exercises in the classroom" on one stem item. The preparation of materials and their application require two different abilities, and respondents may feel secure in one and not the other but still choose a "strongly agree" on the evaluation instrument. This information is virtually worthless to the evaluator.

Classroom observation to assess the frequency and the presence of a learned behavior is another valuable evaluation method. When trained observers are included, when the observation instrument is valid and reliable, and when two or more observers record the frequency and presence of the behavior over time, the results of the observations can be used to make sound evaluation decisions. Some argue that the presence of observers contaminates or influences the observed behavior. Others argue that the standardization of the process controls situational variables that may influence observed behavior. Trained recorders know when correct procedures are used, and their judgment is assumed to be free of bias (Popham, 1988). Any checklist used for observation should provide space for comments, and observers should immediately set up follow-up observation interviews to discuss observed results and to offer suggestions for improvement. (Figure 5.4 shows an instrument which the observers make use of to assess the application of learned behaviors.)

An observation instrument such as that shown in Figure 5.4 should be designed by the instructor(s) and other teachers who make up a panel of experts on the behaviors to be observed. It is important that the panel be knowledgeable and adept in the practical applications of the stated objectives. The panel will ask themselves, "What behaviors should be manifested in the classroom as a result of the learned behavior?" In other words, what should the teacher be doing in the classroom as a result of the mastered objectives in the staff-development activity? Those behaviors should be listed down the left side of the instrument. If there is a large number of behaviors, it is better to divide them into a manageable number (four or fewer). The remaining behaviors should be placed on another observation instrument to be assessed in other observations. Listing too many behaviors may cause the observer to become confused or distracted from the observation of behavior.

The panel should set a minimum period of time during which the observation will occur and divide that time into five-minute segments to aid the observer in the classroom. These five-minute segments will be listed across the top right of the instrument. The duration of the observation should be determined by ascertaining the time period during which the observer can reasonably expect to see the anticipated behaviors.

Structured Observation Instrument
(for a Twenty-Five Minute Observation)

Name of Observed Teacher: _____

Name of Observer: _____ Date: _____

Objective to be Assessed: The teacher promotes instructional engagement through techniques that promote both overt and covert involvement on the part of students.

	Behavior	Five-minute time segments				
		1	2	3	4	5
1.	Varies the type of responses generated.					
2.	Promotes relevant thinking by pausing after questions to allow students to formulate responses or to form mental images.					
3.	Stimulates covert involvement of students with techniques such as directing students to think of an example or asking students to prepare to respond.					
4.	Generates overt responses with techniques such as asking students to respond on scratch paper, asking for signal responses, or directing students to tell another student.					

Date set for follow-up interview and feedback to teacher: _____

Comments: _____

_____

_____

_____

FIGURE 5.4. Structured observation instrument assessing whether or not a learned behavior was correctly applied.

Following the observation, the observer(s) should set up a scheduled session with the teacher to provide a feedback. Additional classroom observation times may be set up at this point.

Change in the affective domain can be evaluated using a Semantic Differential. A variation of a Likert-type scale, the Semantic Differential is composed of bipolar adjectives, with opposite adjectives at each end of a continuum. Because the instrument is designed to elicit attitudinal responses toward a general concept, such as one's attitude toward a workshop, series of response descriptors, such as "strongly agree," "agree," and so on, are not needed. An example of a Semantic Differential to assess respondents' attitudes toward a workshop is shown in the following:

The Workshop

Good . . . . Bad

Dislike . . . . Like

Unimportant . . . . Important

Interesting . . . . Boring

The construct being assessed is presented in one or two words to focus the respondent's thinking on a specific evaluation area. Adjectives that are most appropriate for the construct are selected, and an even number of spaces connect each bipolar adjective. Respondents are asked to react quickly to each bipolar set to capture first impressions. Adjective sets are randomly placed with random placement of reversed bipolars. That is, positive adjectives should not always appear first on each continuum to ensure that the respondent's attention is directed to each assessment continuum. For a complete description of Semantic Differential assessments, see Charles E. Osgood, George J. Suci, and Percy H. Tennenbaum, *The Measurement of Meaning.*

SCORING EVALUATION INVENTORIES

Results from cognitive and affective instruments can be analyzed using descriptive statistics, such as frequency count, mean, and percent, and through inferential statistics such as the t-test, chi-square, and analysis of variance. Descriptive and inferential statistics are commonly used for both pretest and posttest purposes in school situations. The reader is directed to any basic statistical method textbook as a source for selecting the most appropriate statistical technique.

DEVELOPING EVALUATION INSTRUMENTS

Several approaches are recommended when developing evaluation instruments for practical use (Popham, 1988; McMillan and Schumacher, 1984; Borg and Gall, 1983). Generally, the following considerations are of primary importance in the development of an inventory or questionnaire:

(1) Clearly define the assessment objectives.

(2) Translate these objectives into questions to which respondents can respond.

(3) Write questions in clear and concise terms using words that are easy to understand.

(4) Avoid placing more than one concept against a single stem.

(5) Make questions brief to enable respondents to answer them quickly.

(6) Make sure descriptors are appropriate for the stem item.

(7) Avoid biased words or terms that may trigger a reaction to a concept other than the concept being assessed on the stem. For example, the *social acceptability* phenomena is triggered by items that cause respondents to react positively, regardless of their "true" feelings.

(8) Specify the situational constraints asked by the question. For example, use "in my classroom" or "for my students." Do not use a stem item such as: "The use of peer tutors is better than the use of adult tutors." Respondents may think, "That depends on the particular student," and the evaluation response may refer to a different construct than the one intended.

FORMAT OF EVALUATION INSTRUMENTS

The instrument itself will influence the respondents' attitudes toward the importance of the topic being evaluated. Favorable impressions are essential for cooperation and serious mindsets. The following will elicit favorable impressions:

(1) Use quality paper of a pastel color, and print on one side of the paper using only medium-size type.

(2) Provide short, concise directions to avoid respondent confusion.

(3) Make sure spelling and grammar are correct and avoid abbreviations.

(4) Allow enough room for proper spacing of items and make sure questions are logically or sequentially arranged.

(5) Place the most important items at the beginning of the questionnaire and provide examples to illustrate questions that are difficult to understand.

(6) If written responses are necessary, leave adequate space. Often the space for written responses is left blank if the questions appear to be redundant or if the survey is too long.

(7) Proofread the instrument for errors.

REFERENCES

Arends, R. 1990. "Connecting the Uiversity to the School," in *Changing School Culture through Staff Development* B. Joyce, ed., 117–143. Alexandria, VA: Association for Supervision and Curriculum Development.

Borg, W. R. and M. D. Gall. 1983. *Educational Research: An Introduction.* Fourth edition. New York: Longman.

Campbell, D. T. and J. C. Stanley. 1963. *Experimental and Quasi-Experimental Designs for Research.* Chicago: Rand McNally.

Castetter, W. B. 1996. *The Human Resource Function in Educational Administration.* Sixth edition. Englewood Cliffs, NJ: Prentice-Hall.

Deming, W. E. 1986. *Out of the Crisis.* Cambridge, MA: MIT Press.

Deming, W. E. 1993. *The New Economics for Industry, Government, Education.* Cambridge, MA: MIT Press.

Dessler, G. 1991. *Personnel-Human Resources Management.* Fifth edition. Englewood Cliffs, NJ: Prentice Hall.

DuBrin, A. J. 1995. *Leadership: Research Findings, Practice, and Skills.* Boston: Houghton Mifflin.

Duke, D. 1990. "Setting Goals for Professional Development," *Educational Leadership,* 48:71–75.

Dutweiler, P. 1989. "Components of an Effective Staff Development Program," *Journal of Staff Development,* 10:2–6.

Evertson, C. 1986. "Do Teachers Make a Difference? Issues for the Eighties," *Education and Urban Society,* 18:195–210.

Fullan, M. 1990. "Staff Development, Innovation, and Instructional Development," in *Changing school culture through staff development* B. Joyce ed., 3–25. Alexandria, VA: Association for Supervision and Curriculum Development.

Hirsh, S. 1997. *Building Effective Teams.* Reston, VA: National Association of Secondary School Principals.

Joekel, R. 1994. "Nebraska Professional Proficiency Plan," *Design for Leadership: Bulletin of the National Policy Board for Educational Administration,* 5:5–7.

Joyce, B. and B. Showers. 1982. "The Coaching of Teaching," *Educational Leadership,* 40(1):4–10.

Joyce, B. and B. Showers. 1995. *Student Achievement through Staff Development.* New York: Longman.

Killion, J. and B. Kaylor. 1991. "Follow-up: The Key for Training for Transfer," *Journal of Staff Development,* 12:64–67.

Lunenburg, F. C. and A. C. Ornstein. 1996. *Educational Administration: Concepts and Practices.* Second edition. Belmont, CA: Wadsworth.

McMillan, J. H. and S. Schumacher. 1984. *Research in Education: A Conceptual Introduction.* Boston: Little, Brown and Company.

O'Brien, P., P. Heroschak, and D. Eadie. 1990. "Strategic Leadership," *American School Board Journal,* 177:21–22, 36.

Osgood, C. E., G. J. Suci, and P. H. Tennenbaum. 1957. *The Measurement of Meaning.* Urbana, IL: University of Illinois Press.

Osborn, D. and T. Gaebler. 1992. *Reinventing Government: How the Entrepreneurial Spirit is Transforming the Public Sector.* New York: Addison-Wesley.

Rebore, R. W. 1982. *Personnel Administration in Education.* Englewood Cliffs, NJ: Prentice Hall.

Sagor, R. and B. G. Barnett. 1994. *The TQE Principal: A Transformed Leader.* Thousand Oaks, CA: Corwin Press.

Schenkat, R. 1993. *Quality Connections: Transforming Schools through Total Quality*

Management. Alexandria, VA: Association for Supervision and Curriculum Development.

Schmoker, M. J. and R. B. Wilson. 1993. *Total Quality Education: Profiles of Schools that Demonstrate the Power of Deming's Management Principles.* Bloomington, IN: Phi Delta Kappa.

Seyfarth, J. T. 1996. *Personnel Management for Effective Schools.* Second edition. Boston: Allyn and Bacon.

Smylie, M. and J. Conyers. 1991. "Changing Conceptions of Teaching Influence the Future of Staff Development," *Journal of Staff Development,* 12:12–16.

Sparks, B. 1983. "Synthesis of Research on Staff Development for Effective Teaching," *Educational Leadership,* 41:65–72.

Stufflebeam, D. L. 1974. "Alternative Approaches to Educational Evaluation," in *Evaluation in Education: Current Applications.* Berkeley, CA: McCutchan Publishing.

Swift, J. A., J. E. Ross, and V. K. Omachonu. 1998. *Principles of Total Quality Management.* Second edition. Boca Raton, FL: St. Lucie Press.

Wade, R. 1984/1985, December-January. "What Makes a Difference in Inservice Teacher Education? A meta-analysis of research," *Educational Leadership,* 42:48–54.

Warwick, R. 1995. *Beyond Piecemeal Improvements: How to Transform Your School Using Deming's Quality Principles.* Bloomington, IN: National Education Service.

Webb, L. D., P. A. Montello, and M. S. Norton. 1994. *Human Resources Administration: Personnel Issues and Needs in Education.* Second edition. New York: McMillan.

Weller, L. D. 1996. "The Next Generation of School Reform.," *Quality Progress,* 29(10):65–70.

Weller, L. D. and S. J. Weller. 1997. "Quality Learning Organization's and Continuous Improvement: Implementing the Concept," *NASSP Bulletin,* 81(591):62–70

Weller, L. D. and S. J. Hartley 1994. "Total Quality Management and School Restructuring: Georgia's Approach to Educational reform," *Quality Assurance in Education,* 2(2):18–25.

Weller, L. D. 1993. *Total Quality Management: A Conceptual Overview and Applications for Education.* Athens, GA: College of Education, The University of Georgia.

West-Burnham, J. 1993. *Managing Quality in Schools: A TQM Approach.* Harlow, England: Longman Group U.K., Ltd.

Wilmore, E. 1993. "The Management Profile and Site-Based Management," *National Association of Secondary School Principals Bulletin,* 77:84–88.

CHAPTER 6

Promoting Human Resources through Rewards and Recognitions

Rewards and recognitions are vital in building good staff member morale, and good morale is essential for obtaining quality job performance outcomes. Motivational theory is an important conceptual framework used by effective principals to provide a rewards and recognitions system that fosters quality performance and maintains high teacher morale and job satisfaction levels.

REWARDS AND RECOGNITIONS

Rewards and recognitions systems abound and are developed by effective principals who relate these systems to their leadership philosophies and styles. Rewards can provide a safe, secure, and orderly environment and the support and resources needed to produce quality outcomes. Respect and appreciation are shown to staff members for their professional knowledge and skills; and jobs are designed to be personally challenging and professionally satisfying. Staff members are valued for their individual contributions, and creative thinking and innovation are prized, recognized, and continuously supported.

In schools that are effective, staff members have principals who care about their well-being, give them the freedom to exercise their own judgments, and encourage them to make decisions that influence the quality of their work. Staff members are a part of the school governance team and principals continually look for opportunities to promote teachers to positions of authority and responsibility while providing opportunities for their personal growth and development. Specific rewards and recognitions vary, but may include financial assistance, release time, few or no extra duty assignments, recognition and rewards from peers, banquets, plaques, sabbaticals, gift certificates, empowerment opportunities, compensation time, merit pay, and the opportunity for advancement.

143

MOTIVATING STAFF MEMBERS

Many teachers leave the classroom annually in search of more challenging experiences, higher salaries, or career changes. Some move into administration for the challenge, and others seek the move for pay increases. Some find the education field lacking in career opportunities, and others seek salaries greater than those possible as career teachers. Hoy and Miskel (1996) report that teachers with low job satisfaction complain of too much bureaucracy, policies that are too rigid, poor relationships with peers and administration, and little opportunity for advancement. Conley and Levinson (1993) noted that teachers with low motivation had little or no opportunity to make decisions about their professional growth, the curriculum, or the policies and procedures relating to classroom instruction. Lunenburg and Ornstein (1996) relate that poor interpersonal relations with and inadequate supervision of students, inflexible school policies and administrative practices, and poor working conditions are major job dissatisfiers. Costello (1991) found that teacher dissatisfaction stemmed from lack of intellectual stimulation and burnout. Grier (1988) lists teacher job dissatisfiers as being due to alienation from decision making, lack of proper recognition and rewards, poor administrative practices, and lack of administrator support. Finally, Levine (1989) reported that for mid-career teachers, boredom, complacency, and lack of professional and personal challenges resulted in a leveling off of performance and in low morale.

To enhance teacher motivation, principals must find ways to meet the personal and professional needs of their teachers, to maximize their human potential, and to satisfy career expectations. Some principals respond to low teacher morale by providing pay increases and by improving working conditions. Evans (1989) and Costello (1991) noted that although such extrinsic motivators were of help, they were insufficient to maintain high morale among teachers. Cohn and Kottkamp (1993) pointed out that salary was not as highly important or as strong a motivator for many teachers as were intrinsic rewards.

Extrinsic rewards can be broadly defined as promotions, money, and recognition. Money is the most talked about extrinsic reward in education and industry; however, research findings are mixed on the actual importance of this reward (Hoy and Miskel, 1996). Firestone and Bader (1992) relate that teachers who are paid more stay longer in teaching whereas Cohn and Kottkamp (1993) indicate that greater preference is given by teachers to intrinsic rewards. However, this does not mean that teachers are not motivated by money. Firestone and Bader caution that although teachers are not solely motivated by money, they are motivated by the opportunity to earn more, and are motivated by money when their income fails to provide them with their basic needs. Work by Johnson (1986) relates that financial rewards promote teachers' taking on different and more teaching assignments, and agreeing to set and work toward meeting measurable goals.

Intrinsic rewards are those that are mediated within the individual or come from peers and include feelings of achievement, competence, efficacy, and self-actualization (Miskel, 1982). Cohn and Kottkamp (1993) state that teachers, in general, find intrinsic rewards more meaningful and attractive than extrinsic rewards. Miskel states that intrinsic rewards promote teacher motivation, which is fundamental to quality performance in the classroom, higher levels of retention on the job, and higher levels of involvement in committee work. However, Hajal and Dibski (1993) point out that overemphasizing intrinsic rewards at the cost of extrinsic rewards can have adverse effects on teachers. False praise or unmerited recognition or reward also produces adverse effects. Teachers are motivated by a *right mix* of extrinsic and intrinsic rewards and both are necessary to foster and sustain teacher motivation. Firestone (1991), in examining money as a motivating factor, observed that providing extra pay to teachers facilitates the accomplishment of extra duties and that high intrinsic motivators include regular and objective feedback from supervisors, time for teachers to plan and be creative in their teaching, and more control over their professional lives.

EMPOWERMENT AND SHARED GOVERNANCE

During the 1980s, the concept of shared governance in schools through site-based managed models began to spread rapidly. Conley (1993) describes site-based managed schools as schools with a change in structure, authority, and responsibility for teachers within the school. The major stakeholders of the school, namely teachers, parents, students, and community members, share authority to make decisions and enact policy that affect the daily operations of the school and that provide teachers with sufficient autonomy to have professional control over instructional procedure. Conley notes that *site-based management* means different things to different people, but its essence is a bottom-up power structure that allows teachers to make decisions and to be accountable for their outcomes. Moore (1994) relates that teachers gain a sense of "professional maturity" when they gain control by solving problems that exert an influence on their professional lives. They have higher levels of morale when they are involved in making schoolwide decisions, and the overall teaching-learning process is improved. These factors affect school climate positively. Weller (1996) and Weller and Hartley (1994) found that total quality management (TQM) is a school reform, site-based management model that promotes teacher team-shared decision making and problem solving and results in increased teacher morale, self-confidence, and job satisfaction. In these schools, principals adopt the TQM tenet to improve continuously and allow individual teachers to solve problems that affect instructional effectiveness in their classrooms. Teachers are provided more or longer planning time and feel more in control of situational variables that influence student learning. Lanier and Sedlak (1989) note that teachers who share in school decision making and feel they can control their work environment have a sense of personal efficiency and accountability that promotes dedication and self-confidence.

Research on site-based managed schools is not all positive. Malen, Ogawa, and Kranz (1990) examined over 200 reports on site-based management outcomes in Australia, Canada, and in the United States and found that in most cases where shared governance models had failed, principals had limited teacher decision making in general, had failed to address salient issues that affect curriculum and instruction, and/or had provided little or no training on how to operate as a governing body. They concluded that little evidence exists that site-based management improves student achievement. Moore (1994) relates that principals are more involved as instructional leaders in site-based managed schools, but they experience sociopolitical pressures as a result of their delegation of authority to teachers and teacher teams. The idea that the principal is not the only one responsible for daily school operations conflicts with expectations of the job held by certain external publics. Sometimes these pressures lead to the subsumption of delegated powers and the demise of shared governance models. Conley (1991) and Rosenholtz (1989) agree that the way principals structure shared governance procedures is a critical factor in the success or failure of site-based management. They stress the importance of principals researching existing models and determining which model is the most responsive to the goals of the school and the needs of their teachers.

Time is of major concern to teachers, and shared governance places heavy demands on teachers' time. Carnoy (1990) relates that unless principals ease the demands on teachers' time by providing release time, substitute teachers, extended day contracts, or teacher aides, the benefits derived from autonomy and policy making have little meaning.

Costello (1991) and Weller (1996) noted that successful site-based management programs have principals who take the role of instructional leader by planning and coordinating staff development programs that provide the necessary knowledge and skills for teachers to practice shared governance. Topics include time management, conflict resolution, goal and priority setting, problem solving and decision making, and leadership theory.

With site-based management comes the decentralization of the school system's control over independent schools. Redistribution of authority provides principals with more responsibility and direct control over human resource functions. Principals will have to become more knowledgeable in school law, human resource administration and its policies and regulations, and the research on personality theory, motivation, change, and staff development. These new demands are being increasingly realized, and they add to the existing pressures of the principalship. By themselves, these demands create situations that can trigger doubt, cause frustration, and lead to the demise of shared governance (Weller and Hartley, 1994).

TEACHER EMPOWERMENT

Teacher empowerment, the keystone of site-based management models of the 1990s, is a new type of leadership that claims to enhance the quality of decisions, to maximize the leadership skills of teachers, to improve school-based communications, to generate a higher degree of public confidence, and to improve student learning and resource utilization. Although research findings of these outcomes are mixed (Lunenburg and Ornstein, 1996), Hoy and Miskel (1996) indicate that sufficient benefit exists in the empowerment practice to sustain and increase its application in school governance models.

Empowerment of teachers entails sharing administrative authority with teachers and teacher teams. Empowerment is a vehicle to tap teacher creativity for solving problems and making decisions that directly influence their professional lives and work space. McEwan (1997) relates that quality outcomes stem from the individual's ability to make decisions at the level that directly affects the individual's work. TQM's success in industry and education partially results from the practice of allowing employees to make immediate adjustments in their work when adjustments are needed. This idea is based on the tenet that people, not administrators, know their own problems best and how best to solve them. Deming (1993) maintains that empowered teams, trained effectively, improve the process of quality production through their ability to anticipate problems before they occur and to take measures to prevent their occurrence. Moreover, empowered teams create a powerful partnership dedicated to high-quality performance and outcomes, and they build higher levels of personal commitment in the workplace.

Shared authority has distinct advantages says DuBrin (1995). When authority is shared, the leader's influence increases and greater loyalty results. As team members receive more authority, they can accomplish more and provide leaders with more time to coordinate and support employee decisions. Sharing authority also means sharing the credit for success, and team achievements become administrator achievements. Whetton and Cameron (1991) noted that leaders who share authority are perceived as "influential" and influential people attract more influence by the influence perception they radiate.

Empowering employees is not difficult or costly. Conger (1991) provides the following essentials to maximize effectiveness in empowered teams:

- Provide training in team building and team work skills and create a positive emotional environment that supports team work, team decisions, and radiates with leader dedication to team efforts.
- Provide teams with the necessary time, moral support, and resources to accomplish their tasks.
- Reward and recognize the merits of teamwork and constantly encourage teams to be creative in solving problems and to be innovative in designing new programs.
- Increase team responsibility and authority as successes occur and initiatives are taken.
- Encourage team members to practice self-leadership, the heart of empowerment, by allowing teams to set their own goals and objectives, evaluate their own performance, and recommend their own rewards. This creates an atmosphere of "no bosses, but many leaders," which builds self-confidence and self-leadership among team members.

Effective school principals find new and creative ways to use empowered teacher teams. Costello (1991) provides the following examples: (1) designing new instructional programs, courses, and curricular materials; (2) interviewing and selecting new teachers; (3) making staff assignments, setting the school calendar, and planning beginning teacher induction programs; (4) developing the school budget and allocating resources based on departmental and teacher needs; and (5) recommending and drafting school policies concerning student discipline, teacher evaluation, and criteria for working with student teachers, teacher aides, and parent volunteers.

Although many positive outcomes result from empowered teacher teams, rewards are primarily limited to the intrinsic. Unlike industry, meritorious performance in education is not recognized by promotions, salary increases, bonuses, larger offices, or individual expense accounts. Recognition, therefore, must come from the appreciation expressed by principals, peers, and parents; the personal and professional challenges provided; the freedom for creativity; and the limited extrinsic rewards, such as duty-free lunch and bus assignments, substitute teachers, teacher aides, or extra planning periods. Rewards such as these promote job satisfaction and the retention of good teachers in classrooms.

Providing teachers with rewards and recognition is essential in promoting teacher morale and job satisfaction. Many principals have a rewards and recognition system, whereas others lack a formal system. Some, unfortunately, recognize teacher efforts and accomplishments sparingly. The following gives excerpts from case studies on how principals attempt to enhance teacher morale and job satisfaction through rewards and recognitions.

"Employee of the Month" is a commonly used system that targets recognition for those teachers who excel in classroom performance or exemplify school spirit. Generally, teachers are nominated and elected by peers; however, some principals select these teachers. Rewards vary but usually consist of an engraved plaque, a gift certificate (from $20 to $100), a parking space, a picture in the trophy case, and a written description of merit for achieving the reward, which is read to the faculty at staff meetings and framed for each teacher.

"Teacher of the Year Award" is commonly given and the type of award varies among schools. Usually, teachers receive a parking space, a recognition certificate and a plaque, a picture in the local newspaper, and a gift certificate ranging from $300 to $1,000.

"Caught Being Good" rewards are presented by some principals for teachers doing "good deeds." This award focuses on service performance for students, parents, teachers, and community members. The recipients, usually presented at monthly faculty meetings, are recognized in the school paper or in general letters to the faculty. Academic recognition does not fall within the scope of this reward.

"End of School Picnic" is a reward and recognition ceremony practiced by some principals. The school's budget provides all the essentials along with rewards and recognitions for academic and other achievements. Plaques, certificates of appreciation, gift certificates, and parking space awards are demonstrations of appreciation.

Other less formal rewards and recognition systems include allowing teachers to leave early from school, thank you notes, recognition at faculty meetings, and verbal praise throughout the year. However, some principals have no system for rewarding teachers. One principal characterized his way of providing teachers with rewards and recognition this way: "Teachers are expected to perform well and should derive satisfaction from doing a good job. When they do not do their job, then I recognize them by making suggestions for improvement."

Despite the benefits to teacher morale, some principals fail to provide a formal system for rewarding and recognizing achievement, hard work, and dedication. A few principals fail to acknowledge teacher performance altogether, apparently thinking that teachers should feel lucky to be employed.

MOTIVATIONAL THEORY

Traditionally, job satisfiers are those identified by Herzberg (1966), who focused on the work environment rather than on the individual and maintained that certain motivators are essential for promoting quality outcomes. Motivators include satisfaction from the job itself, achievement and recognition from peers and supervisors, responsibility and advancement, and opportunities for personal and professional growth. Environmental factors, such as safety and security, good interpersonal relations with peers, and pleasant facilities, are motivators and job satisfiers (Maslow, 1954). Each of these job satisfiers can be controlled either directly or indirectly by the principal.

Role theory, part of social systems theory, strongly influences the idea of motivation and job satisfaction. Getzels and Guba's classic model on organizational behavior (1957) describes how individuals attempt to meet their needs as they interact with the organization's environment that comprises policies, role definitions, and outcome expectations. Individual behavior in organizations results from the roles individuals are assigned to play, the expectations of each role, and the personality and need disposition of the individual. Figure 6.1 presents a modification of the Getzels and Guba model of the organization as a social system.

As presented in Figure 6.1, the organization defines the roles and expectations for the system whereas the individual interacts with the system according to personality and need disposition. The continuous interaction between the organization and individual yields observed behaviors. When congruency exists among these variables, job satisfaction, motivation, and outputs are high. Getzels and Guba (1957) use the term *equilibrium* to describe a *quid pro quo* relationship that produces a satisfying, lasting, and productive agreement. Principals have direct influence on the organizational aspect of the model and thereby influence teacher job satisfaction, motivation, and the rewards and recognitions they receive. Because principals help define the organization, they have the responsibility to describe *accurately* the job requirements essential for each teaching position in their school. Principals also have the responsibility to recruit and hire teachers who have the personality and job requirements for each teaching position available. Job requirements and the culture of the school define the role and role expectations for each teacher, at each school, and serve as a template during the recruiting and screening process with which the personality and need disposition of the job candidates are matched.

Role expectations take many forms but primarily include both the job description and the major components of the school's culture. Hiring considerations should include the school's values, mission, norms, morals, traditions, and educational beliefs. School cultures that have a positive influence on student learning have productive, harmonious working relationships among peers

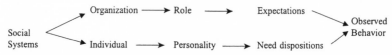

FIGURE 6.1. Modified Getzels-Guba model of the organization as a social system.

and administrators alike. However, when the personality of the individual conflicts with the assigned or expected role outcomes, social tension results among peers, parents, administrators, and students, and the needs of the individual and the organization are not met. Modification of role expectations and the personality or behavior of the individual must take place for equilibrium to be restored.

Conflict can also occur when the individual's needs are not met by the role or role expectations of the organization. Role requirements may not allow the individual to meet the inherent needs described by Maslow (1954) or those attributed to professional growth and development that include the need for autonomy and creativity. Goffman (1961) believes that roles are performances people play as they interact with superiors and peers, and the "actor's" performance is based partly on role expectations of superiors who attempt to control the environment or to provide stability within the organization. Various organizational factors determine the kinds of performance required from the roles in the organization. Peers also regulate actors' behavior. Teachers act as teachers should act in classrooms and in parent conferences, but they "act" differently with peers outside the formal environment. In other words, a double standard of behavior is expected—one behavior set for "professional" activities and another set for group/teamwork and social interaction.

Principals who exercise an authoritarian leadership style, for example, define teacher roles and expectations in accordance with the traits of that leadership style. That is, work is accomplished through rigid rules and regulations; strong control over others is viewed as being essential; solutions to problems are governed by administrative authority or policy; and decision making is the prerogative of leadership. Teachers who seek creative alternatives to accomplish tasks, question rules or regulations, or seek input through shared governance models are viewed as threats to power and control with little respect for the rules of the organization. These teachers have role conflicts with the organization. They view their roles differently than does the organization and have needs different from those of the principal. If role modification or reciprocal role relationships take place, equilibrium is attained; if not, tension continues until one party either adopts a new role and role expectations or leaves the organization. When individuals are forced to assume roles and role expectations that run counter to their personalities and need dispositions, tension in the organization occurs, job satisfaction ceases, morale plummets, and behavior becomes unpredictable and inconsistent (Boguslaw, 1965). Forced role modification can also lead to the performance/actor analysis described by Goffman (1961), which can ultimately lead to dysfunctional behavior for the organization.

Role theory can be applied to teamwork as well. Bennis (1966) noted that leaders in organizations have distinct role expectations for work teams and that team members have personalities and needs as they perform the role of team member. Leaders have the responsibility to create environments wherein team members can express themselves openly and honestly, have the autonomy to perform in accordance with their mission, and have the authority to set standards of behavior and work expectations. Leaders are expected to coordinate the work of teams, to make positive contributions to the ideas of teams, to keep them goal focused, and to provide the time and resources necessary to complete their tasks. Team members also have expectations and needs from teamwork. These include rewards and recognitions for their work and achievements, required autonomy to achieve their goals, moral and fiscal support, and implementation or acceptance of the task upon completion. When congruence or reciprocal role relationships exist, job satisfaction results and effective and efficient outcomes are evidenced. However, when role and role expectations run counter, conflict results, the quality of work suffers, and goals may not be achieved.

The two-factor model of motivation, developed by Herzberg (1982), has direct implications for principals. By adding *job enrichment* variables and reducing *hygiene* factors (those thwarting job satisfaction and motivation), principals can better promote (1) individual psychological growth needs and (2) more satisfying interpersonal relations. Job enrichment focuses on work itself and when individuals are well treated, are recognized or rewarded for their contributions, and are valued for their knowledge and skills, their morale and job satisfaction increase. Job enrichment also implies that when people have the opportunity to use their full range of knowledge and skills, they are motivated to maximize job performance. The six components listed by Herzberg central to job enrichment are as follow:

(1) jobs should be client-oriented and provide services (satisfiers) to clients;
(2) jobs should provide knowledge of the quality of services provided to clients;
(3) jobs should provide employees with new knowledge and skills, and provide meaningful work experiences and rewards;
(4) jobs should allow employees the necessary resources to do their jobs effectively;
(5) jobs should allow employees the timely and necessary information to do their work;
(6) jobs should have a built-in mechanism to allow employees personal responsibility for job results.

The quality of work life, a social norm, is a recent extension of the work of Herzberg (1982), which maintains that employees are entitled to certain working conditions and expectations from organizations. Among the expected quality of work life factors are adequate salary, job security, safe and clean working conditions, adequate and nonthreatening supervision, reasonable work policies, and a system of rewards and recognition (Massarik, 1992). Research on applying Herzberg's (1966) work to teachers is minimal; however, Sergiovanni (1967), in replicating Herzberg's work, found teachers to be motivated by personal achievement, recognition from peers and supervisors, and increased responsibility. Hygiene factors included poor interpersonal relations with peers, students, parents, and administrators; rigid and inflexible school policies and administrative behavior; and inadequate supervision practices. Miskel (1982) reports that teachers have a high need for security and recognition and are dissatisfied with hygiene factors that directly influence their classroom performance. Owens (1998) reports that school administrators would benefit greatly from practicing three main concepts suggested by Herzberg: (1) *enrich the job* (redesign the job to tap individual knowledge and skills thereby providing personally rewarding and challenging tasks), (2) *increase autonomy on the job* (involve teachers in decision-making processes and teamwork that affect their work life), and (3) *expand personnel administration* (provide human resources practices that provide safe and orderly environments, a system of rewards and recognitions, and a program to promote job satisfiers and decrease hygiene factors).

Expectancy Theory

The expectancy theory of motivation incorporates components of other motivational theories and is based on the rational-economic view of human behavior. That is, the amount of effort an individual expends depends on the reward the individual expects to get from the effort expended (Mento, Locke, and Klien, 1992). Individuals are presented with alternatives from which to choose, and the choice depends on one's perception of which alternative one has the "best" chance of attaining and with the greatest reward. The theory maintains that individuals want to maximize their rewards and will choose alternatives that they believe they have the best chance of getting with the greatest personal success. Their goal is zero loss. Motivation is viewed as rational behavior, and choice between alternatives and corresponding rewards is viewed as economic benefit.

Expectancy theory models by Vroom (1964) and Porter and Lawler (1974) have wide application for profit and nonprofit organizations. Vroom's theory states that individuals join organizations to meet their needs and to attain certain benefits from the organization. They also make conscious choices on how they will behave depending on what they can get from the organization. People, therefore, join organizations to meet their needs and will make efforts to be productive. However, people will be more productive when they perceive that a strong relationship exists among the effort expended, the performance required, and the value of the reward. Personal choices are made for personal gain. Central to the expectancy theory is the *value* one places on the reward. The effort that is expended depends on the reward's value *and* the probability that the reward will be provided. Rewards *must* be provided when effort and performance meet the criteria for the reward. Failure to provide the reward thwarts motivation and attempts to perform at maximum capacity. Both intrinsic and extrinsic rewards interplay in expectancy theory models.

Expectancy theory models have the following four basic parts:

(1) *Expectancy.* The belief that certain behaviors will provide predictable outcomes. If no opportunity for success is perceived, no effort will be expended to perform at a certain level.

(2) *Valence.* The degree of preference one has for a reward. Valence is associated with one's need and the personal appeal of the reward.

(3) *Outcomes.* The consequences of the behavior and/or the end result of the effort expended.

(4) *Instrumentality.* The strength of the relationship between the amount of effort necessary to achieve the reward and the value of the reward to one's personal or professional goals. If an individual is convinced that superior performance will result in a significant salary increase and a higher salary is important to the individual, the individual will put forth the required effort and performance to achieve the reward.

Another variation of expectancy theory is presented by DuBrin (1995). This is a quantitative model in which individuals assign probability values to the effort-performance-reward decision. First, individuals determine whether the reward is achievable given their knowledge and skills. This is the *effort-to-performance* decision, and the probability of success ranges from 0 to 1 with 1 being one's complete faith in reward attainment. Having the self-confidence and the perceived knowledge and skills to attain the reward are essential in deciding whether the pursuit of the reward is worth the effort required to perform. Second, individuals assess the likelihood that performance will lead to the reward. *Performance-to-reward* expectancy is a self-assigned probability of 0 to 1 with 1 being the belief that the reward *will* follow the required behavior. *Valence* is the personal attractiveness or aversion to an outcome. Individuals can be motivated to either seek or not seek an outcome. A valence has a motivational range of ± 1 with zero indicating no motivation. Before motivation begins, individuals must believe the reward *will be* received and that the expended effort is worth the offered reward.

Teachers working on advanced degrees to gain administrative positions are confronted with decisions concerning effort and rewards. Earning an advanced degree will provide greater income through the school system's salary scale, but there is little guarantee that they will be selected for an administrative position in their school systems. Decisions to pursue outcomes are a series of trade-offs, with the individual choosing the pursuit of rewards having the greatest personal value.

Principals can apply expectancy theory to rewards and motivate teachers through various intrinsic and extrinsic motivators. First, principals must recognize that teachers are individuals and are motivated by different satisfiers. Knowing what motivates individual teachers is essential to providing reward options that are enticing and satisfying. Second, principals must provide opportunities for teachers to achieve awards and recognition. Providing opportunities for teachers to be leaders or advising and recommending them for administrative positions are teacher satisfiers. Third, teachers must know that rewards and recognition will be forthcoming. This means that a trusting relationship has to be established through consistently fulfilling promises and praising achievements. The positive and negative aspects of the outcome should always be explained. Allow the teachers to make the decision if the outcome offsets any negative factors associated with the reward. Finally, provide ongoing moral support and the resources necessary to achieve the outcome. Quinn, et al. (1990) note the importance of the Pygmalion effect in increasing motivation with teams and individuals. The fact that teachers can communicate well raises their expectation levels, which in turn increases their levels of performance. Care is taken not to encourage teachers to pursue outcomes for which they lack the essential knowledge and skills. Intentions may be good, but setting individuals up for failure or for partial success can have lasting negative effects.

Research on teachers shows that schools having a highly centralized structure have teachers with low expectancy motivation (Herrick, 1973), and that principals who hold high expectations for staff members have staff members with high expectancy motivation (Pulvino, 1979). Miskel, McDonald, and Bloom (1983) report that expectancy motivation is positively correlated with student and teacher attitudes, student achievement, and communication between teachers and principals. In addition, Straw and Cummings (1990) observed that some individuals engage in much thought and make cognitive calculations concerning the amount of effort required to pursue an outcome. The key factors are the time required, their ability to achieve, and the availability of adequate resources to achieve the outcome. Others, they maintain, make impulsive decisions to pursue an outcome and are enticed solely by the value of the reward.

Equity Theory

Equity theory has great importance to principals who are concerned about being fair in their rewards and recognition system. Adams (1965) relates that employees perceive equitable rewards that are central to their job satisfaction as promotions, adequate salary, good working conditions, and job security and personal safety. People contribute to the organization through their knowledge, skills, attitude, and effort. People expect the ratio of their inputs to outputs (rewards and recognition) to be fair or equitable. Fairness or equity is evaluated by social comparison. That is, people compare the input-output ratio with a *comparison other* who is perceived as a peer or an equal in the ratio comparison. When the ratio is perceived as fair or equal, equity is achieved and contributes to a high morale and strong job satisfaction. When the ratio is perceived to be unequal, the inequity has a negative effect on morale and job satisfaction. Perceptions are personal judgments; they are based on correct or incorrect information. Regardless of the information presented by someone else, the perception of the comparison will remain the same for the individual. Individuals respond to perceived inequity in various ways, but the individual is motivated to restore equity on the job.

Individuals attempt to restore equity on the job in the following ways:

(1) Alter inputs by contributing less effort and time

(2) Alter outcomes by demanding more pay, better working conditions, more recognition, and greater responsibility

(3) Cognitively distort inputs or outputs and thereby rationalize the incompatibility to reduce personal tension

(4) View differently the inputs and outputs of the comparison other, encourage the other to alter his or her behavior, or leave the organization

(5) Change the comparison other to one who is perceived to be more or less equal in the area of concerned inequity

(6) Leave the organization when rationalizing, changing the comparison other, or equity is not restored (Steers, 1991).

Others have examined work behavior using equity theory and have found that inequity negatively influences employee motivation, morale, and job satisfaction. Greenberg and Leventhal (1976) report that pay increases will motivate employees and will reduce feelings of inequity, and Carrell and Dettrich (1976) observed that underpaid employees have low morale, low job satisfaction, and higher rates of absenteeism and job turnover. Huseman, Hatfield, and Miles (1985) and Steers (1991) report that equity can be restored through a variety of overt and covert methods, and that the manager has to determine which method to use to restore the perception of equity. Rewards and recognitions and performance are inextricably linked, says Mayes (1978), and fair and equitable treatment is essential, regardless of the extenuating circumstances, if managers want to maintain employee perceptions of equity in the organization. Rewards and recognitions that match effort and performance are essential, and care should be taken to provide equal extrinsic and intrinsic motivators under similar conditions with similar achievements.

REFERENCES

Adams, J. S. 1965. "Inequity in Social Exchange," in *Advances in Experimental Social Psychology.* L. Berkowitz ed. Vol. 2, 267–299 New York: Academic Press.

Bennis, W. G. 1966. *Changing Organizations.* New York: McGraw-Hill.

Boguslaw, R. 1965. *The New Utopians: A Study of System Design and Social Change.* Englewood Cliffs, NJ: Prentice-Hall.

Carrell, M. R. and J. E. Dettrich. 1976. "Employee Perceptions of Fair Treatment," *Personnel Journal,* 55:523–524.

Carnoy, M. 1990. "Restructuring Has a Downside, Too," *Education Week,* 32, pp. 2–3.

Cohn, M. M. and R. B. Kottkamp. 1993. *Teachers: The Missing Voice in Education.* Albany, NY: State University of New York Press.

Conger, J. A. 1991. "Empowered Employees: Rhetoric or Reality?" *Personnel,* 15: 17–25.

Conley, D. T. 1991. *Restructuring Schools: Educators Adapt to a Changing World.* Trends and Issues Series, No. 6. Eugene, OR. ERIC Clearinghouse on Educational Management. 57 pp.

Conley, D. T. 1993. *Roadmap to Restructuring: Policies, Practices, and the Emerging Vision of Schooling.* Eugene, OR: ERIC Clearinghouse on Educational Management.

Conley, S. and R. Levinson. 1993. "Teacher Work Redesign and Job Satisfaction," *Educational Administration Quarterly,* 29(4):453–478.

Costello, R. T., ed. 1991. *School Personnel Administration: A Practitioner's Guide.* Boston: Allyn and Bacon.

Deming, W. E. 1993. *The New Economics: For Industry, Government, Education,* Cambridge, MA: MIT Press.

DuBrin, A. J. 1995. *Leadership: Research Findings, Practice, and Skills.* Boston: Houghton Mifflin Company.

Evans, R. 1989. "The Faculty in Midcareer: Implications for School Improvement," *Educational Leadership,* 46:10–15.

Firestone, W. A. 1991. "Merit Pay and Job Enlargement as Reforms: Incentives, Implementation, and Teacher Response," *Educational Evaluation and Policy Analysis,* 13(3):269–288.

Firestone, W. A. and B. D. Bader. 1992. *Redesigning Teaching: Professionalism or Bureaucracy.* Albany, NY: State University of New York Press.

Getzels, J. W. and E. G. Guba, 1957. "Social Behavior and the Administrative Process," *The School Review,* 65(4):423–441.

Goffman, E. 1961. *Encounters.* Indianapolis, IN: The Bobbs-Merrill Company

Greenberg, J. and G. Leventhal. 1976. "Equity and the Use of Overreward to Motivate Performance," *Journal of Personality and Social Psychology,* 34:179–190.

Grier, T. B. 1988. "15 Ways to Keep Staff Members Happy and Productive," *Executive Educator,* 10:26–27.

Hajal, V. J. and D. J. Dibski. 1993. "Compensation Management: Coherence between Organizational Directions and Teacher Needs," *Journal of Educational Administration,* 31, (1):53–69.

Herrick, H. S. 1973. "The Relationship of Organizational Structure to Teacher Motivation in Multiunit and Non-Multiunit Elementary Schools," Technical

Report No. 322. Madison, WI: Wisconsin Research and Development Center for Cognitive Learning, University of Wisconsin.

Herzberg, F. 1982. *The Managerial Choice: To be Efficient and to be Human* (Rev. Ed.). Salt Lake City, UT: Olympus.

Herzberg, F. 1966. *Work and the Nature of Man.* Cleveland, OH: World Publishing Company.

Hoy, W. K. and C. G. Miskel. 1996. *Educational Administration: Theory, Research, and Practice.* Fifth edition. New York: McGraw-Hill.

Huseman, R. C., J. D. Hatfield, and E. W. Miles. 1985. "Test for Individual Perceptions of Job Equity: Some Preliminary Findings," *Perceptual and Motor Skills,* 61:1055–1064.

Johnson, S. M. 1986. "Incentives for Teachers: What Motivates, What Matters," *Educational Administration Quarterly,* 22:54–79.

Lanier, J. and M. Sedlak. 1989. "Teacher Efficacy and Quality Schooling," in *Schooling for Tomorrow: Directing Reform to Issues that Count,"* T. Sergiovanni and J. Moore, eds. Boston: Allyn and Bacon.

Levine, S. L. 1989. *Promoting Adult Growth in Schools: The Promise of Professional Development.* Needham Heights, MA: Allyn and Bacon.

Lunenburg, F. C. and A. C. Ornstein. 1996. *Educational Administration: Concepts and Practices.* Belmont, CA: Wadsworth.

Malen, B., R. T. Ogawa, and J. Kranz. 1990. "What do we Know about School-Based Management? A Case Study of the Literature—A Call for Research," in *Choice and Control in American Education, Vol. 2: The Practice of Choice, Decentralization and School Restructuring,* W. H. Clune and J. F. White, eds. 289–342. New York: Falmer Press

Maslow, A. H. 1954. *Motivation and Personality.* New York: Harper & Row.

Massarik, F., ed. 1992. *Advances in Organizational Development,* Vol. 2. Norwood, NJ: Ablex Publishing.

Mayes, B. T. 1978. "Some Boundary Considerations in the Application of Motivation Models," *Academy of Management Review,* 3:51–55.

McEwan, E. K. 1997. *Leading your Team to Excellence: How to Make Quality Decisions.* Thousand Oaks, CA: Corwin Press.

Mento, A. J., E. A. Locke, and H. J. Klien, 1992. "Relationship of Goal Level to Valence and Instrumentality," *Journal of Applied Psychology,* 21:395–405.

Miskel, C. 1982. "Motivation in Educational Organizations," *Educational Administration Quarterly,* 18:65–88.

Miskel, C., D. McDonald, and S. Bloom. 1983. "Structural and Expectancy Linkages within Schools and Organizational Effectiveness," *Educational Administration Quarterly,* 19:49–82.

Moore, J. A. 1994. "Meeting the Challenges of the Principalship in a Complex Society," *National Association of Secondary School Principals Bulletin,* 78:91–97.

Owens, R. G. 1998. *Organizational Behavior in Education.* Sixth edition. Boston: Allyn and Bacon.

Porter, L. W. and E. E. Lawler. 1974. *Behavior in Organizations.* New York: McGraw-Hill.

Pulvino, C. A. F. 1979. *Relationship of Principal Leadership Behavior to Teacher Motivation and Innovation.* Doctoral Dissertation, University of Wisconsin.

Quinn, R. E., S. R. Faerman, M. P. Thompson, and M. R. McGrath. 1990. *Becoming a Manager: A Competency Framework.* New York: Wiley.

Rosenholtz, S. J. 1989. *Teachers' Workplace: The Social Organization of Schools.* White Plains, NY: Longman.

Sergiovanni, T. J. 1967. "Factors that Affect Satisfaction and Dissatisfaction of Teachers," *Journal of Educational Administration,* 5:66–82.

Steers, R. M. 1991. *Motivation and Work Behavior.* Fifth edition. New York: McGraw-Hill.

Straw, B. M. and L. L. Cummings. 1990. *Research in Organizational Behavior,* Vol. 12, New York: JAI Press.

Vroom, V. H. 1964. *Work and Motivation.* New York: Wiley.

Weller, L. D. and S. H. Hartley. 1994. "Total Quality Management and School Restructuring: Georgia's Approach to Educational Reform," *Quality Assurance in Education,"* 2(2):18–25.

Weller, L. D. 1996. "The Next Generation of School Reform," *Quality Progress,* 29(10):65–70.

Whetton, D. A. and K. S. Cameron. 1991. *Developing Management Skills.* Second edition. New York: Harper Collins.

NECESSARY SKILLS AND KNOWLEDGE FOR THE DEVELOPMENT OF HUMAN RESOURCE POTENTIAL

CHAPTER 7

Maximizing Human Potential through Conflict Management

Conflict is ubiquitous because it is an outcome of human and human-organizational interaction. Principals cannot avoid conflict, but proactive leaders can take measures to prevent or to minimize the potential of issues or situations developing into confrontational outcomes. Conflict can produce both positive and negative social and psychological results. Conflict, broadly defined, refers to disagreement between two or more individuals or groups over an issue in which both parties have a vested interest or seek favorable outcomes for their own best interests. Conflict resolution is a multidisciplinary, analytical, problem-solving approach to resolve conflict that will yield maximum results, satisfaction, and agreement among conflicting parties.

UNDERSTANDING CONFLICT

Conflict exists whenever two or more people come together with divergent views or needs. Conflict is rooted in disagreement over issues or needs, the way to address issues or achieve needs, and the reconciliation of differences in personal aspirations behind the issues of needs. "The potential for conflict permeates the relations of humankind, and the potential is a force for health and growth as well as destruction. . . . No group can be wholly harmonious . . . for such a group would be empty of process and structure" (Burns, 1976, p. 37). In organizations, cooperative effort is essential to achieve both individual and organizational goals, and harmony and collaboration are key to the success of teacher empowerment and shared governance in schools.

Conflict arises over personal desires that stem from personal and professional needs. People experience internal tension when they perceive their personal values and goals being compromised, or when they are asked to behave

163

in contradiction to their own betterment or the betterment of others whom they support. Conflict causes stress, fear, anxiety, anger, and aggression.

Conflict can destroy interpersonal communication, inhibit group cohesion, and rupture interpersonal relations. The positive effects of conflict are creative stimulation and opportunities for problem solving, innovation, change, and organizational cohesion. The manner in which conflicts are resolved is the key to promoting the positive effects that can result from conflict situations.

Conflict can be resolved in many ways, ranging from formal written contracts to tacit agreements. Causes of conflict include misunderstandings over roles, responsibilities, policy, values, goals, resources, and authority. More specifically, conflict is intrapersonal, interpersonal, and intergroup in nature. Conflict may be visible or hidden, but the successful resolution of conflict is attributed to the knowledge, skills, and management style used by the leader.

Robbins (1974) states that conflict is "antagonistic interaction" that is oppressive to one or more people. Thomas (1976) notes that conflict is behavior resulting from divergent views or incompatible views that result in antagonistic or negative behavior, and Owens (1998) discusses conflict as a win-lose situation, a hostility that is dysfunctional to the individual and organization.

This hostile action can be physical or emotional and malevolent or non-malevolent (Boulding, 1972). Malevolent behavior is designed to hurt an individual or group with little concern over the consequences for the target or for the attacker. Non-malevolent hostility is action taken to worsen the position of others and to improve the position of the attacker. Owens (1998) notes that attacks designed to harm others can focus on persons, issues, and views through the use of hostile language, statements, and emotional expressions. Conflict may lead to constructive outcomes and can be viewed as being necessary to sustain organizational health and productivity. The difference between malevolent and constructive conflict lies in the motivation behind the action. Legitimate or constructive conflict is positive in nature; for example, disagreement over personal philosophies, interpretation of research findings, or other areas where open, honest, and professional debate takes place for the betterment of the individual, group, or organization is constructive. Conflict can provide new knowledge, information, and data that are central to good decision making and problem solving. Maurer (1991) notes that legitimate conflict in teams strengthens their values and norms and leads to better decisions through a more thorough understanding of root causes of problems.

Both negative and positive outcomes can result from individual or team conflict or both. Lippitt (1983) views negative outcomes as being instrumental in preventing individual and organizational growth and views positive outcomes as opportunities for individual and organization renewal. Negative outcomes bring about the following:

- Destroys morale and polarizes individuals and groups.
- Thwarts cooperative action and decreases productivity.
- Creates suspicion, distrust, and hostility.
- Produces irresponsible behavior and deepens differences among conflicting parties.

The positive outcomes of conflict include the following:

(1) Brings to the surface views, issues, or root causes of problems that need to be resolved.
(2) Increases involvement and allows for the expression of different ideas and points of view.
(3) Improves solutions to problems and promotes necessary change.
(4) Improves working conditions, programs, policies, and other issues negatively affecting the promotion of effective and efficient outcomes.

Maidment (1987) relates that conflict is a valuable source of organizational renewal and that when legitimate conflict is encouraged by principals, it provides a healthy environment for constructive development. Maidment also notes that principals should realize teachers have the right and responsibility to challenge or resist, in a legitimate way, policies they perceive as being detrimental to their jobs and performance outcomes.

Sources of Conflict

Disagreement over values, facts, goals, ethics, philosophies, and policies can all be sources of conflict. Conflict also occurs over personal likes and dislikes, programs, rules and regulations, budget, textbooks, and curriculum. These are the most frequent sources of conflict, and they can be either constructive or destructive in nature (Katz and Lawyer, 1993).

Other sources of conflict, according to Smith and Piele (1997), are communication problems, organizational structure, limited resources, and cultural diversity. Owens (1998) includes denial, avoidance, and control as sources of conflict. Communication is a major source of conflict because of inadequate feedback, vague or unclear directions, poorly defined expectations, and lack of communication from superiors.

Organizational structure as a source of conflict may result from either too much personal freedom or too much administrative control or supervision. Shared governance, allowing teachers to make decisions and solve problems, can be a source of legitimate conflict through the expression of concerns or discussion of areas of dissatisfaction. Constructive conflict in site-based managed schools is facilitated by team members with knowledge and skills in group dynamics, decision making, and conflict resolution.

Personality conflicts, differences in personal goals, needs, and values, can be a major source of conflict. Some individuals seek power and have a need to control others or to dominate a situation. Smith and Piele (1997) report that certain "personality traits have been found to correlate with increased conflict and are high authoritarianism, high dogmatism, and low self-esteem" (p. 391). The need to protect one's "turf" is another source of conflict that arises over perceived infringement of what people see as rightfully or historically "theirs." In schools, areas of curriculum and instruction for teachers and decision-making authority for department heads are major areas for "turf" battles.

Limited resources trigger conflict. Competition for materials that are essential or perceived as extras to do the job cause tension that may lead to dissatisfaction or jealousy. Consistently fair treatment and the assignment of resources though a teacher-principal agreed-upon priority system can reduce this type of conflict.

Cultural diversity, says Katz and Lawyer (1993), is a potential source of conflict. With greater ethnic, racial, and religious diversity, more and different values, norms, and customs are infused into the workplace. Lack of understanding of or appreciation for these differences can trigger conflict. Tolerance of and appreciation for these differences can be achieved by learning about these different represented cultures.

The goal in managing negative sources of conflict is to reduce or eliminate its causes. Smith (1998) relates that school administrators must be ever cognizant of potential conflict sources and seek to resolve it when early signs of conflict are detected. Some conflict can be resolved, whereas some cannot. Managing conflict is the next best step to resolving conflict. Diagnosing conflict entails ascertaining whether conflict actually exists or simply appears to exist. Often what appears to be a conflict is actually a misunderstanding. Conflict is evident when the two parties are pursuing incompatible goals (Owens, 1998). Misunderstandings usually result from poor or no communication and lead to distorted perceptions among the parties. Ensuring that the parties have the necessary information to resolve their distorted perceptions is an effective way to clear up misunderstandings.

MANAGING CONFLICT

Conflict management methods are almost as numerous as sources of conflict. Smith (1998) views conflict management as a means of promoting collaboration among conflicting parties, thereby preventing the conflict from becoming irresolvable or affecting others. One model for managing conflict presented by Smith begins with diagnosing the way in which each individual has conceptualized the conflict issue. In this model, two important goals exist for the conflict manager: (1) to instill in conflicting parties a spirit of cooperativeness and (2) to discover the root problems of the conflict. The following steps can help conflict managers achieve these ends.

(1) Promote an atmosphere of empathy and focus on achieving an outcome that is fair and mutually acceptable.

(2) Require open and honest communication among all parties in the conflict management conference (including the communication of the conflict manager).

(3) Discover ways in which parties have similar and dissimilar goals. Emphasize the positive aspects of mutually agreed-upon goals and look for a "bridge" to reconcile dissimilar goals.

(4) Develop a plan to achieve improved working relationships by identifying ways to achieve mutual goals. Develop a time frame for goal achievement and specify exactly how progress is to be evaluated in achieving these agreed-upon goals.

Managing conflict can also be accomplished by using authority. Robbins (1974), Nebgen (1978), and Seyfarth (1996) state that although decisions made by the authority can end open conflict quickly, they cannot resolve initial differences, which may lead to more widespread conflict. Use of authority should be applied judiciously in light of potential negative ramifications, and with the understanding that the application of authority is not as important as how the authority is applied.

The use of authority to settle conflict may be necessary when both parties are deeply committed to their beliefs or goals and when job performance is being sacrificed. Also, authority may be necessary when parties are unwilling to compromise, when threats are made, or when the potential for a physical altercation is likely. Seyfarth (1996) notes that principals in site-based managed schools should consult peers or teachers before using authority because of the serious consequences to morale and the possible subsequent questioning of the principal's commitment to shared governance procedures. Finally, "forcing" parties into an agreement usually creates dissatisfaction and unless the root causes can be identified and resolved, future conflict is always possible.

Avoidance behavior is the most natural way to deal with conflict (Robbins, 1974). Principals who seek to avoid emotional turmoil do so by withholding information or opinions, procrastinating, isolating themselves, ignoring the issue or situation, or "soothing" or making light of the conflict (Blue, 1988). Maidment (1987) sees positive outcomes in ignoring and procrastinating when confronted with conflict situations. At times, conflict reaches its own state of equilibrium, with administrator involvement being counterproductive. Procrastination often allows time for conflicting parties to reconcile differences on their own terms or through peers who may see the conflict as an unwanted intrusion on their time and emotional health. Ignoring and procrastinating should be used only as short-term management strategies and must be seriously questioned if the conflict affects work performance or the physical safety of the involved parties or others. In the following case study, the principal had tried to "soothe" the conflict situation at the expense of all parties:

> Principal Wright found himself mediating a large number of conflicts stemming from parental and student complaints about the teaching, communication, and interpersonal skills of Mr. Warren, a social studies teacher on his staff. He received at least two calls per month from parents who wanted their children to be removed from Mr. Warren's class, and at least one student visited his office each month with another complaint concerning Mr. Warren's teaching. The complaints were all centered around the following concerns:

> (1) Mr. Warren does not care enough about his students to be able to diagnose their strengths and weaknesses so that when parents call or set up conferences with him to identify how their children can improve their performance in his classroom, he has no specific suggestions for improvement. In fact, parents point out that Mr. Warren cannot even remember his students' names. To make matters worse, when a student's name does not come to mind, he simply makes up a nickname that is, more often than not, a disparaging one. The worst example of this in Mr. Wright's notes is when Mr. Warren referred to a hefty female student in his class as "Buffalo Butt."

> (2) Mr. Warren does not make directions or expectations for assignments or activities clear to students. When parents call him seeking clarification, the parents cannot seem to pin him down on specific directions either.

> (3) When parents call Mr. Warren about problems their children are facing in the classroom, he refers to other "bad influences in the classroom" whose behavior may be "rubbing off" on their children, and he refers to these bad influences by name.

> Needless to say, the parents who call Mr. Wright are quite distressed and demand immediate removal of their children from Mr. Warren's classroom. Mr. Wright's manner of handling this has been as follows:

> (1) He takes careful notes of parent complaints and concerns.

> (2) Most parents who have called with complaints have requested that their names be kept confidential because they have heard from other parents who have complained directly to Mr. Warren that their children are thereafter singled out for sarcastic remarks related to their parents' phone calls. Mr. Wright has honored these requests for confidentiality.

> (3) Following each complaint made by a parent or student Mr. Wright holds a conference with Mr. Warren. However, Mr. Warren always vehemently denies each incident. Because Mr. Wright cannot reveal parent or student

names, Mr. Warren spends most of the time during each conference trying to guess which student or which student's parents have complained.

Mr. Warren realizes that his manner of dealing with these conflicts is ineffectual, and he decides to approach the situation in an entirely different way. He sets up the following guidelines for his plan:

(1) Any parent who calls with a complaint must be willing to come in and discuss the complaint with Mr. Wright and Mr. Warren. Depending on the circumstances the student may also be asked to attend the meeting. If parents hesitate about making a complaint directly to Mr. Warren, Mr. Wright explains that the situation cannot be resolved unless all parties are willing to sit down and talk about it. He also explains that because he has not had an opportunity to hear Mr. Warren's side of the story he cannot come to any conclusion without being unfair to the teacher. However, if he goes to the teacher without the parent being present and Mr. Warren has a completely different perspective of the situation, Mr. Wright still cannot resolve the problem because he must then go back to the parent and explain Mr. Warren's perspective. In short, Mr. Wright explains, his own role becomes one of running back and forth between the two parties. Sitting down together, he explains, will resolve this difficulty.

(2) Any patterns of behavior that are revealed during a conference or conferences will be discussed with Mr. Warren privately. If these patterns of behavior indicate deficiencies that need to be remediated, Mr. Wright will develop an improvement plan for Mr. Warren.

(3) All conferences with parents, Mr. Warren, and Mr. Wright will be documented by Mr. Wright with a summary of the conference which will include any directives with which Mr. Warren has been asked to comply. Mr. Warren will be provided with a copy of the summary and directives and will be asked to sign the copy. If Mr. Warren disagrees with all or part of the written record, he will be given the opportunity to attach a written account of his version of the discrepancies.

When Mr. Wright implements the plan, he begins to see an immediate change in Mr. Warren's behavior. Mr. Warren becomes much more receptive to accepting responsibility for incidents occurring in his classroom that result in complaints. When Mr. Wright was asked to summarize how the new guidelines he had implemented added to this change on Mr. Warren's part, he offered the following reasons:

(1) Initially it was easy for Mr. Warren to deny the incidents because Mr. Wright was not present and had no first-hand knowledge of the incident. When Mr. Warren heard the complaints directly from parents and students, he found it much more difficult to deny all responsibility.

(2) Having Mr. Warren hear complaint after complaint directly from parents and

students made it much easier for Mr. Wright to point out patterns of inappropriate behavior to Mr. Warren and for Mr. Warren to understand how Mr. Wright had arrived at these conclusions. Mr. Wright could refer to specific incidents, language, and behavior that both Mr. Wright and Mr. Warren had heard described by students and parents.

(3) Because Mr. Wright was able to identify specific areas for remediation for Mr. Warren and because he had documentation related to specific parents and students, Mr. Warren began to accept the fact that he must work on his problems. Under the terms of his improvement plan, failure to do so could result in termination.

Making light of conflict situations is not a recommended solution. Eventually, a resolution must be reached, and it is better for principals to be proactive and use a conflict-management strategy early in a conflict situation so that parties can continue their work, and the effects of the conflict can be contained (Blue, 1988; Katz and Lawyer, 1994).

Myers and McCaulley (1985) observed that people with similar personalities tend to have less conflict and a better understanding of how others react in situations. Some principals, however, see hiring teachers with similar personalities as a negative strategy. Concerns focus around the absence of divergent thinking, differences of opinion, and different ways to solve problems or analyze information. Use of personality inventories, such as the Myers-Briggs Type Indicator, to help people understand their differences, however, can be extremely beneficial. (See Chapter 3 for an in-depth explanation of this instrument.)

Another way to view the management of conflict can be seen in the power model of French and Raven (1968), who present administrative power as *reward power, coercive power, referent power,* and *expert power. Reward power* comes from the power to use rewards to shape behavior. Desirable behavior results when rewards are personally enticing or satisfy the needs of individuals. The power to control the budget, to make favorable class or grade-level teaching assignments, and to assign extracurricular responsibilities provides principals with reward power. *Coercive power* is punitive in nature, is associated with the authoritarian management style, and is derived from the legitimate or positional power of the office. Here, the potential for or actual application of power controls behavior. Hoy and Miskel (1996) relate that principals apply coercive power to manage conflict by withholding preferred teaching assignments, by issuing official reprimands, and by strictly enforcing school policy. Coercive power can be viewed as a form of reward power depending on the situation and the individuals involved. That is, obeying out of fear of punishment may lead to future rewards through acts of accepted behavior.

Referent power, the ability to influence behavior through the leader's personal attributes (like charismatic leadership), has mitigating effects on organizational conflict. The leader's personal qualities are respected and admired, and followers seek identification with the leader by modeling his or her exemplary qualities and personal characteristics. Modeled behavior is expected and rewarded by the leader and affects the culture of the organization. Finally, *expert power* is the leader's ability to influence behavior through knowledge and skills. The cognitive expertise necessary for managing conflict includes human relation skills, listening skills, and conflict management and resolution skills. The use of expert and referent power are closely tied to the leader's leadership style, personal values and beliefs, and interpersonal knowledge and skills. The leader who has such power is more likely to manage conflict successfully and to lessen the likelihood of conflict situations in the organization than the leader who depends on reward and coercive power.

STAGES OF CONFLICT

Conflict has generic stages, and different management techniques are required at different stages. Maurer (1991) describes the "smoke" state where conflict events begin to surface and signal tension or dissatisfaction. Words or behaviors suggest that something is "not right," or the leader's intuition signals the realization that equilibrium is no longer present. Talking to people is a way to detect "smoke" before it turns into fire. Often tension results from misunderstandings and can be remedied through the dissemination of accurate information. The "discussion" stage follows the "smoke" stage and results from procrastinating or ignoring the situation. Discussion makes the sources of the conflict widespread and formally recognized, with individuals taking sides and polarizing the workplace. Administrators have to "run to catch up" in order to identify the causes of the conflict and then seek to mediate it.

The "fire" stage develops when conflict erupts into the open as a result of verbal accusations or unprofessional behavior, and administrative action is required immediately through the process of conflict resolution before total disruption occurs. During this stage, people "take sides," emotions run deep, and the conflict requires all involved parties to spend time and energy on the issue. Work is often disrupted, and the administrator is frequently viewed as being partial to one side or the other, which results in a possible lose-lose outcome among the individuals.

The "ashes" or final stage is a period of reassessment or natural healing. Here, the administrator must determine the root cause of conflict and take measures to negate its recurrence. Owens (1998) suggests that lessons learned from conflict be used to bring about immediate, positive changes. Thomas and Bennis (1972) suggest establishing a grievance committee or a formal procedure whereby parties in conflict have an early avenue to pursue resolution before conflict escalates into widespread discontent and employee polarization.

CONFLICT: PROCESS AND STRUCTURAL CONSTRUCTS

Process construct of conflict is viewed as a sequence of events that explains the interactions of two or more parties engaged in dynamic interaction. Viewed as a series of episodic events, the behavior of one party triggers the behavior of another with the degree of the reaction being dependent upon the significance of the impact. Reaction follows after consideration of the impact. The reaction will be highly subjective and will reflect the assessment of impact (Thomas, 1976). Conflict is viewed as a win-lose situation and escalates over time with responses depending on the personalities involved. Pondy (1967) observed that in process situations, cooperation is essential in resolving conflict and that mutually satisfactory outcomes must be reached or latent conflict areas will trigger later conflict between the two parties. This "conflict aftermath" can be more serious than initial conflict episodes.

Structural construct conflict maintains that conflict results from conditions that influence behavior. Structural causes may be organizational policies, authoritarian practices, cultural or group norms, or other perceived dysfunctional practices of the organization. People also contribute structural conflict factors with their personality traits and expectations of others' behaviors. Peer or team norms of conduct are also structural factors. Anderson (1993) reported that when principals allow teachers to make decisions, involve teachers in team problem solving, promote a culture that values open dialogue and divergent opinion, and allow teachers to share in setting up school policy, structural conflict is less frequent and less intense. Katz and Lawyer (1994) report that team decision making in shared governance models decreases conflict situations in schools, but that team members can become sources of conflict themselves. In these cases, conflict will result from lack of agreement or follow-through on agreement reached both within and among teams.

Resolving Team Conflict

Team conflict has many causes, but "the irony of the empowered team concept is that many people ignore what they know about human nature when they become empowered and involved in team exercises. Teams are made up of individuals with their own idiosyncrasies, human frailties, and personal values. The idea of being a team player is second to the inbred notion of self-reliance and individualism" (Weller, 1995, p. 46). As such, conflict among individuals is inevitable, and learning how to handle interpersonal conflict is essential to quality decision making. Consider, for example, the following case study of empowered teams in a conflict situation:

> The principal of a large urban high school suggested that the social studies and language arts departments develop and implement a plan for the interdisciplinary teaching of these two subject areas. The two departments, however, continuously sought to achieve their own ends and to stress their own disciplines rather than to move toward an interdisciplinary approach to teaching language arts and social studies. Teams refused to plan jointly the interdisciplinary curriculum or to develop goals and objectives that combined the two disciplines for teachers to implement in their classrooms. The best interests of the students, the overarching goal, were placed in jeopardy, and the principal sought a solution to the conflict with the department heads. Neither department head wished to make concessions on the position that the interdisciplinary approach did not promote student learning, despite convincing research to the contrary and the positive support for the interdisciplinary approach by many department members. The principal determined that time was of the essence and until the conflict could be resolved, he asked that a coordinator be chosen by the two faculties to assume the leadership and administrative responsibilities of the two departments as related to the development of the interdisciplinary curriculum. The position of coordinator was designed to be on a rotating basis every two years, and the coordinator organized a team composed of volunteers from both departments to develop the interdisciplinary program's goals and objectives. Over a six-month time frame, the principal and department heads worked together to resolve the original conflict. In the meantime, teachers in both departments became more willing to work with the new curriculum and to support the working team. Eventually, both departments agreed that the department heads should be replaced by a coordinator. The conflict was resolved when teachers from both departments voted to replace the department head structure with a rotating coordinator. In this case, the structural organization of the two departments, each with a department head "protecting" individual "turf" for personal reasons, was working against the idea of a unified team made up of both departments.

Conflict in empowered teams has two root causes: (1) the goals of the team and (2) the collected "negative stamps" of team members. Conflict can lead to passive aggressive behavior such as procrastination, delay, and avoidance. Verbal attack, avoiding responses, and denying the existence of conflict are disruptive and conflict-causing behaviors. Team conflict can result from unclear goals, weak or nondirective leadership, poorly organized meetings, unrealistic deadlines, inadequate resources, perceived inequities, or lack or perceived lack of administrative support. Katz and Lawyer (1994) relate that disagreement can be minimized by (1) resolving the problem through open discussion, with all parties clearly understanding and agreeing upon the task or solution; (2) clearly stating and circulating copies of the agreement for discussion; and (3) agreeing on a system for monitoring the solution or task. Breach of terms should be resolved immediately among the involved parties.

Team conflict can also be caused by principals who show favoritism with financial resources; who unfairly assign heavier workloads or increased responsibilities; and who award recognition, benefits, or privileges inequitably (Seyfarth, 1996). Redeker (1989) provides a model to resolve team conflict that can be applied by team leaders or principals. Redeker's model contains the following four steps:

(1) Discuss the issues in an open forum and get to problem clarification with all team members present. Additional information, not previously known, should be presented by all parties involved. This leads to the identification of root causes that are often personal in nature.

(2) Identify overarching goals to gain common agreement, and identify mutually shared values as a way to focus the group's attention on achieving its task.

(3) Engage group members in brainstorming for solutions to the problem. Solutions should come only from the leader, not from the group members.

(4) Decide on a solution agreeable to both parties. The solution does not have to be ideal, but it should be one both parties can live with.

Solutions that work do not always have to be of the win-win outcome proposed by Covey (1989). A win-Win outcome, such as that proposed by West-Burnham (1993), is often a more ideal solution to problems. Here, although team members and leaders share mutual benefits, the leaders do not *always* receive equal (win–win) or greater (Win-win) benefits as a result of their authority or power.

Resolving conflict by identifying common values promotes commitment through people's personal belief systems. Values are universally accepted behaviors, not codes of conduct or doctrine. Principals and team leaders who model their values place the best interests of people first and seek solutions that maximize human potential and resolve conflict to their benefit and satisfaction.

Team conflict can also result from role-expectation conflict when leaders and subordinates have incongruous role expectations for themselves and for others. Role-expectation conflict is explained in the Getzels and Guba (1957) social systems model, which maintains that people in organizations have roles defined by the organization and by themselves. When the leader's role is compatible with the expectations of the followers, conflict is minimal and can be managed by clearly defined roles and expectations. Role definitions and expectations must be clearly defined and agreement must be reached before the goal can be attained.

Resolving Conflict between Two or More Parties

Resolving problems between two or more parties requires objectivity and open and honest discussion. Facts must be separated from supposition, areas of disagreement must be clearly identified, and both parties must mutually agree on the facts and areas of disagreement. Those resolving conflict must focus on the *problem* and not on the *personalities* of those involved. Robbins (1974) maintains that good listening skills are important for conflict resolution and that a certain amount of time must pass before individual differences can be resolved. Thomas (1976) stresses the importance of reaching a compromise through a natural progression of exchange of facts and feelings and notes that compromise should not result from a sense of obligation or force.

Interpersonal conflict can result from the following behaviors:

(1) Attacking others by arguing, enjoying put-downs, finding fault, blaming, threatening, or ganging up on them.

(2) Avoiding others by ignoring, refusing to participate, or being frequently absent or tardy.

(3) Avoiding conflict by pretending nothing is wrong, refusing to take a side or defend a point of view, or refusing to take the task or issues seriously.

Leaders can implement a commonly used five-step model to resolve interpersonal conflict as follows:

(1) Meet with conflicting parties at the first sign of conflict in a nonthreatening environment and create a pleasant atmosphere.

(2) Initiate the conversation in a blame-free manner by describing the "perceived" conflict. Lefton, Buzzotta, and Sherberg (1980) suggest that the leader use the "I" approach with a description of the leader's feelings, followed by examples of observed behaviors that cause the feelings.

(3) Discuss the causes of the conflict with others presenting their points of view. Careful listening is essential to detect areas of potential agreement and to understand root causes of the conflict. Ask open-ended questions such as "What do you think?" or "What do you think the causes of the problem are?" Stimulate dialogue and provide additional information.

(4) Determine a series of possible solutions through a mutual give-and-take session, and then have the parties agree on the "best" possible solution for both parties.

(5) Develop a plan for implementing the solution, a time line, and methods for assessing improved behavior.

Sometimes conflict cannot be resolved in this manner. When deadlock occurs, the leader can resort to the following techniques:

(1) Shift from "I" to "We" and acknowledge the resistance and its sources. Be honest and forceful in the analysis and use specific facts or describe specific behaviors. Pay attention to what is said and seek clarification.

(2) Probe for further understanding while showing empathy.

(3) Readdress the conflict issue and then focus on the problem(s) causing deadlock. Frequently the two problems are related.

(4) Allow the "stalling" party time to suggest alternative solutions.

(5) Use peer intervention when appropriate.

(6) Present an ultimatum. This may require assistance from higher authority and may be viewed as failure or intimidation. Allow the other party to choose among the alternatives. Freedom of choice allows the other party to take responsibility for the consequences.

Analyzing Conflict Management Styles

Internal organizational issues over power and politics are a major source of conflict between people (Hoy and Miskel, 1996). Resolving the conflict between individual needs and organizational expectations requires administrators to mediate differences in a way that provide satisfaction for the individual and effective outcomes for the organization. Thomas (1976) presents a model for analyzing conflict management styles for conflict situations. In Thomas's model, conflict has two primary sources: (1) individual needs and (2) organizational expectations. The administrator focuses on meeting organizational expectations and uses the following conflict management styles to resolve conflict:

(1) *Competing style.* The administrator sets up a win-lose outcome. The administrator is highly uncooperative and highly assertive and uses authority to win.

(2) *Avoiding style.* The administrator displays highly unassertive behavior and is highly uncooperative. The administrator hopes the conflict will resolve itself. When forced to act, the administrator resorts to bureaucratic policy.

(3) *Accommodating style.* The administrator displays an unassertive and highly cooperative behavior toward conflict resolution by favoring appeasement or focusing on the needs of the individual. The expectations of the organization are placed second to individual needs to achieve harmony and good working relationships.

(4) *Collaborating style.* The administrator exhibits a highly assertive and highly cooperative behavior. Conflict resolution is viewed as a win–win outcome with the desire to meet needs of the individual *and* expectations of the organization. The basic stance of the administrator is that conflict can be fully resolved only through mutual satisfaction.

(5) *Compromising style.* The administrator emphasizes negotiation by looking for trade-offs between the two parties. Common points of agreement are sought and the administrator is mildly assertive and mildly uncooperative. Because both parties leave the conflict less than completely satisfied, conflict is apt to emerge later from deeper sources of conflict.

Thomas (1977) relates that effective application of the five styles depends on the situation. Examples of the five conflict management style situations are as follows:

(1) *Competing style* is best used for emergency situations when quick, independent action is needed or when unpopular decisions have to be made, the welfare of the organization is threatened, or employee actions can harm others.

(2) *Avoiding style* is most appropriate when the issues are minor, when others can best resolve the conflict, when more data are needed to resolve the conflict, or when conflict calls for a cooling-off period.

(3) *Accommodating style* is best used when building or maintaining harmony is the most important outcome, when there is an administrative error, when good relations are essential for future joint efforts, or when an issue is most likely to be defeated and it is necessary to "save face."

(4) *Collaborating style* is best used when consensus and commitment are important, when problems have to be identified, when strong, healthy future relationships are essential for personal and organizational well-being, when creative ways are needed to resolve problems, and when job performance and job satisfaction are important considerations.

(5) *Compromising style* is best used when time is limited to reach an agreement, when a temporary settlement of a highly disruptive conflict is needed, and when competing and collaborating styles will yield unsatisfactory outcomes.

Combs (1987) presents three common conflict types and ways to manage the conflict:

(1) *Individuals have incompatible goals or values. Principals are viewed as representatives of the organization and are perceived to be aligned with one of the conflicting sides.* A third party is needed to resolve the conflict to attain mutual satisfaction.

(2) *Individuals seek different outcomes but must abide by one solution.* Reaching a win–win solution is difficult, but the principal can ensure each party has gained something to provide a foundation for future, positive relationships.

(3) *Individuals want different outcomes but only one outcome can be satisfied.*

Emotions can trigger escalating actions leading to violent outcomes because self-interest is involved. The principal can use a negotiations model to stop the current conflict, but the collaboration conflict resolution style will be needed in the future to reach a satisfactory outcome.

Because attitudes affect both our and others' behaviors, they are often sources of conflict. People place the behavior of others in perspective to their own behavior and their expectations of others' behavior and then act accordingly. Attitudes, according to Katz and Lawyer (1993), filter or screen our images of behavior, determine the information we accept or reject, and provide a picture of the world. We respond to others, therefore, based on our filtered perceptions. These "self-fulfilling prophesies" cause conflict because attitudes assign meaning and allow us to "make sense" of others' behaviors. Changing attitudes is difficult and requires a predisposition to change. It begins with the willingness to find common areas of agreement, to develop a positive attitude toward the strengths of others, and to respect the perceptions of others.

The conflict resolution model presented next is a variation of the Katz and Lawyer (1993) model and is an interpersonal process for modifying perceptions.

(1) Practice reflective listening. Listen to others' points of view and how they perceive the conflict—give them plenty of "air time."

(2) Listen for points of agreement and remember to respect others' points of view. Try to empathize with and understand the perceptions and the behaviors that shaped these perceptions.

(3) Establish rapport by demonstrating an understanding of others' perceptions and provide examples for clarification. Explain the reasons for your behavior within the context of the situation and seek the understanding of others.

(4) Summarize others' points of view to their satisfaction and then have the other parties summarize your point of view to your satisfaction. Although minor points are not important, understanding the attitudinal reasons for perceptions is essential.

(5) The tension level is reduced through this understanding of attitudinal reasons, common points of agreement are identified, and empathy now exists for the different perceptions. A mutual agreement is then reached on a solution to the conflict issue.

Using a Third Party to Achieve Compromise

When conflict cannot be resolved to the full satisfaction of the parties in conflict, achieving compromise through a third party is imperative. Maidment (1985) and Seyfarth (1996) point out that principals who resolve conflict through compromise using a problem-solving model are successful. A model frequently used is a variation of Drucker's (1974) model, developed by a leading organizational theorist in industrial management. The problem-solving model has six steps, which are as follows:

(1) Jointly define the problem
(2) Jointly identify the root causes of the problem
(3) Jointly identify possible solutions to the problem
(4) Jointly determine the best solution to the problem
(5) Jointly develop an action plan to solve the problem
(6) Implement and evaluate the results

Compromise requires a mutual give and take between both parties and an *understanding* that the ultimate goal is to reach an agreement that *best serves* both parties. The principal's role as the third party is to facilitate the objective analysis of the problem, to keep the conversation focused on the problem and away from personality traits, to reach an agreement that benefits both parties, and to monitor progress toward achieving the agreed-upon outcomes. When the principal is a part of the conflict issue, a third party, who is neutral and mutually agreed upon, should act as the mediator.

When should principals intervene in conflict situations? Maidment (1987) argues for early intervention before other staff members begin to take sides and groups begin to polarize. When behavior begins to affect performance negatively or to disrupt others in the school, action should be taken. Even misunderstandings, often not classified as conflicts, can influence performance and should be addressed by the principal.

Two intervention strategies are popular among principals for effective outcomes. One strategy is to discuss the issue with the joint parties involved to assess perceptions and facts and to then seek compromise. The other strategy entails meeting with the conflicting parties separately to understand their perceptions and gather facts and then meeting jointly to resolve the conflict through a mutually agreed upon process. In both strategies, the term *reasonable* is stressed and used as a criteria for compromise. It is essential to be fair to both parties; however, both parties must understand that give and take is expected if compromise is to be achievable and workable. Principals must make it clear that the authority of the principal does not lie in *forcing* the terms of compromise.

Building Consensus

Gaining consensus is a way to prevent conflict. Katz and Lawyer (1994) relate that conflict occurs within teams or groups, between teams or groups, or between an individual and a team or group and is not strictly between two or more individuals. Consensus, they maintain, does not mean that all people have to approve the outcome 100 percent, but it does mean that each group member accepts and can abide by the outcome. Katz and Lawyer present the following steps to achieve consensus:

(1) The issue should be presented in a rational, nonemotional way that emphasizes positive and negative aspects of the issue factually and objectively.
(2) All parties should listen carefully and objectively to others.
(3) All parties should present their views in an objective and fact-based way and a proposed solution should be solicited by the facilitator.
(4) The facilitator should call for and gain consensus or seek another solution if consensus cannot be reached.

Consensus building is more natural in organizations with cultures whose norms, values, traditions, and mores are shared and strongly supported (Deal and Kennedy, 1983). These cultures build mutual trust and respect, and dialogue and debate are encouraged to promote continuous improvement. Owens (1998) notes that schools with a Systems 4 leadership style emphasize consensus building and promote win–win outcomes. Debate and diversity of opinion are encouraged, but unity or commitment is in place when the debate is concluded. Owens also relates that Systems 4 leadership style, a variation of McGregor's Theory Y style (1960) developed by Likert (1979), supports group decision making, promotes supportive relationships among employees, and sets high-performance goals for the organization. Systems 4 leaders have open communication systems, build morale through rewards and recognition, and delegate responsibility to employees.

Reaching consensus is not always easily achieved or quickly accomplished. Original positions or expectations often require modification. Flexibility in thinking and making concessions to other points of view are required. Maurer (1991) maintains that concession giving leads to counteroffers which, in turn, provide additional avenues to explore to help develop congruence. When attempting to reach consensus, the long-range or overall goal must remain the target. Making small concessions is an expected part of the human negotiation process and serves to strengthen consensus among those seeking unified outcomes.

SKILLS TO RESOLVE CONFLICT

Conflict resolution skills are many, but some are more salient to principals who attempt to resolve conflict quickly and who strive for win-win outcomes. Principals should be aware that there are some people who are not interested in seeking mutual gains or resolving conflict if their interests are not fully satisfied, and there are others who will use tactics to stall mediation or to refrain from entering into a conflict resolution process altogether. Some refer to those who use tactics such as guile or deceit as Machiavellian (named after the sixteenth-century Italian political theorist Niccolo Machiavelli). Christie and Geis (1970) relate that those who have strong Machiavellian traits are prone to lie and use deceit and similar tactics to gain concessions. Those with weak Machiavellian traits use these tactics less often to seek gain, and they are more concerned about the effect of an outcome on themselves or on others. However, people with even weak Machiavellian traits lie and deceive for personal benefit or as delaying tactics.

Although lying is only an occasional practice for some, there are others for whom it is a common practice (Lewicki, 1983). Goleman (1988) relates that according to mental health professionals lying is a part of normal development because it is a part of social and work life. Reasons for lying vary as do the categories of the lie. *White lies* are told most commonly, and they are often viewed as facilitators of mutual benefit with no malice behind the motive. *Feel-good lies* are "helping" lies to assist another feel better without overly distorting the truth. These lies boost morale, delay the possibility of bad news, or encourage optimism. *Pathological lies,* says Goleman, are told by those with mental problems and their lies have little or no basis in facts. Their reality is often self-made and serves their personal ends. *Self-benefit lies* are those designed to damage others, to achieve personal benefit, or both. These lies are intended to hurt others by distorting facts or by creating untrue stories about their behavior.

Unless principals know how to detect lies, resolving conflict in "good faith" and with trust becomes difficult. Lewicki (1983) relates that most people have an intuitive sense that someone is lying. Liars also have problems with maintaining consistent facts or with describing situations consistently. Certain types of body language, voice pitch, facial expressions, and eye contact can be indicators of dishonesty. For example, being restless, sweating, and having dry lips and mouth, which cause thirst or change in voice inflections, are consistent with lying. Other indications are high voice pitch or a loud and forceful tone associated with defenses. Frequent loss of sustained eye contact, expressions of disgust, or fear may also suggest that someone is lying.

Three options exist when lying is detected. These are as follows:

(1) *Ignore* the lie. Ignoring indicates that the facts are either unimportant or erroneous and that questioning the facts may lead to larger problems or loss of focus on the current issue.

(2) *Realize* the lie exists. The facts influence you directly but not enough to seriously damage your reputation or work. Realizing that the lie exists and letting others know you discovered the lie gives others an opportunity to explain their reasons for lying, thereby saving face by substituting a "good" reason for the lie.

(3) *Confront* the lie. The facts presented are personally or professionally damaging and action must be taken. Facts must be used to confront the liar, but neither an attack on the other's character nor punitive actions should be taken. Losing face may result, but unless the lying is settled in a nonconfrontational way, future conflict may result and damage relationships.

Because principals model the expected behavior of their teachers, students, and staff, lying becomes a central issue in interpersonal relations. The authority of the office should be no excuse to deviate from the personal values and behavior codes one has, nor should it be an excuse for double standards.

Negotiating

Negotiating strategies abound, with each strategy requiring involved parties to present their demands on conflict issues, to acknowledge the legitimacy of the demands and issues, to develop a cooperative working relationship, and to conclude with mutually agreed-upon outcomes to the satisfaction of all involved parties. When principals enter into negotiations, they do so in good faith and run the risk of losing some inherent authority, but not legitimate or legal authority granted by the board of education or state statutes. Schoonmaker (1989) relates the importance of knowing when not to enter into negotiations with employees because negotiation implies a potential win–lose outcome and the use of adversarial strategies. Therefore a quasi-negotiations approach is recommended in many situations to resolve conflict. The use of the quasi-negotiations approach is to avoid the use of authority or having authority tested, and to achieve the outcomes of mutual respect, mutual satisfaction, and mutual commitment. The quasi-negotiations model is successful in resolving conflict when (1) a common interest exists for both parties, (2) a strong desire to maintain a continuous, friendly relationship exists, (3) mutual trust exists, (4) the resolution of the conflict may not be difficult or overly emotionally disturbing, and (5) the parties are willing to solve the conflict in good faith by openly discussing problem areas.

Negotiations is a process that takes the divergent needs and expectations of people and, through mediation, facilitates an acceptable solution more quickly and harmoniously than does an interpersonal conflict resolution model. Fisher and Ury (1983) relate that negotiation is a rational process and proceeds best when emotional levels are reduced. A variation of the negotiations model presented by Fisher and Ury is as follows:

(1) Both parties identify their interests individually by writing a position statement of two or more paragraphs. The idea is to determine the real motives behind their interests, which can be achieved by analyzing the key words and the emotions used to express their interest statement.

(2) Both parties provide a joint oral summary of the interest statement, and a list of similarities and differences are placed on a flip chart by the facilitator or mediator. Emphasis is placed on similar interests that are expressed. Sometimes an agreement is reached at this stage if an agreed-upon solution can be identified.

(3) The mediator develops a problem statement, which is agreed upon by both parties, and asks both parties to brainstorm possible solutions to the problem. Each proposed solution must be treated with respect by all involved in the negotiations process if open and honest discussion is to take place.

(4) The mediator places solutions on a flip chart but does not ask for their evaluation. Ideas for solution can be merged when points of agreement exist. If mutual interests are met at this stage, the problem is then solved and the negotiation process ends. If not, the process continues with Steps 5-7.

(5) The mediator asks both parties to evaluate the statements and to decide on a proposed solution by placing each solution in rank order. The optimal solution may not exist, but the solution providing the greatest satisfaction to both parties is the goal of negotiation.

(6) The mediator takes the solution identified by both parties, and encourages them to develop an action plan with specific activities for each party to initiate and implement toward the agreed-upon solution. The mediator helps the parties arrive at a time frame for implementing the action plan and procedures for evaluating progress.

(7) The mediator conducts periodic reviews of progress toward the solution through meetings where progress is discussed and any new issues are resolved.

Communication Skills

Good communication skills minimize the potential for conflict situations to arise. Katz and Lawyer (1994) found that establishing trust and rapport were essential for successful conflict resolution: "Rapport is a shared psychological state between people who are responsive and attentive to each other. The mutual state of rapport describes a state of trust between people" (p. 4). Rapport is characterized by cooperation and agreement of views, dependability, and comfort in another's company. Rapport is the first requirement for effective communication.

Communication is defined as words, voice tone, and body language used to convey meaning. Kowalski (1996) discusses the functions of nonverbal language as a means of expressing emotions, conveying interpersonal attitudes, presenting one's personality to others, and emphasizing verbal communication. Visual communications include facial expressions such as eye contact and movement, gaze, smile, eyebrow lift, and frown. Other communication methods involve hand, leg, and feet movements. Kindred, Bagin, and Gallagher (1990) discuss verbal communication and relate the importance of word choice, voice inflection, and their corresponding body language as being important for effective communication. Listening skills, they maintain, are as important as effective communication skills. (See Chapter 3 for a discussion of effective communication skills.)

Listening Skills

Good listening skills are essential for good communication. Rice (1998) observed that listening skills enhance job quality and effectiveness, personal relationships, and social exchanges. Effective listening calls for intellectual and emotional involvement and correlates with the purpose and expected benefits derived from the communication. Adopting a positive attitude toward the sender, being willing to listen, and maintaining interest in the topic are essential prerequisites for good listening. Believing that the message is personally important and beneficial and having respect for the sender are also vital to good listening. When the receiver has empathy with the sender, effective listening takes place. (See Chapter 3 for a more complete discussion of listening skills.)

Barriers to effective listening include lack of mental concentration, lack of emotional commitment, and "noise." Effort is required to filter out "noise," which is any distracting element that causes a lapse in concentration and that interferes with message decoding. Examples of sources of distractions include light, dress, mannerisms of the other person, or loud or annoying sounds. Screening out noise requires practice and effort. Rice (1998) presents the following examples of noise or barriers to effective listening:

(1) Being preoccupied with personal matters while listening to others.
(2) Thinking of a response before the sender finishes the message. The brain can process 400–600 words a minute, whereas speech flow maximizes at 124 words a minute.
(3) Using acronyms or word choice that causes confusion and loss of attention.
(4) Creating dysfunctional or threatening environments that cause inattention and emotional defensiveness.
(5) Participating in rushed meetings where more attention is paid to time than to the content of the message.

Overcoming Listening Barriers

Good listening requires dedicated effort, a positive attitude toward the sender, an atmosphere devoid of noise and threat, and a belief that the message

is personally important or beneficial. These intellectual and emotional fundamental preparations supplement the following skills:

(1) Asking for periodic feedback from the receiver as the message is being
    conveyed.
(2) Allowing the listeners to take notes to help them concentrate and slow
    down the pace of the message being sent.
(3) Asking the receiver to repeat the central ideas or concepts of the message
    to the satisfaction of the sender.

REFERENCES

Anderson, P. L. 1993. "Conflict: How to Beat the Odds," *School Business Affairs,*
    59(9):4–8.

Blue, M. 1988. "Conflict: Educational Administrators Must Learn to Manage It,"
    Thrust for Educational Leadership, 17(4):46–48.

Boulding, K. E. 1972. *Conflict and Defense: A General Theory.* New York: Harper and
    Brothers.

Burns, J. M. 1976. *Leadership.* New York: Harper & Row.

Christie, R. and F. L. Geis. 1970. *Studies in Machiavellianism.* New York: Academic
    Press.

Combs, C. H. 1987. "The Structure of Conflict," *American Psychologist,* 42:355–363.

Covey, S. R. 1989. *The Seven Habits of Highly Effective People,"* New York: Simon and
    Schuster.

Deal, T. E. and A. A. Kennedy. 1982. *Corporate Cultures: The Rites and Rituals of
    Corporate Life,* Reading, MA: Addison-Wesley.

Drucker, P. F. 1974. *Management: Tasks, Responsibilities, and Practices.* New York:
    Harper & Row.

Fisher, R. and W. Ury. 1983. *Getting to Yes: Negotiating Agreement without Giving In.*
    New York: Penguin.

French, J. R. P. and B. H. Raven. 1968. "Bases of Social Power," in *Group Dynamics:
    Research and Theory* D. Cartwright and A. Zander, eds. 259–270. New York:
    Harper & Row.

Getzels, J. W. and E. G. Guba. 1957. "Social Behavior and the Administrative Process,"
    School Review, 65:423–441.

Goleman, D. 1988. "Lies Can Point to Mental Disorders or Signal Normal Growth,"
    New York: *New York Times,* p. C1.

Hoy, W. K. and C. G. Miskel. 1996. *Educational Administration: Theory, Research,
    and Practice.* Fifth edition. New York: McGraw-Hill.

Katz, N. H. and J. W. Lawyer. 1993. *Conflict Resolution: Building Bridges.* Thousand
    Oaks, CA: Corwin.

Katz, N. H. and J. W. Lawyer. 1994. *Resolving Conflict Successfully: Needed
    Knowledge and Skills.* Thousand Oaks, CA: Corwin.

Kindred, L. W., D. Bagin, and D. R. Gallagher. 1990. *The School and Community Relations.* Fourth edition. Englewood Cliffs, NJ: Prentice Hall.

Kowalski, T. J. 1996. *Public Relations in Educational Organizations: Practice in an Age of Information and Reform.* Englewood Cliffs, NJ: Prentice-Hall

Lefton, R. E., V. R. Buzzotta, and M. Sherberg. 1980. *Improving Productivity through People Skills.* Cambridge, MA: Ballinger Publishing.

Lewicki, R. L. 1983. "Lying and Deceit: A Behavioral Model," in *Negotiating in Organizations* M. H. Bozerman, ed., 68–90. Beverly Hills, CA: Sage Publications.

Likert, R. 1979. "From Production and Employee-Centeredness to Systems 1–4," *Journal of Management,* 5:147–156.

Lippitt, G. L. 1983. "Can Conflict Resolution Be Win–Win?" *School Administrator,* 40(3):20–22.

Maidment, R. 1987. *Conflict! A Conversation about Managing Differences.* Reston, VA: National Association of Secondary School Principals.

Maurer, R. E. 1991. *Managing Conflict: Tactics for School Administrators.* Boston: Allyn and Bacon.

McGregor, D. 1960. *The Human Side of Enterprise.* New York: McGraw-Hill.

Myers, I. B. and M. H. McCaulley. 1985. *Manual: A Guide to the Development and Use of the Myers-Briggs Type Indicator.* Palo Alto, CA: Consulting Psychologists Press.

Nebgen, M. K. 1978. "Conflict Management in Schools," *Administrators Notebook,* 26(6): 6.

Owens, R. G. 1998. *Organizational Behavior in Education.* Sixth edition. Boston: Allyn and Bacon.

Pondy, L. R. 1967. "Organizational Conflict: Concepts and Models," *Administrative Science Quarterly,* 12:296–320.

Redeker, J. 1989. *Employee Discipline: Policies and Practices.* Washington, DC: Bureau of National Affairs.

Rice, E. J. 1998. "Are You Listening?" *Quality Progress* 31(5):25–29.

Robbins, S. P. 1974. *Managing Organizational Conflict: A Nontraditional Approach.* Englewood Cliffs, NJ: Prentice-Hall.

Schoonmaker, A. N. 1989. *Negotiate to Win.* Englewood Cliffs, NJ: Prentice-Hall.

Seyfarth, J. T. 1996. *Personnel Management for Effective Schools.* Second edition. Boston: Allyn and Bacon.

Smith, R. E. 1998. *Human Resources Administration.* Princeton Junction, NJ: Eye on Education.

Smith, S. C. and P. K. Piele. 1997. *School Leadership.* Eugene, OR: ERIC Clearinghouse on Educational Management.

Thomas, K. 1976. "Conflict and Conflict Management," in *Handbook of Industrial and Organizational Psychology* M. D. Dunette, eds., 889–936. Chicago: Rand McNally.

Thomas, K. 1977. "Toward Multi-Dimensional Values in Teaching: The Example of Conflict Behaviors," *Academy of Management Review,* 20:486–490.

Thomas, J. M. and W. G. Bennis. 1972. *Management of Change and Conflict:* Baltimore: Penguin Books.

Weller, L. D. 1995. Quality teams: Problems, causes, solutions. *The TQM Magazine,* 7(3), 45–49.

West-Burnham, J. 1993. "Managing Quality in Schools," London, England: Longman Group U.K., Ltd.

CHAPTER 8

Recruitment, Selection, Retention, Dismissal, and Reduction

Recruitment, selection, and retention of personnel require both short- and long-range planning and are the most challenging and difficult tasks faced by principals who seek to make their schools high-performing, quality-producing learning organizations. Dismissal means that failure of the recruitment, selection, and retention process has failed, whereas turnover usually refers to failure in the area of leadership. In each of these five areas, the principal has the ultimate responsibility for achieving success or failure.

RECRUITMENT, SELECTION, RETENTION, DISMISSAL, AND REDUCTION: AN OVERVIEW

Recruiting, selecting, and retaining staff members require short- and long-range planning which focuses on the vision and goals of the school, the demands of the curriculum and instructional delivery system, and the needs of the students. Recruitment's purpose is to attract quality applicants, based on current and projected needs, and it requires a proactive plan to acquire a pool of applicants whose backgrounds and interests closely match the needs of the school.

Selection is a consideration of the worth or overall value of an applicant in making positive contributions to the school's vision and goals. Selection should be based on both *person* and *position* requirements. Primary considerations in selecting personnel include human relations skills, personality, initiative, and the knowledge and skills to perform the requirements of the position.

Retention, maintaining employee stability, is primarily a result of job satisfaction, which is influenced by the principal's leadership, the induction process, the school's culture, and the opportunities for personal and professional development. The recruitment and selection of excellent teachers must be followed with the support needed to retain them.

Dismissal, the involuntary termination of employment, is the final phase in an unsuccessful process to strengthen or remediate deficiencies or to satisfy the goals of the school and the needs of the individual. Turnover, voluntary separation from employment, can indicate dissatisfaction with school policies and leadership or failure to meet the personal or professional needs of the teacher. Turnover may indicate failure in the selection process as well. Both dismissal and turnover provide opportunities to reevaluate job descriptions and requirements and to ascertain specific reasons for employment separation. This information should be used to strengthen the school's recruitment, selection, and retention practices.

RECRUITMENT OF PERSONNEL

Planning for recruitment is the essential first step in achieving quality educational outcomes. Recruitment is a multidimensional process that involves the following: identifying current and future staffing needs, considering budgetary needs, targeting recruitment areas, monitoring external and internal environmental trends, preparing informational literature, and planning visits for recruitment. Evaluation of the recruitment process using input from teachers and newly hired personnel is the responsibility of the principal.

Recruitment comprises the dual functions of promoting the school's *image* and *reputation* and "selling" the accomplishments and opportunities of the school to prospective teachers. Principals must point out to potential employees the positive characteristics that set their school and employment opportunities apart from competitors. In essence, the school must have *appeal* and *promise*.

In general, recruiting teachers is more difficult than recruiting for vacancies in industry or in the health professions. Low salary, low job esteem, and increases in school violence have made teaching less attractive than other vocations. Recruitment practices have to be aggressive, and should offer fact-based and enticing information to interest quality teacher candidates. Reputation, image, and the potential for success are major selling points principals must stress when recruiting new teachers. Most often, teacher candidates express interest in a school's academic program and reputation, its history of violence and discipline problems, its geographic location, its salary potential, and its student population. Some are interested in a school's athletic and extracurricular programs whereas others have interest in retirement and benefit packages, opportunities for advancement and personal growth, and support networks such as peer coaching or mentoring programs. Teacher candidates have concerns over affordable housing, commuting distance, insurance, and cultural and fine-art events. Recruitment must provide fact-based information about all these concerns and present it in an attractive, eye-catching package that stimulates interest in reading about and considering the school as a highly desirable employment opportunity.

Short- and Long-Range Recruitment Planning

Short-range planning focuses on needs that continuously exist and can be met primarily from resources within the school and the community itself. Long-range planning is designed to provide for quality personnel to meet the future needs of the school's existing and expanding programs (Castetter, 1996). Short-range planning focuses on openings occurring through promotion, turnover or dismissal, retirement, or position elimination or creation. Usually, these openings are quickly filled from within the school or school system, but if the openings are filled "temporarily," permanent replacement becomes a concern and a long-range planning issue.

Long-range planning is future oriented and anticipates changes with respect to school size, instructional programs, and governance structure. Potential employees must be identified to meet the school's needs, and external recruitment remains the best solution (Castetter, 1996). Long-range planning is a structured, systematic, and comprehensive strategy to identify and recruit the best applicants available. Efforts will include recommendations and nominations from external and internal sources, visits to college campuses, and circulation of position announcements to college placement offices, college professors, newspapers, and teachers and support personnel within the school. Review of applications on file is another source for potential quality personnel. Having a comprehensive and multidimensional approach to recruitment greatly increases the probability of hiring the *best qualified* person for the job, which is the ultimate goal of the hiring phase of the employment process. Consequently, recruitment is a planned, organized, and continuous process.

In site-based managed schools, department heads and teachers take on responsible roles in the recruitment process by helping principals develop job qualifications and descriptions. Teachers know best the current demands of their positions, with evolving new technology, school governance requirements, and extracurricular assignments. Accurate descriptions of the skills and knowledge required for teaching positions complement the interpersonal skills necessary for teachers to function effectively in the classroom and with colleagues.

Although requests for new personnel need approval from the superintendent, requests accompanied by a data-based rationale for new or replacement personnel, an updated job description and qualifications list, and salary request are essential for serious consideration. Superintendents also look for a needs statement showing the direct relationship and importance of the position to the school's strategic improvement plan and to the overall goals of the school system. Importance and relationship are best demonstrated through documentation indicating that the knowledge and skills essential for the job are continuously monitored, that the requirements for local training to fill the job vacancy would be of considerable expense to the school system, and that the position will directly benefit students and the curriculum. Recruitment policies must clearly demonstrate compliance with law and procedures, and application packets must contain copies of the school system's employment practices.

Public Employment Practices and Recruitment

Discriminatory employment practices of the past have yielded legal reforms through legislation, regulations, and court decisions to correct these abuses. Seyfarth (1996) notes that public employment policies are antidiscriminatory in nature, and that public organizations must adhere to existing federal, state, and local policies when recruiting and hiring personnel. The goal of these mandates is to ensure that applicants will be considered based on their *abilities* and *qualifications* without regard to race, color, gender, religion, or national origin. Discrimination laws have been increasing in number with new legislation and court decisions, and principals have to be aware of changes in recruitment and hiring policies. The local school board attorney is the best source for current law and court rulings on nondiscriminatory recruitment and hiring practices.

Generally, employment discrimination falls under three broad categories, namely racial, employment, and gender. McCarthy and Cambron-McCabe (1992) relate that racial-discrimination complaints usually focus on hiring, recruitment, assignment, promotion, and dismissal practices. Gender-discrimination complaints usually center on compensation, sexual harassment, employment conditions, pregnancy policies, and retirement benefits. Employment-rights complaints may arise from age, handicap, drug use, health, obesity, privacy, performance appraisal, religious, and wrongful dismissal issues.

Affirmative Action and Recruitment

"The intent of affirmative action is to open job opportunities that have traditionally been closed to minorities and women" (Seyfarth, 1996, p. 218). Castetter (1996) states that the intention of "affirmative action plans initiated by the federal government has been to accord preferential treatment in recruitment, hiring, promotion, and development of groups against whom discrimination has been practiced" (p. 93). The preferential treatment issue is much debated and litigated. Currently, the issue of affirmative action is under renewed attack with the 1996 passage of California's Proposition 209, which bans racial and gender preferences, and the state of Washington's ban on preferential treatment passed in 1998. The argument central to the California and Washington bans on allowing racial and gender preferences is that treatment preference of any kind, regardless of any previous injustices or other presented reasons, voids the idea that equal and fair treatment exists. When one individual is given preference over another because of race, color, creed, or gender, fair and equal treatment cannot exist by definition of terms. In other words, making up for perceived wrongs does not "make a right" if the method of attempting to achieve equality for some violates equality for others.

Regardless of the current or future status of affirmative action, current laws apply to the human resources function in educational institutions, as do those under the Equal Employment Opportunity Commission (EEOC) regulations of Title VII of the Civil Rights Act of 1964, as amended. The EEOC prohibits discrimination regarding compensation and terms and conditions of employment based on race, color, sex, religion, or national origin. This legislation also prohibits classifying, limiting, or segregating applicants or employees in ways that may deprive them of employment opportunities or negatively affect their employment status.

Central to the recruitment process are considerations of fair and equal treatment. McCarthy (1983) provides the following criteria for evaluating employment practices, which can serve as guidelines for principals planning recruitment programs and for the hiring of personnel:

- Qualifications for hiring must be based only on bona fide occupational qualifications and not on sex, age, religion, race, or national origin.
- Employment prerequisites must be valid indicators of success for the job in question.
- Policies cannot adversely affect certain classes of employees in performing their work.
- Questions used in job interviews must directly relate to the individual's ability to perform the job.
- Recruitment, hiring, promotion, and job-assignment decisions must be based on qualifications, merit, and performance.

Additional Recruitment Considerations

Principals must be knowledgeable of school board policies that concern residency requirements and nepotism. Some school systems have policies that call for filling vacancies from within the system before recruiting from outside the system, whereas others call for a global recruitment process. Limiting recruitment to currently employed personnel negates the possibility of finding the *best* qualified candidate, and the limitations of hiring from within can become one of the greatest detriments to achieving school effectiveness.

Prospective candidates should have access to copies of position announcements that give clear definitions of the necessary personal and professional qualifications and that accurately reflect the requirements of the job. Applicants should be encouraged to ask questions, and be given telephone numbers so that they can call to acquire additional information. Sometimes applicants have questions that, when answered, lead to voluntary withdrawal of job consideration, whereas others may find that they do not meet the minimum requirements when questions are clarified.

When applicants are required to submit supporting information along with their applications, careful thought should be given to what is *absolutely* essential for the selection process. Standard information includes a letter of interest and a statement of how the applicant's qualifications coincide with the required qualifications listed in the job announcement. A completed application, résumé, and references provide the essential information for initial consideration. Requiring candidates to provide copies of official transcripts at this stage of the employment process is unnecessary and an added expense for the applicant. Transcripts should be asked for before offering the candidate a contract. A quick call to the applicant's college advisors or registrar's office can verify information deemed essential. Sometimes the applicant's consent is needed for this information, and this can be accomplished through consent forms that are included in the application packets.

When applications are received, a personal letter acknowledging receipt of the application, with a personal signature and the applicant's name, should be mailed rather than a form letter. The personal touch creates a positive impression and promotes a favorable image. Letters should inform candidates of their status in the selection process and a time line for interviewing candidates should be provided to those selected for interviews. Those not selected for interviews should receive personal letters that include an expression of appreciation for their interest, an explanation that not being selected for an interview in no way reflects negatively on their credentials, and a request for permission to keep their applications on file for future consideration.

In recruitment, as in other stages of the employment process, principals should give primary importance to professional courtesy and applicant convenience. Recruitment is a form of selling the school to others and it provides a first-time "snapshot" of the school and its principal.

SELECTION OF PERSONNEL

Selection, the second stage of the employment process, "is the focal point of the personnel function" (Castetter, 1996, p. 71). The goal is clearly to select the *best* candidate for the job, the one who holds the highest promise of succeeding in the face of the demands and requirements inherent in the job.

Longevity of personnel indicates an effective selection process, whereas turnover is ineffective in terms of personnel time, effort, and finances. Selection provides the greatest opportunity to enhance the school's overall program by hiring quality people who can enhance the curriculum, the culture, and the instructional delivery system. Redeker (1989) clearly states that "when you hire a problem you will have to fire a problem" (p. 6). Therefore, selection becomes the most important process management can perform to promote and sustain quality outcomes.

Screening Indicators for Selection

The screening of applicants is an important process; however, there is no single "best" method for doing so (Cascio, 1989). Consistency in the selection process is essential to avoid litigation. Castetter (1996) maintains that pre-screening tests must have a direct relationship to job requirements, and be free of potential negative influence on minorities. Bible and McWhirter (1990) caution that test results must remain confidential, and when results of personality, psychological, and medical tests are discussed with supervisors, it must be done in the context of "good faith" as it relates to job requirements and responsibilities. Redeker (1989) advises administrators to use only those tests with which they are familiar. Tests should be directly relevant to the screening process and should have substantial test validity and reliability. Requiring applicants to take an array of tests to have data on file is unnecessary, costly, and inconvenient to the applicant.

The screening criteria for applicants should be both situation specific and standardized. Castetter (1996) reports that knowledge of the subject matter and the ability to manage classrooms and relate well with students are essential, generic requirements for teachers. Seyfarth (1996) discusses the following relative or situational criteria that serve as screening variables: community expectations, character, commitment, communication and interpersonal skills, persistence, and attitude toward authority. Weller (1998) notes that total quality management (TQM) schools include flexibility, receptiveness to change, self-motivation, creativity, and the ability to work cooperatively with others as highly desirable teacher attributes. In site-based managed schools, many of these criteria are essential for teamwork and shared decision-making responsibilities. When criteria have been determined to be "predictors" of success, and are "reasonable" job requirements, they are less likely to be litigated, even though some fall within the area of subjective judgment.

The Importance of Job Descriptions in the Selection Process

Selection criteria for positions are reflected in job descriptions that identify the duties and responsibilities of the positions. Performance responsibilities should include those that are essential to achieving the goals of the school and to meeting the needs of students. All teaching positions are not alike and vary depending on subject matter, grade level, and student characteristics; therefore, job descriptions should reflect these differences in specific ways. Dailey (1982) emphasizes the importance of job descriptions or *job models* as being results oriented so that the selection process can be more focused on desired outcomes. Both positive and negative aspects of the job should be presented to provide applicants with a realistic and honest picture of the duties and responsibilities.

Job descriptions should describe the *desired results* of the job or what teachers are expected to accomplish. Some refer to desired results as performance-based outcomes required for the job that focus on the most important tasks to be performed. Job descriptions should also contain the *refined tasks* that must be performed, and these tasks should correlate with those duties and responsibilities within the desired-results section. The third part of the job description is the *job-environment* section, which describes the school and community and those characteristics that serve to facilitate or detract from completing job performance requirements (Dailey, 1982). Job descriptions or job models should be developed with the input of those actually performing the tasks and should include a description of job demands that accompany the job duties and responsibilities. Demands may include being a club sponsor, attending athletic events, or serving on committees outside shared governance responsibilities.

Screening Applications in the Selection Process

A careful review of each application will determine if an applicant meets the minimal qualifications as stated in the job description. Those meeting minimal qualifications will be required to submit letters of reference and other supporting material for careful examination. Key words provided in references, such as *cooperative, tactful, sensitive, independent,* and *energetic,* should be noted and examined in their context.

A background check provides verification of information and is the second step in the screening process. The information solicited should be a balance between "need to know" and the privacy rights of the applicant. State and federal law and court decisions concerning background checks should be consulted before soliciting information, and information received should be "in good faith" and directly related to the duties and responsibilities of the job.

Reference checks should be made with the applicant's knowledge and permission. The most valuable information often comes from past or current supervisors who know the applicant's work habits, work-related knowledge and skills, and interpersonal traits. A negative report should be explored further because of personality conflicts or other unknown circumstances that may have resulted in a less than fair and honest assessment of the candidate. When a negative reference appears to lack substance, it is debatable as to whether the applicant should be informed about the reference. One way to approach the situation without betraying confidentiality is to ask the applicant to reexamine his or her selection of references.

When checking references by telephone or mail, a prepared form should be used to provide the predetermined, essential information and to ensure consistency. Questions may vary but should be related to the job description and the duties, responsibilities, and demands of the job. In site-based managed schools, questions focus on attributes proven necessary to be a successful member of a shared governance school. One question often asked is whether a reference would rehire the applicant. Should the answer be "no," *specific* reasons should be given for the negative answer. It is possible that one supervisor does not value certain qualities in an employee that may be valued by another.

Nepotism and Politics in Screening Applicants

Some states and school systems have policies concerning the hiring of relatives. With or without these statutes, a principal may be placed under pressure to hire a friend or a relative. In some school systems, nepotism is clearly defined and the working relationships with relatives are spelled out; for example, some school systems approve of husband and wife employment as long as one does not supervise the other in the same school or department. Some forbid nepotism under any condition, and others will have policies concerning the hiring and supervising of sons, daughters, grandchildren, brothers and sisters, and in-laws. Generally, if a relative is the *best* candidate for the job, the applicant can be hired as long as there is no direct supervision involved. Nepotism increases the possibility of conflict of interest or violations of ethical or professional conduct.

Political pressure is sometimes applied to principals to hire family members, friends, or relatives of school board members or community power agents. Principals are placed in compromising situations, and their jobs can be in jeopardy by being "caught in the middle." Using committees of teachers in both the screening and interviewing process and requiring a two-thirds vote over a simple majority vote when hiring an applicant can further remove the principal from compromising ethical or professional standards.

Using Tests in the Selection Process

Disagreement exists as to the exact value of tests as a screening device. Alexander (1990) believes that testing is a high-predicting variable of applicant success when job requirements match test content. Aldag and Stearns (1990) reported that screening tests were valuable for predicting job satisfaction, reducing absenteeism, and lowering turnover rates. Tests, they maintain, are less biased than are interviews and letters of recommendation. Castetter (1996) states that when selecting personnel, supervisors should consider the use of tests and, depending on the job requirements, may wish to use intelligence, aptitude, interest, and/or personality tests. Others, such as Fischer, Schimmel, and Kelly (1991), note that care should be taken in using tests for screening candidates. Violation of Title VII of the Civil Rights Act of 1964 is a key concern in testing job applicants. To be allowed by the courts, tests have to be significantly related to successful job performance and be reliable and valid to avoid litigation for discrimination.

Screening tests that have high validity and reliability are the National Teacher Examination (NTE), which is an achievement test, the Miller Analogies Test (MAT), which is an aptitude test, and the Wechler Adult Intelligence Scale, which measures general intelligence. The Myers-Briggs Type Indicator (MBTI) is a personality characteristics measure and is useful for assessing personality traits important for on the job success. Castetter (1996) points out that tests, used as *one* indicator, can support other screening indicators, can allow for a more complete picture of the applicant's potential, and result in a more intelligent hiring decision. Caution should be used on relying too heavily on any one test result because some individuals naturally perform below their ability on standardized assessment measures. For this reason, tests of intelligence and aptitude, if required, should receive a low priority indicator rating.

The Selection Committee

Members of the selection committee should include the principal; an assistant principal; the immediate supervisor, department head, or team leader; and two or three teachers who know the demands, duties, and responsibilities of the job. Committee members should be trained in interviewing techniques; should review the specific interview questions, which will be asked of all candidates, ahead of time; and should have a standardized recording procedure to assess each candidate's responses. Interview questions should be based on the duties and requirements of the job to elicit essential information related to the successful performance of the job. Follow-up questions or probing questions are helpful to gather additional information.

Interviewing for Selection

Interviewing is not only the most widely used screening method, but it is also the most widely misused for reasons that will be explained. Interviewing five or six candidates for an opening is desirable if the pool of qualified candidates is sufficiently large. Two types of interviews are frequently conducted: (1) a preliminary interview and (2) a final interview. Principals may choose to forego the preliminary interview step, which is designed to develop first impressions, to "get-acquainted," to meet members of the interview committee, and to tour the facilities. The preliminary interview is time consuming and costly. The final interview is conducted by the selection committee with the intention of offering a contract to one of the prescreened applicants.

Shortcomings of Interviews

Some believe that interviews are poor predictors of job performance (Lunenburg and Ornstein, 1996). Dessler (1991) lists five problems associated with interviews and the use of committee members.

(1) Involving interview committee members who are unfamiliar with the job and its requirements. These interviewers do not ask the right questions, spend time on matters of personal interest, and have a poor grasp of the information provided by the candidate.

(2) Making premature decisions about the applicant. Decisions are usually made within a few minutes of the interview, and interviewers spend the rest of their time confirming their first impressions.

(3) Emphasizing negative information. Interviewers tend to search for negative information and rely more on negative comments than positive ones. When interviewers change their minds, they tend to shift from a positive to a negative view.

(4) Emphasizing personal biases. Some interviewers have preconceptions about people and others have prejudices. Some choose candidates with similar backgrounds and values, whereas others place importance on how one dresses, speaks, looks, and other non-job related qualifications or characteristics.

(5) Hiring based on quotas. When committees are given hiring quotas, they tend to give higher ratings to interviewees who qualify under quota guidelines. Pressure to hire influences the interviewer's judgment of the applicant and detracts from the overall purpose of the interview process.

In addition, interviewers who are not trained in detecting meanings of nonverbal behavior can easily mistake the body language of those considering answers to difficult or sensitive questions. Interviewers also tend to develop a stereotype of the best candidate for the job and seek a match, and some hold expectations they themselves cannot attain. Also, when an average candidate is interviewed before two or more candidates with similar qualifications, the first candidate becomes "above average" in the minds of some interviewers.

Finally, training and interviewing experience have minimal effect on selection judgment (Rebore, 1987).

At a minimum, however, members of the selection committee should be trained in the types of interview questions that could lead to charges of discriminatory employment practices. Consider the following case study, which contains an exercise used by a principal with selection committee members:

The principal begins the training by asking the committee members: "What kinds of questions do you ask in an interview?"

Committee members usually respond that interview questions are concerned with the educational background of the applicant, work experience, and the skill and knowledge areas required for the job, and so forth.

The principal acknowledges that these are appropriate interview topics, but notes that there are inappropriate interview topics as well. She states:

"Let's see if you can tell the difference between appropriate and inappropriate questions for interviews and for job applications. Take out a sheet of paper. I'll read a possible question for the application or the interview situation and you write *yes* if you think it's a permissible question or *no* if you think it's not. There are twenty questions."

   (1) What is your maiden name?
   (2) Do you own or rent your home?
   (3) How old are you?
   (4) What is your birth date?
   (5) When did you attend and complete elementary and high school?
   (6) How did you acquire the ability to speak a foreign language?
   (7) What language was most commonly used by your parents in your home during your childhood?
   (8) How may children do you have?
   (9) Are you married?
 (10) What kind of provisions for child care do you have?
 (11) What are the names and addresses of your children?
 (12) With whom do you reside?
 (13) What is your height and weight?
 (14) What is your health condition?
 (15) Have you ever received Workers' Compensation?
 (16) Do you have any physical disabilities or handicaps?
 (17) Do you go to church?
 (18) Have you ever been arrested?
 (19) Have you ever served in the military?
 (20) Do you belong to any clubs or organizations?

The principal reads each question and has the committee members indicate by a show of hands their *yes* or *no* answers. A committee member tallies the *yes* and *no* answers for each question.

The principal then explains that *all* twenty questions are inappropriate to ask on an application or in an interview.

The principal notes that there is usually some surprise that all twenty questions are inappropriate, and this surprise is a good lead-in to a discussion on *why* the questions are inappropriate and how they could be rephrased to make them more appropriate.

An explanation of the reason each question is unacceptable and an acceptable way to ask a question on the same topic follows:

(1) The question as written indicates an inappropriate interest in the marital status of the applicant. What the questioner really wants to know is whether any of the applicant's records are listed under a different name, and what that name is so the records or information can be requested.
Acceptable: Have you ever used another name?

(2) This question as written indicates an inappropriate interest in the socio-economic status of the applicant.
Acceptable: What is your address?

(3) This question as written indicates an inappropriate interest in the age of the applicant, which could lead to complaints of age discrimination. The question may have been included because the interviewer needs to ensure that the applicant was over the age of eighteen. Instead, people over the age of forty may view the question as an attempt to screen out older applicants.
Acceptable: If you are under the age of eighteen, can you, after employment, submit a work permit?

(4) Same as (3).

(5) Same as (3).

(6) The question as written implies that the national origin of the applicant may be inappropriately used as a screening device for applicants.
Acceptable: Which languages to you speak?

(7) Same as (6).

(8) The question implies that whether an applicant has children is being used as a screening device for applicants.
Acceptable: None. If an applicant is later hired, the names of children or dependents can be secured for insurance or tax purposes.

(9) Same as (8).
Acceptable: None.

(10) Same as (8).
Acceptable: None.

(11) Same as (8).

(12) The question implies that the marital status or living arrangements of an applicant are pertinent to whether the applicant is qualified for the job.
Acceptable: What is your address?

(13) The question implies that an applicant's height and weight are pertinent to whether the applicant is qualified for the job.
Acceptable: None.

(14) The question asks the applicant to reveal health-related issues that may not be related to the applicant's ability to perform the job.
Acceptable: Do you have any condition that limits your ability to perform the job you have applied for? Are there accommodations that can be made for this condition that would allow you to perform the job?

(15) Same as (14).

(16) Same as (14).

(17) The question implies that whether an applicant attends church will impact the hiring decision, which could result in complaints of religious discrimination.
Acceptable: None.

(18) The question implies that an arrest disqualifies an applicant.
Acceptable: Have you ever been convicted of any felony or misdemeanor other than minor traffic offenses? If so, please explain.

(19) The question implies that military service is being used inappropriately as a screening device.
Acceptable: None. If an applicant mentions having served in the military, it is acceptable to ask what types of skills or knowledge were acquired that could be used in the job for which the applicant applied.

(20) Asking an applicant for this information could result in the naming of clubs and organizations that indicate race, national origin, age, and so forth.
Acceptable: Are you affiliated with any professional organizations relevant to the job for which you have applied?

A Process to Negate Interview Shortcomings

The following guidelines developed by Yate (1993) enhance the interviewer's goal of selecting the best candidate:

(1) A structured format, which consists of prepared written questions, should be used by all interviewers. All applicants should be asked the same questions, questions should be job related, and a standardized rating scale should be used for individual interviewer responses. Comments or notes should be made on a separate paper for each candidate for responses not pertaining to the standardized questions.

(2) A discussion of recorded observations made by each interviewer should take place, as soon as possible, after the interview. Tape recording the interview serves as a reference check for the discussion. Areas of disagreement should be highlighted, specific reasons provided, and areas of conflict resolved before interviewing subsequent applicants.

(3) An interview team whose members know their duties, responsibilities, and demands of the job should be appointed. Using several interviewers will provide an array of feedback that will allow for greater confidence in

selecting the "best" candidate when consensus is reached. The candidate's immediate supervisor should be on the interview team, with each member's vote having equal weight.

(4) Interviewers should be trained in interviewing techniques to enhance the validity and reliability of the process. Staff development or seminars can be used to train interviewers in developing listening skills, asking probing questions, using rating instruments, observing body behavior, and confronting personal bias.

(5) A good rapport must be established at the beginning of the interview to increase the probability that the candidate will share personal insights and information not contained in résumés or references, which are often vital for making a "good" selection.

(6) The interview should be supplemented with other selection criteria such as test results and reference checks. A second interview may be necessary depending on the results of the selection committee.

Types of Interviews

THE PILOT INTERVIEW

Advantages exist for conducting trial or pilot interviews with the selection committee members before the formal interview process. Castetter (1996) advocates using the simulation technique whereby experienced teachers act as interviewers and assist committee members in clarifying questions asked to candidates, in recommending specific questions to be asked by specific interviewers, in providing the committee with an approximate length of time needed for applicant interviews, and in developing response indicators that are key in hiring the "ideal" candidate. Pilot interviews can also assess if the candidate will feel comfortable in the interview setting, if the committee provides professional and courteous treatment, and if committee members appear open and friendly. They can also provide the means for an overall evaluation of the interview process. Because first impressions do count, the best candidate for the job may refuse a job offer if negative impressions or treatment from the selection committee exist.

THE FORMAL AND THE OPEN-ENDED INTERVIEWS

Two types of interviews are most often used for screening applicants. These are the formal interview and the open-ended interview. Formal or structured interviews follow set procedures, have standardized questions, and provide interviewee response sheets for comparison of candidate responses.

The open-ended interview is less structured and focuses on general questions that allow the candidate to respond freely to interview questions. Probing questions allow interviewers to gather more specific information from the candidate's responses. The purpose of both types of interviews is to acquire specific information about the candidate's knowledge, skills, values, beliefs, attitudes, and interpersonal skills (Fear, 1990). In open-ended interviews, responses should be recorded and questions should focus on position requirements and previous experiences that are relative to job responsibilities. Questions may also include case studies or sets of scenarios for applicants to answer. Responses to case studies or scenarios allow interviewers to assess applicants' abilities to "think on their feet" and to draw on their educational training and experience to solve problems which affect their ability to perform job-related tasks.

A Prototype of the Interview Process

Atmosphere is an essential consideration in the interview setting. Interviews should be conducted in surroundings that are pleasant, free from distractions, and comfortable. Applicants should be made to feel at ease and encouraged to stimulate a free-flowing dialogue that promotes a candid exchange of information between interviewers and interviewee.

Interviews should have opening, middle, and concluding sections. The opening part of the interview should include the following:

- The committee chairperson should provide an introduction of committee members, their positions, and job assignments.
- The committee chairperson should provide a brief review of the job description, job responsibilities, and job demands.
- The candidates should provide a brief biographical sketch of their backgrounds including academic preparation, professional accomplishments, work experience, and career goals. This allows the candidates to talk about themselves and promotes confidence.
- When applicants begin to feel comfortable with committee members, questions relating to position requirements can be asked and the middle point of the interview process begins.

The middle part of the interview can be viewed as being behavioral in scope. Fear (1990) relates that questions relevant to job requirements and responsibilities, prepared in advance, should explore the candidate's qualifications based on predetermined criteria. These criteria are specifically related to those behaviors that are necessary to successfully accomplish the job. Deming's quality theory (1986) states that behaviors most desirable in candidates must reflect those encompassed in the vision and goals of the school. These translate into the behavioral expectations necessary to attain the outcomes of the school's educational programs. Castetter (1996) maintains that interviewers should pose questions that fully explore candidates' work backgrounds and accomplishments as well as those areas pertaining to academic preparation and related experiences. Careful attention should be paid to areas of strengths and weaknesses.

Questions posed to candidates in a behavioral setting are situation specific. However, Castello (1991) provides the following guidelines for those who want to construct interviews on job-related criteria.

- Questions should be written that directly relate to specific job criteria and the goals of the school. Criteria should consist of those listed on the position announcement and those found in actual practice by the interview committee.
- Questions should be pretested by one or more teachers performing these job-related tasks and be revised according to suggestions.
- Questions should relate to each area of competency and be coded to designate which interviewer will ask the question. The degree of importance of each question should be noted and assigned a weight.
- Questions should be ordered randomly, and responses should be recorded during the interview and compared *immediately* after the interview. Comparison of responses allows the detection of possible bias or problems related to the recording of answers, listening ability, the *halo effect,* the identification of strengths and weaknesses of the candidates, and the consistency of answers.

Different types of questions can be asked in an interview to allow for several types of response modes that allow interviewers to observe how candidates react to a variety of hypothetical situations. Seyfarth (1996) states that *criteria questions* can detect possible problems that call for more information from the candidate or from the candidate's references. A criteria or behavior important to assess might be: "The candidate is able to work in a team and group environment." The question would then be: "What experience have you had in working with teacher teams and groups, and how do you perceive your role as a member of an instructional team and a problem-solving group?"

Other response mode questions for interviews are as follows:

- *Case study or situational questions.* These are beneficial in that they allow committee members to observe body language and hear immediate responses as to how candidates would react in a real-life situation. Usually, situations are recent happenings in the school, with the end result already known to the interviewers. How candidates arrive at the solution to the problem provides insight into how they think, their knowledge and skills, and their compatibility with the thinking and methods of solving problems with others within the school.

- *Opinion or philosophy questions:* These allow committee members to determine the overall view held by the candidate on a particular topic or issue. For example, when addressing the issue of student motivation, candidates often provide insight into their philosophies of education, their perceptions of the nature of the learner, and the role and responsibilities of the teacher.
- *Experience questions:* These allow candidates to reveal how they have confronted difficult problems, what led to the problems, and whether the problems were resolved to their satisfaction. Here, committee members can assess factors such as blaming others, accepting responsibility, and working with or seeking the opinions of others.
- *Professional judgment questions:* These allow committee members to explore the areas of professionalism and ethical behavior. "Forced choice" questions can be used to explore the degree of conviction a candidate has in a critical area of education. A question such as "Which is more important, covering the required course of content or selecting knowledge and skills essential for the student's overall success as a learner and applier of knowledge?" may not have a single solution and may be effectively argued both ways. The response can be judged on the candidate's ability to defend the answer with documentation, on how well the candidate articulates a defense, and on how the candidate responds to an immediate challenge by a potential peer.

The concluding section of the interview should allow candidates to ask questions about any concerns they may have about the position and to "follow-up" on any responses they had made to previous interviewer questions. Candidates should feel as though they have had an opportunity to adequately present their qualifications for the position and that their experience, knowledge, and skills were properly recognized. The interview should end on positive observations, with the chairperson highlighting some of the candidate's strengths, but refraining from making any commitments to the candidate that cannot be fulfilled. The candidate should be told when the hiring decision will be made, who will make the final hiring decision, and the salary and beginning date of employment.

Offering Contracts to Selected Candidates

Successful candidates should be notified by telephone, with contracts being signed within a week of notification. Each new hire should receive a comprehensive employment packet consisting of school board policies, faculty and student handbooks, a school calendar, and other information pertaining to school and faculty regulations and events. Information should be discussed with new faculty members in a preinduction seminar early in the summer before scheduled new staff member orientation sessions. Sometimes new staff members find certain policies inconsistent with their expectations, and timely decisions to seek other employment allows principals time to re-advertise the position or return to the original pool of applicants.

Notifying unsuccessful candidates is unpleasant at best. Debate exists as to whether telephone calls should be made to each candidate. Although personal telephone calls demonstrate professional courtesy and foster good public relations, they do take time and are best made by the principal. It is unnecessary to go into a great deal of detail with the unsuccessful candidate; generally, a brief description of the qualifications of the candidate who has *accepted* the position is sufficient. Form letters sent to unsuccessful candidates convey an impersonal impression and do little to assist them in understanding why they were not selected. Personal conversation can assist the unsuccessful applicants in understanding where their strengths lie, and suggestions can be made as to how they can strengthen their weaknesses.

RETENTION OF PERSONNEL

Retaining qualified personnel is a major concern of all administrators. Retaining highly qualified teachers requires effort, and effective school principals turn to research to help develop the skills needed to facilitate the personal and professional development of teachers and to provide avenues that make teaching a continuously rewarding and satisfying experience.

Successful principals fuse theory with common sense and experience to retain good teachers. Job satisfaction concerns among teachers have been identified as concerns about workload, frequent and varied new assignments, lack of adequate resources, inadequate administrator support, lack of adequate supervision for instruction, principal leadership style, stress, and lack of career opportunities (Haggart, 1990). Principals can successfully address many of these concerns by changing grade level or course assignments, by designing staff development programs around teacher needs, by instituting seminars or self-improvement programs, by encouraging teachers to attend conferences or workshops, by aligning or changing the curriculum, and by providing teachers more planning periods. One of the best ways principals can provide job satisfaction to teachers is to *reflect* on their own teaching experiences and take steps to eradicate those policies and practices that thwarted job satisfaction when they were teachers.

Research on motivation also provides principals with a conceptual framework to make teaching more rewarding and satisfying. Work by Maslow

(1970), Herzberg, Mausner, and Snyderman (1959), and others mentioned throughout the text have reported that intrinsic and extrinsic motivators promote job satisfaction. For example, achievement on the job, recognition for work accomplishments, job advancement, and increased responsibilities are job satisfiers. Adequate salary; a secure, safe and orderly environment; clean and updated facilities; a system of recognition and rewards; and the freedom to be creative are essential motivators for job satisfaction and personal development.

Herzberg, Mausner, and Synderman (1959) and Lunenburg and Ornstein (1996) point out that poor relationships with peers and supervisors or insecure feelings about one's position inhibits job satisfaction. People thrive on the known, on routine, even if they are dissatisfied with existing conditions. Fear of the unknown or uncertainty detracts from a secure environment and causes tension and dissatisfaction. When individuals are unsure about their future or are required to change their work routine too frequently, they become *disengaged* from active involvement and support for the organization's vision and goals, and they either explore other employment possibilities or extend their tension and dissatisfaction to others. Disengagement can ultimately lead to internal decay of the school's culture.

The values, beliefs, traditions, and other artifacts associated with organizational culture help perpetuate relationships and reinforce the school's environment. When relationships are free of conflict, threats, and confrontations, positive attitudes and a healthy environment help promote the school's vision and goals. When a culture reinforces the value of teachers through rewards and recognitions, allows for autonomy, and fosters mutual and self-respect, job satisfaction is a natural outcome. Central to promoting the positive aspects of school culture is the principal who models and perpetuates the satisfying variables essential for high morale, teacher engagement, and quality performance (Weller, 1998).

RETENTION THROUGH ORGANIZATIONAL STRUCTURE

Changes in school governance systems can improve the quality of the school environment. Site-based management models, such as TQM, have embraced many of the ideas found in motivational theory and in the research on effective leadership. Site-based management is a significant departure from the traditional bureaucratic structure of school governance and its leader autonomy, rigid rules and regulations, and disregard for the needs and expectations of employees. Most site-based models empower teachers to make decisions and to solve problems through school governance teams. Teachers have autonomy to make decisions regarding the school's curriculum and classroom instructional practices, the school's budget, and its operational policies.

From a human resources perspective, site-based management uses the full range of human potential through shared decision making, teamwork, the development of leadership skills, the opportunity to be creative and innovative, and peer collaboration (Prasch, 1990). The National Education Association (1991) reports that higher morale, more open communications, higher trust levels, and more innovations come from site-based managed schools than from those schools with traditional governance structures. In site-based managed schools, professional development programs address teacher needs through teacher-directed programs, and policies that affect classroom instruction are initiated and approved by teachers. Principals, however, have to be dedicated to site-based management for it to yield its promised results. Lunenburg and Ornstein (1996) caution that principals who pay "lip service" to shared governance practices and do not actively support the work of teacher teams create morale problems and promote distrust between teachers and administrators.

Teacher Turnover

Teacher turnover refers to teachers leaving the teaching profession or leaving one school for employment in another. Haggart (1990) relates that one teacher out of four remains in teaching after fifteen years of employment and attributes the high turnover to stress, isolation, powerlessness, low salary, lack of appreciation, and poor working conditions. Seyfarth (1996) comments on teacher dissatisfaction variables as being reasons for turnover and identified such variables to be boredom, lack of resources, lack of administrative support, and poor working conditions. Schlechty and Vance (1983) note that approximately fifteen percent of the teaching force leave the profession during their first two years as teachers and over forty percent leave the profession within their first seven years. They attributed teacher dissatisfaction to poor working conditions, low salary, lack of autonomy, excessive paperwork, extra duties, and student discipline problems.

Principals have little control over the salary scale, but they do have influence over other job dissatisfiers. Principals can do much to reduce teacher turnover by applying the findings of motivational theory, involving teachers in site-based decisions, establishing a rewards and recognition system, and having ongoing dialogues with teachers to determine their individual needs and expectations.

DISMISSAL OF PERSONNEL

Dismissal is a psychologically and emotionally difficult process. To avoid litigation, the principal must follow due process procedures. Lengthy proceedings and high legal and court costs make dismissal an option of last resort for principals and school boards. State statutes specify dismissal procedures, and the school system's attorney should be consulted before any action is taken to initiate dismissal proceedings. Most common grounds for teacher dismissal are incompetence, neglect of duty, insubordination, immorality or unprofessional conduct, and (in some states) for "good or just cause." Seyfarth (1996) relates that teachers have been dismissed for poor classroom discipline, abuse of children, refusal of assistance to enhance job performance, excessive absences and tardiness, and lack of self-control. Courts generally side with teachers in litigation, reasoning that the burden of proof lies with the school board to convince the courts of the charge(s). The basic legal concept is to protect the rights of the individual and to ensure each individual fairness and due process. When school systems act without regard for the rights of the individual, their actions may be viewed by the courts as being arbitrary and capricious (Alexander and Alexander, 1992).

School systems should have a systematic termination process which clearly delineates the reasons and procedures for the dismissal of personnel. Usually found in the system's personnel handbook, such a process provides a uniform approach to be applied to all employees. Dismissal is more difficult for tenured personnel than it is for non-tenured personnel.

Castetter (1996) and Rebore (1987) observed that ineffective performance as a reason for dismissal requires strict adherence to local, state, and federal regulations. When immoral or insubordinate acts are committed, the behavior leaves little doubt for grounds for dismissal, and the legal process is more clear than it is for dismissal for ineffective performance.

Dismissal for ineffective performance is a multifaceted problem. First, the system used for recruitment and selection may need to be reevaluated to detect more effective ways to screen and hire applicants. Second, variables associated with the school's culture or policies have to be examined. For example, teacher workload, supervision policies and practices, administrator support, opportunities to develop both personally and professionally, and safe and secure working conditions are institutional variables associated with regressive performance. Castetter (1996) points out that until the organization provides its best efforts to assist individuals in becoming effective, dismissal is unjust and should not be considered.

Options other than dismissal should be carefully explored. One option is to *retain* the teacher and have requirements that include behavior modification through assistance such as peer coaching or staff development. This option can include changing or modifying duties or responsibilities or assigning the individual to another position. The second option is to *sever* the teacher from the school. Suboptions include early retirement (voluntary or involuntary), transfer to another school, or termination from the school system with placement assistance (Castetter, 1996).

A decision to terminate employment should follow legal guidelines with reasons for termination fully documented as set forth in policy and statutes. Time lines for notification of intent to terminate must be adequate and in accordance with policy, and time should be provided to allow the individual to seek other employment. Dismissal hearings, under the due process clause of the Fourteenth Amendment, are usually held with written notice of intent to terminate. Dismissal charges are provided before the hearing. Teachers should have adequate time to prepare a response and to present evidence against the accusations. Attorneys and witnesses may assist the defendant, and a written record of the proceedings must be retained in case the teacher exercises the option to appeal an unfavorable decision.

Generally, courts are concerned with several key issues in cases of teacher dismissal: that the individual had adequate warning of the consequences of his or her conduct; that policy and procedures were followed leading up to the decision to terminate employment; that the rules, policies, and penalties were fairly applied without discrimination and that the individual was treated fairly; that the individual had knowledge of the policies and procedures of the school or school system; and that the school system followed due process procedures. Knowledge of school board policy can be addressed by providing teachers with copies of the system's rules and regulations in faculty handbooks and in new teacher orientation sessions. Concerns over legitimate duties and responsibilities required of the job, fair and equal treatment, and conduct and consequences can be addressed through formal evaluation procedures and written documentation. Due process procedures should be followed exactly as outlined by the attorney for the board of education.

Incompetency

Incompetency has been defined as a lack of adequate skills or subject knowledge, poor classroom management practices, outright neglect of duty, poor or inadequate teaching methods, and physical or mental disability that prohibits the ability to perform the job (Alexander and Alexander, 1992). Proof of incompetency lies with the school board, and testimony from parents, students, peers, and supervisors may be used to support the charge of incompetence. Evidence presented by the supervisor is given the greatest weight, and it must be substantial and compiled over time. Documented evidence must be based on standards used to evaluate other teachers in similar positions with similar responsibilities, and not on ideal, abstract criteria. Further, the evidence for dismissal must demonstrate a pattern of behavior, and not just a single incident.

Charges of incompetence come from all quarters. Parents or community members who have little direct contact with the classroom performance of teachers may complain about the incompetence of teachers. Such complaints should, of course, be investigated, especially when complaints are frequent or when there is a discernable pattern underlying frequent complaints. Students also make complaints concerning teacher incompetence. Because students sometimes exaggerate and negative personal experiences can bias their perceptions, it is necessary to determine the roots of their dissatisfaction. In many cases, supervisors are in the best position to provide information on charges of incompetence. Supervisors work closely with subordinates, are trained and skilled teachers themselves, and evaluate performance on valid and reliable instruments. Should remediation be needed, supervisors are responsible for notifying the teacher (in writing) of areas that need improvement, for assisting the teacher in developing a plan for remediation with delineated goals, for allowing adequate time for improvement strategies to take place, and then for evaluating the teacher on the same evaluation instrument initially used for performance assessment.

When areas needing remediation are identified, teachers may request additional observations or evaluations from peers trained in using the assessment instrument. To thwart charges of administrator bias, a comparison of peer and administrator evaluation results should be conducted. A good practice is to have two or more teacher evaluation observations with two or more different evaluators. Composite results provide a pattern of behavior that usually presents an accurate picture of performance.

Neglect of Duty

Neglect of duty differs from insubordination in that insubordination is the *refusal* to follow policies or procedures or to obey a direct and lawful order from a superior, whereas neglect of duty is the *inability* to perform job requirements. Physical or mental disabilities are grounds for dismissal. In determining whether dismissal is justified, the question to be asked is "Does the disability prevent the person from meeting the demands of the job?" If the impairment hinders adequate job performance, dismissal or reassignment is justified. Schneid (1992) relates that employers must make "reasonable accommodations" to assist the disabled in performing the "essential" responsibilities of the job. The Equal Employment Opportunities Commission (EEOC) provides guidelines for job modifications, and these must be followed to ensure that qualified personnel have the opportunity to perform those requirements that are essential to fulfill their contractual obligations.

Disabilities such as failing eyesight or hearing may be grounds for dismissal or reassignment in certain cases. Risk of infectious disease (contamination) is another reason for dismissal, but courts have ruled that the disease *must* pose a "significant risk" of contamination, which requires strong medical evidence. Rulings from courts on disabilities that relate to employment are based on the

Americans with Disabilities Act of 1990 (ADA), which extends to all phases of employment, from recruiting to dismissal.

Mental or emotional illness, which produces dangerous or bizarre behavior, may be grounds for dismissal. Offers of medical assistance must be provided, but if treatment is refused and there is an insistence on working while illness exists, grounds for dismissal may exist.

Immoral and Unprofessional Behavior

Moral behavior or good conduct has both universal and situation-specific (local) standards. Local standards of moral conduct are those perpetuated by local norms, beliefs, values, and mores. Court decisions have also defined moral conduct for educators. *Morals* pertain primarily to good conduct and give guidance to human acts or codes of behavior deemed acceptable by others. Put another way, universal morals define *good* conduct, whereas local or situation-specific morals define *good* conduct within locally accepted codes of behavior. Courts have been the primary source to determine what constitutes moral behavior in educational situations.

Relationships between teachers and students that exceed the "normal" bounds of friendship, such as dating, is considered to be inappropriate behavior. Sexual acts between teacher and student are causes for immediate suspension, whereas allegations are investigated (Rebore, 1987). Rebore notes that unconventional lifestyles such as homosexuality, wife swapping, and cohabitation without marriage do not affect one's ability to perform on the job and, because of media coverage, have limited influence on students and community members. However, when teachers advocate unconventional lifestyles in schools, and these lifestyles go against the local standards of acceptable behavior, teachers may be in danger of dismissal because they are viewed as exemplars and their conduct is highly scrutinized by the community.

Behavior that results in arrest may be grounds for suspension with pay but may not constitute grounds for dismissal. However, conviction of moral turpitude may be grounds for termination of the contract. Alexander and Alexander (1992) relate that a *nexus* must exist between personal conduct and the ability to teach, the conduct must have a negative effect on the school, or the conduct must have sufficient notoriety to warrant dismissal. In all cases, allegations of misconduct must be supported by facts and clearly documented.

Other causes for dismissal may include sexual misconduct with nonstudents, talking about sex with students outside the context of the curriculum, dishonesty, and use of profane language. Possession and use of controlled substances may be grounds for suspension and eventual dismissal. In general, cases of immoral conduct resulting in court decisions have balanced the rights and personal freedom of the individual with the interests of the schools and students.

Dismissal for Just Cause

Dismissal for *good* or *just cause* is a general concept, and reasons vary for instituting dismissal proceedings on these grounds. Generally, dismissal proceedings in these cases are initiated for the good of the school system. Some grounds for good or just cause are neglect of duty, unprofessional conduct, and conduct unbecoming a teacher. Castello (1991) states that just cause provisions in contracts protect non-tenured teachers, who are usually on a two- or three-year probationary period, from arbitrary and capricious reasons for dismissal. Sometimes teacher contracts specify reasons for just cause dismissal, but there is no universally accepted definition or test of good or just cause that can be applied. Usually, good or just cause dismissal issues revolve around the following situations:

(1) Job performance: Behaviors that influence classroom competency and are evidenced in evaluation results of job performance.

(2) Neglect of duties: Behaviors that are against or do not fulfill the requirements of the job as explained, as provided in the contract, or as stated in the job description.

(3) Unprofessional behavior: Behaviors defined by the school system as unbecoming a teacher or member of the teaching profession (Castello, 1991)

Insubordination

Insubordination is more than outright refusal to comply with an administrative directive or to obey an administrative order. Insubordination is also interpreted as a refusal to perform "reasonable" and/or job-related responsibilities. Seyfarth (1996) and Castello (1991) relate that insubordinate acts may include excessive absenteeism and tardiness, failure to complete required reports or projects, refusal to assume newly assigned duties, repeated uses of profanity, and the use of corporal punishment in violation of school board policy. Courts have generally ruled that newly assigned duties that are reasonable and relate to the instructional program and that are not overly time consuming or burdensome are within the prerogative of administrators. However, assigned duties must be commensurate with the teacher's abilities and be related to the school's programs. Refusal to perform tasks outside these qualifiers are seldom sustained by courts as lawful grounds for dismissal.

In insubordination cases, courts tend to favor school boards when the following conditions exist: repeated offenses of the same violation occur; the behavior is deemed irremediated; and the behavior is exhibited with knowledge of the policy or directive (Fischer, Schimmel, and Kelly, 1991). Fischer et al., report that willful and deliberate neglect or violation of policy or an administrative directive are grounds for dismissal, within the following guidelines: (1) the policy or directive must fall within the legal rights of the school board or administrator and (2) the policy or directive must be *clearly stated* and *reasonable.* Insubordination cannot be charged when a teacher refuses to obey a policy or directive that violates that teacher's constitutional rights.

Lunenburg and Ornstein (1996) relate the importance of school principals' seeking legal counsel before initiating charges against staff members. Generally, litigation that involves teachers and school boards centers around the First Amendment, Fourth Amendment, Fifth Amendment, and Fourteenth Amendment rights of the federal Constitution. The First Amendment focuses on free speech rights and rights of expression, the right to assemble, and the right to file a petition for redress of grievances. The Fourth Amendment rights pertain to unreasonable searches and rights to privacy, whereas the Fifth Amendment addresses due process rights. The Fourteenth Amendment pertains to issues involving tenure and discrimination regarding race, sex, age, and handicaps.

OTHER ISSUES

Academic Freedom

Academic freedom is a tradition that stems from our democratic heritage, and it centers on freedom of expression and thought. Freedom to learn implies freedom to teach, and threats to one endanger the other. Some definitions of academic freedom are more liberal than others. Some maintain that academic freedom pertains to both teachers and students and others believe academic freedom "refers to the liberty to inquire, to discuss, and to interpret any aspect of culture at all levels" (Castetter, 1996, p. 349).

The essence of academic freedom seems to be a condition for free inquiry, which is essential for unobstructed learning. Although the definition has been revised over time through court decisions, the First Amendment provides for freedom of speech, and courts have ruled on academic freedom cases under this constitutional guarantee. Consequently, academic freedom is held to be limited by those generally accepted standards placed on responsible scholarship as they pertain to expression, investigation, and discussion.

Sexual Harassment and Maternity Leave

Sexual harassment, as defined under Title VII of the Civil Rights Act of 1964, focuses on unwelcome sexual advances or sexual requests, or other verbal or physical conduct of a sexual nature that falls within the context of employment conditions and impedes one's work performance or contributes to an offensive or hostile work environment. Lunenburg and Ornstein (1996) report that courts recognize two separate forms of sexual harassment: (1) *Quid pro quo,* which involves sexual favors for employment benefits. (2) *Hostile work environment,* which consists of unwelcome or offensive conduct that creates an environment that unreasonably interferes with work performance or creates an atmosphere of hostility or intimidation.

Courts look for a pattern in charges of sexual harassment, including frequency and severity of activity, and whether the behavior provides a psychological threat or humiliating experience. Recently, courts have held that sexual harassment must be behavior that inflicts "tangible psychological injury" rather than behavior that is deemed offensive (Hubbartt, 1993).

Maternal discrimination cannot be conducted under the Pregnancy Discrimination Act of 1978. An extension of Title VII of the Civil Rights Act of 1964 states that pregnancy must be treated as any other temporary medical condition (Hubbartt, 1993), and school boards cannot require set periods of time for maternity leave (either before or after birth). Maternity leave policies that are not arbitrary and are designed with the intent of "fulfilling a legitimate goal of maintaining continuity in instruction in a school system" are upheld by the courts (Lunenburg and Ornstein, 1996, p. 382).

The period of maternity leave varies from four to six weeks before and after the date of birth of the child. The Family and Medical Leave Act of 1993 requires a maximum of 12 work weeks of unpaid leave during a calendar year for child birth or adoption. Childbearing leave must also apply to males, and the employee is entitled to his or her original job or an equivalent job with original pay and benefits upon return.

DEMOTIONS, REASSIGNMENTS, AND REDUCTION IN FORCE

A teacher undergoes a demotion when a decrease in salary or responsibilities occurs, when a teacher is transferred to another job and the job requires less knowledge and skill than the previous job, or when a teacher is reassigned to teach a grade level or a subject without proper certification or no significant recent experience. Demotions are generally upheld by the courts when they have been made for the efficient management of resources or to discipline an employee (Webb, Montello, and Norton, 1994). Management of resources as a reason for demotion usually follows declining student enrollments or an unexpected loss of revenue.

Demotion, according to Castetter (1996), is "a form of transfer or reassignment involving a decrease in salary, status, responsibility, privilege, or opportunity" (p. 396). Demotions may arise from staff reductions, overly qualified personnel, or incorrect initial placement. When demotion occurs, due process procedures must be followed lest demotions deny rights granted an individual under the First, Fifth, and Fourteenth Amendments. Unwarranted demotion can cause administrators severe legal problems, and other alternatives, such as job transfer (without loss of pay or status) and incentives for early retirement, should be considered first. Ineffective job performance is a primary reason for demotion, but other reasons include behavior in violation of standards, behavior causing the institution loss of image, elimination of the position, and ideological differences between the individual and the organization. When demotion is contemplated, legal advice should be sought and strictly followed.

Reassignment or *transfer* is clearly within the prerogative of the school board. Reassignment to another position requires certification for the position, and it cannot be done capriciously, arbitrarily, or in violation of established school board policy. The definition of reassignment refers to the transferring of personnel from one position, department, or school to another. Reassignments can be voluntary (requested by personnel) or involuntary (initiated by school or central office administrators).

Voluntary reassignments can be requested by personnel for better working conditions, to work closer to their homes, for advancement or increased compensation, to work in schools that are not in low-income areas, to leave hostile working environments, and for physical reasons. Involuntary reassignments initiated by administrators may result from opening new schools; from court decisions seeking a balance in race, gender, experience, or talent; from friction in personal relationships; from needs of the school system; and from better use of talent (Castetter, 1996).

Reduction in force (RIF) should be carried out in accordance with school board policy, which should be designed to ensure fair, efficient, and consistent procedures. Release of excess employees may be a result of declining enrollments, school consolidation and reorganization, financial emergencies, and curriculum discontinuations. Some states allow RIF for "just" or "good cause." Courts tend to focus on two issues when RIF is instituted by school systems: (1) whether the release of the employee is *bona fide* and (2) whether the release is *justified*. The burden of proof resides with the school board. McCarthy and Cambron-McCabe (1992) relate that there must be an absence of bias on the part of the school board (evidence of discrimination and violation of constitutional rights) in releasing employed personnel. Courts deem boards to act in good faith and generally uphold force reduction policies.

Generally, courts hold that employees have no right to positions deemed unnecessary by school boards. However, reasons for RIF must be reasonable and clearly documented. The positions vacated must also be abolished. Policies on reducing the employee work force should be stated in board policy and employee contracts. Considerations of tenure, seniority, talent, and skills may be used as preferences for employee retention. Courts have been mainly consistent in ruling that neither tenure nor seniority is a guarante for job security or job recall unless stated in the board's policy or in the employee's contract (McCarthy and Cambron-McCabe, 1992).

For reduction in force, Seyfarth (1996) provides the following seven-step process to determine whether reduction should be implemented:

(1) Document through facts that a surplus exists. Small excesses may be taken care of by normal attrition.

(2) Determine the surplus by position and certification.

(3) Review and document alternatives to RIF (e.g., early retirement, unpaid leave of absences, half-time employment, retraining, and the location of other employment opportunities for employees).

(4) Determine those specific personnel who will be laid off. Use board policy and contract agreements to identify the pool of personnel to be laid off (the school board attorney should be consulted in this step and the three subsequent steps).

(5) Review certification credentials for possible reassignment and look for those with special talents and skills that cannot be assumed by others. Some school boards use performance ratings as criteria for maintaining employment as well as tenure, seniority, extra duty assignments, and additional certification.

(6) Review the rank-ordered list of employees slated for reduction and follow the board's policy for preparing reduction in force notices

(7) Prepare letters signed by the superintendent and specify the date the reduction takes effect. Advise the employees of their rights and the appeal process.

In site-based managed schools, some principals have been given much latitude in exercising reduction in force procedures. Consulting the superintendent and the school board attorney are the best practices. What remains different in RIF practices initiated at the school district level and those at site-based managed schools is the school's ability to make decisions that concern budgeting and hiring procedures to meet their own needs (Odden and Picus, 1992). In these schools, when budget cuts occur, school councils play vital roles in making decisions, and they may choose to reduce the number of teacher aides, to transfer monies from one account to another, or to purchase instructional materials from personal funds rather than RIF teachers. More importantly, if site-based managed schools plan their recruitment and hiring needs effectively, the probability that a reduction in force will occur is minimal because each school is a central entity and can best judge its own short- and long-range needs.

REFERENCES

Aldag, R. J. and T. M. Stearns. 1990. *Management.* Second edition. Cincinnati: South-Western.

Alexander, I. E. 1990. *Personology: Method and Content of Personality-Assessment and Pscyhobiography,* Durham, N.C.: Duke University Press.

Alexander, K. and M. Alexander. 1992. *American Public School Law.* Third edition. St. Paul: West.

Bible, J. D. and D. A. McWhirter. 1990. *Privacy in the Workplace: A Guide for Human Resource Managers.* New York: Quorum Books.

Cascio, W. F. 1989. *Managing Human Resources: Productivity, Quality of Work Life, Profits.* Second edition. New York: McGraw-Hill

Castello, R. T. 1991. *School Personnel Administration: A Practitioner's Guide.* Needham Heights, MA: Allyn and Bacon.

Castetter, W. B. 1996. *The Human Resource Function in Educational Administration.* Sixth edition. Englewood Cliffs, NJ: Prentice Hall.

Dailey, C. A. 1982. "Using the Track Record Approach: The Key to Successful Personnel Selection." New York: AMACOM.

Deming, W. E. 1986. *Out of the Crisis.* Cambridge, MA: MIT Press.

Dessler, G. 1991. *Personnel—Human Resources Management.* Fifth edition. Englewood Cliffs, NJ: Prentice-Hall

Fear, R. A. 1990. *The Evaluation Interview.* Fourth edition. New York: McGraw-Hill.

Fischer, L., D. Schimmel, and C. Kelly. 1991. *Teachers and the Law.* Third edition. New York: Longman.

Haggart, B. 1990. "Who is at Risk—Students or Teachers?" *Thrust,* 19 (5):42–44.

Herzberg, F., B. Mausner, and B. Snyderman. 1959. *The Motivation to Work.* New York: Wiley.

Hubbartt, W. 1993. *Personal Policy Handbook.* New York: McGraw-Hill.

Lunenburg, F. C. and A. C. Ornstein. 1996. *Educational Administration: Concepts and Practices.* Second edition. Belmont, CA: Wadsworth.

McCarthy, M. M. 1983. "Discrimination in Employment," in *Legal Issues in Public School Employment.* Joseph A. Beckham and P. A. Zirkel, eds., Bloomington, IN: Phi Delta Kappa.

McCarthy, M. M. and N. H. Cambron-McCabe. 1992. *Public School Law: Teacher's and Student's Rights.* Third edition. Boston: Allyn and Bacon.

Maslow, A. H. 1970. *Motivation and Personality.* New York: Harper and Row.

National Education Association 1991. *Site-based Decision Making: The (1990) NEA Census of Local Associations.* Washington, DC: Author.

Prasch, J. 1990. *How to Organize for School-based Management.* Alexandria, VA: Association for Supervision and Curriculum Development.

Rebore, R. W. 1987. *Personnel Administration in Education: A Management Approach.* Second edition. Englewood Cliffs, NJ: Prentice-Hall.

Redeker, J. R. 1989. *Employee Discipline: Policies and Practices.* Washington, D.C.: The Bureau of National Affairs.

Schlechty, P. and V. Vance. 1983. "Do Academically Able Teachers Leave Education? The North Carolina Case." *Phi Delta Kappan,* 63:106–112.

Schneid, T. 1992. *The Americans with Disabilities Act: A Practical Guide for Managers.* New York: Van Nostrand Reinhold.

Seyfarth, J. T. 1996. *Personnel Management for Effective Schools.* Second edition. Boston: Allyn and Bacon.

Webb, L. D., P. A. Montello, and M. S. Norton. 1994. *Human Resources Administration: Personnel Issues and Needs in Education.* New York: Macmillan.

Weller, L. D. 1998. "Unlocking the Culture for Quality Schools: Reengineering," *International Journal of Educational Management,* 12(6):250–259.

Yate, M. J. 1993. *Hiring the Best: A Manager's Guide to Effective Interviewing.* Fourth edition. Cambridge, MA: Adams House.

CHAPTER 9

Promoting Human Potential Through Performance Appraisal

Principals are legally responsible for evaluating staff performance. Performance appraisal represents judgments about individual performance on objective criteria that accurately reflect the requirements of the job and the overall goals and objectives of the school. The primary purpose of performance evaluation is to improve the teaching-learning phenomena to maximize student achievement.

Unless assessment instruments are valid and reliable, assessment results lack meaning and remediation programs based on these results will be counterproductive to the individual and to the organization. Appraisals should be both formative and summative in scope and be diagnostic in nature. Assessing the *effectiveness* of individual performance relative to job-related objectives and organizational goals allows administrators to make decisions on needed staff development and individual improvement plans, employment status, promotions, and salary increases.

APPRAISAL SYSTEMS

In quality-producing organizations, performance appraisal is used to improve individual performance and to meet the goals of the organization. Appraisal procedures should be formative, summative, and diagnostic in nature and should focus on assessing the *effectiveness* of the individual in performing specific, job-related tasks.

Designed properly, appraisal systems can promote positive attitudes toward performance evaluation and integrate the interests of the individual with those of the organization. Additional advantages of the appraisal process are mutual goal setting, professional development, and the freedom to be creative and innovative within a system that promotes continuous improvement. These benefits promote an affinity between the individual and the organization as both pursue a "fit" that satisfies needs, expectations, and mutual goals.

The Purpose of Appraisal

The most important purpose of performance appraisal is to enhance job performance. As a part of a valid and reliable instrument, the objective criteria should serve as a diagnostic tool to assist administrators in maximizing the potential of teachers. However, assessment instruments can be used in both positive and negative ways. Rebore (1995) notes that positive outcomes of teacher appraisal include identifying needs for staff development and individual professional growth plans; making promotion or job reassignment decisions; deciding on employment retention and/or tenure; recommending salary increases; recognizing achievement; motivating teachers; and realigning job descriptions and job requirements. Castetter (1996) emphasizes the importance of using appraisal findings to remove barriers to effective teaching and student learning.

Negative outcomes of performance appraisals fall under the "control factor"—using appraisals to make teachers conform to organizational expectations, to punish or belittle teachers, or to "motivate" through threat. Castetter (1996) notes that when administrators exert their authority to control teacher behavior through performance appraisals, they may thwart the inclination of teachers to be creative and innovative. Seyfarth (1996) relates that teachers become dissatisfied in and distrustful of the appraisal process when teachers are evaluated on unrealistic criteria, performance criteria are not correlated to job requirements, or when administrators make subjective judgments.

Emotional overtones and personalities can interfere with objectivity in the evaluation process. The quality and type of relationship between the evaluator and the evaluatee may influence assessment outcomes. When this happens, the goals and value of the evaluation process are violated. Difficult as it may be, professional evaluation has to be objective and fair, and accurate data have to be collected on valid and reliable criteria if performance appraisal is to be meaningful and if it is to improve the teaching-learning process.

Teacher Response to Performance Appraisal

Evaluation can be conducted in a perfunctory manner rooted in obligation or policy, or it can be conducted with the goal of improving the teaching and learning environment of the classroom. Many administrators view teacher evaluation as lying somewhere between these bipolars. Teachers also have dichotomous views of evaluation. Some view evaluation as a routine, a necessary evil that they may or may not fear. Others are indifferent and some welcome the opportunity for feedback and improvement suggestions. Some teachers face evaluation with trepidation, high anxiety, and fear. Darling-Hammond (1986) noted that in many schools, evaluation has little effect on teacher performance even though teachers stand to benefit or lose from performance evaluation results. She notes that some fear reprisal through evaluation, whereas others view it as an opportunity to demonstrate their skills. However, the overall effect of evaluation on teachers "contributes to their weariness and reinforces their skepticism of the bureaucratic routine. . . ." (pp. 531–532). Administrators, she relates, view evaluation as an added task and often conduct the minimum number of teacher observations that are required by policy; results of evaluation are usually high; and the quality of feedback on their performance varies from school to school.

Moreover, the style the evaluator adopts during the evaluation process can contribute to a threatening or dissatisfying experience or make it personally rewarding and professionally beneficial. The attitude of the evaluator toward the teacher, and the process in general, affects the teacher's disposition toward the evaluation process; and the manner in which the evaluator conducts the evaluation influences the behavior of the teacher.

School Culture and Performance Appraisal

Culture, defined by Greetz (1973), is "the historically transmitted pattern of meaning embodied in symbols" (p. 109) that includes written and unwritten messages that convey the values, beliefs, traditions, and norms of expected behavior. Heckman (1993) describes school culture as those commonly held beliefs and daily codes of conduct that guide the interaction of teachers, principals, and students. Deal and Peterson (1990) relate that these shared values and beliefs form patterns of behavior that promote a bond of trust among students, teachers, and administrators. Central to this trust relationship are a shared vision and mission that focus on the commonly held quality management goals of constancy of purpose and continuous improvement (Weller, 1996). Cunningham and Gresso (1993) reported that quality-producing schools have cultures that radiate teacher trust, self-confidence, cooperation, and a commitment to continuous improvement. Teachers strive to do their best, to promote a team spirit, and to work with principals who model key cultural behaviors. These factors promote a positive and healthy attitude toward performance appraisal.

In these schools, principals and teachers view performance appraisal as a way to improve teaching and to develop more fully as professionals. Assessments are used as diagnostic indicators to bring about personal and professional development, and principals create positive attitudes toward assessment by emphasizing the positive aspects of evaluation for both teachers and students.

The kind of relationship teachers have with the principal and the manner in which performance appraisal is conducted affect teacher attitudes toward evaluations and the principal. Teachers who view principals as being professional, competent, and having their best interests at heart are more likely to value recommendations for improvement and treat evaluation results more seriously than do teachers who view principals as being incompetent or conducting evaluations as a policy requirement (Duke and Stiggins, 1993). Hoenack and Monk (1990) note positive correlations between teacher evaluation results and teacher improvement when good working relations exist between the teacher and the principal and when performance appraisal results are considered as being fair and accurate. However, when teachers view the evaluation results as being unfair or invalid, they feel threatened, are less open to improvement suggestions, and have low morale. When teachers perceive that personality is a factor in evaluation results, their respect for the principal decreases and they have high anxiety over the evaluation process and low morale and job satisfaction. Castetter (1996) notes teacher concerns over questions of the evaluation instrument's validity and reliability. In addition, when evaluation results are presented by the principal, in writing, before postevaluation conferences, teachers feel frustrated and angry because they perceive that few options exist for clarifying or explaining points of disagreement.

DEVELOPING AN APPRAISAL SYSTEM

Processes for evaluating professional personnel are established through state and/or local school board policy. Legally, these procedures must be followed, but often evaluation policies are broad enough to allow principals some latitude in how certain processes can be conducted at the school level. In states prescribing procedures for evaluating teachers, assessment instruments are usually prescribed, as are specific requirements for assessment. This includes the number of observations, the conditions under which evaluation is to take place, and the criteria being used to assess performance.

Evaluation of Certified Staff

Criteria vary for assessing teacher performance but usually focus on five common areas and address two major questions. The five criteria areas are (1) knowledge of the subject, (2) planning for instruction, (3) implementing and managing instruction, (4) evaluating student learning, and (4) managing the classroom. The two major questions concerning teacher performance are

(1) "Is the teacher able to demonstrate adequate performance on the assessment criteria?" and (2) "Does the teacher apply the knowledge and skills in an appropriate manner?" The first question requires the evaluator to assess the knowledge or the ability of the teacher, whereas the second question calls for judgment decisions by the evaluator on the "appropriateness" of use. Teachers must first understand the criteria being assessed and then demonstrate those specific criteria during the observation. Unless the evaluator is willing to consider the goal and objectives of the lesson, the types of students being taught, and the fact that instruction is a cumulative condition and not an incremental process, judgments made by evaluators may be erroneous. When evaluation instruments call for recording specific degrees of behaviors, training is often required to strengthen the reliability of evaluation results. Lack of or inadequate training in the use of evaluation instruments calls into question the reliability of evaluation findings, and principals are cautioned about the weight they give these results.

Many models exist for developing an appraisal process, but there is general agreement regarding certain procedures to ensure a fair and professional approach to employee evaluation. An example of an appraisal process that ensures a fair, informative, and holistic evaluation for certified staff members follows.

STAGE ONE

Meet all teachers during the preplanning stage and discuss your evaluation philosophy and the purpose of performance evaluation. Go over the evaluation instrument(s) and provide all teachers with copies of the instrument(s). Questions should be addressed to teachers' satisfaction and a time line for evaluation visits should be circulated.

Philosophies differ regarding announced and unannounced observations. This and the number of observations are usually prescribed by local and/or state policy. One argument supporting announced visits is the ability to see teachers perform at their best. Those favoring unannounced visits believe that teachers should be performing at their best all the time. Unannounced visits, however, can cause much anxiety among beginning teachers and among some experienced teachers as well.

STAGE TWO

Before classroom evaluations, meet individually with teachers (usually a week before the observation) and obtain a copy of their weekly lesson plans. Review the assessment criteria and discuss any personal problems teachers may have or specific problems they may have with students in class.

Sometimes teachers are reluctant to share problems, and a meeting such as this often provides teachers the opportunity to discuss openly factors influencing their performance.

STAGE THREE

Observe each teacher using the agreed-upon evaluation instrument and follow the prescribed evaluation procedures discussed with teachers during preplanning.

STAGE FOUR

Meet with the observed teacher within two days of the observation and jointly discuss evaluation results using a copy of the coded instrument to foster discussion. Present positive findings first and then discuss those that are deemed less than satisfactory. Allow teachers time to present their perspective of the lessons and be willing to revise your instrument responses if appropriate. Make immediate suggestions for improvement and, if necessary, arrange for special assistance with teacher input. Sometimes another observation is appropriate in a week or two, especially for first-year teachers.

STAGE FIVE

Provide teachers with a signed and dated summary of the post-observation conference results and discuss formal improvement plans if necessary. Plans should be mutually agreed-upon and signed by both parties. Principals must provide adequate support, time, and resources while teachers are undergoing improvement plan activities.

STAGE SIX

For those teachers working under remediation or improvement plans, subsequent observations will follow that focus only on areas needing remediation as agreed-upon in the improvement plan. Any adjustment in the plan should be mutually agreed-upon, documented in writing, and signed by both parties.

Aside from classroom observations, principals should periodically discuss teacher progress and difficulties encountered while working on improvement plans. Periodic conferences with department heads, peer teachers, or peer coaches should supplement teacher conferences. Providing an ongoing support and communication network allows principals to continuously monitor teacher progress and to demonstrate commitment to assisting teachers in maximizing their potential.

Evaluation of Noncertified Staff

Procedures for evaluating noncertified personnel should closely model the evaluation process for teachers. Staff members should know their duties and responsibilities as outlined in their job requirements. Essential to effective performance evaluation outcomes is a knowledge of the criteria upon which performance is to be evaluated. If assessment instruments are unavailable, they should be developed with staff member input and should include any additional expectations the principal may have. Agreement over these criteria must be mutual with the job requirements serving as the foundation for evaluation criteria.

Many times, one or two formal assessments are impractical for a given position. Ongoing assessment may provide more accurate evaluation results with periodic conferences and written documentation of the conferences. For example, office personnel or custodians perform expected tasks daily and the results of their work or attitudes are readily observed. Areas that need improvement should be brought to their attention, plans for remediation should be mutually agreed-upon and signed, and a time line for improvement and criteria for improvement should be developed jointly.

Building the "Freedom to Fail" into the Appraisal System

If teachers are to improve, principals must allow them the freedom to fail. Learning from previous mistakes is one of the best learning exercises that one can have. Freedom to fail without the threat of reprisal encourages creativity and innovation. Being able to experiment leads to greater learning and promotes feelings of personal satisfaction and autonomy. Herzberg, Mausner, and Snyderman (1959) note that personal satisfaction and autonomy are central to personal development and promote greater job satisfaction and job effectiveness.

Teacher improvement plans should have inherent flexibility to allow teachers to experiment with new and different approaches for improvement. Principals should encourage and support creative improvement approaches and require only that teachers learn from their unsuccessful outcomes. In this way, principals accomplish a dual purpose: (1) they allow teachers the opportunity to satisfy personal growth interests by encouraging them to experiment with ideas of personal interest and (2) they allow teachers to work toward self-improvement in an environment that is free of undue stress and the threat of failure. Personal interests frequently dovetail with areas that need improvement and with the goals of the organization. Bennis (1990) talks about a "committed partnership" that is essential for individual job satisfaction and for organizational goal attainment. Allowing employees to be creative, innovative, and responsible for their own successes and failures allows for risk taking and promotes greater job effectiveness. Greater job effectiveness and employee satisfaction are goals of organizations and yield a committed partnership.

SOME APPRAISAL CONCERNS

Many school systems use their own teacher appraisal instruments as supplements or as replacements of state mandated instruments to assess performance. In evaluating teacher performance, the major concerns are over instrument validity and reliability, questions that professional testing houses have addressed in their published instruments. These concerns will be discussed later in this chapter. Other concerns are ones with which principals should be familiar in terms of their influence on the appraisal process. These include the differences in and the appropriate use of formative and summative evaluation and appraiser style.

Formative and Summative Evaluation

Evaluation has two major processes with which to assess results on investigated variables. These are the formative and summative methods and each requires a different evaluation design and technique. Formative evaluation assesses the effect or quality of a treatment while the experiment is in progress to determine its intermediate impact before conclusion. Results allow for modification of the process so that the desired end outcomes can be achieved. Popham (1988) describes formative evaluation as a proactive process where one makes decisions to adjust the process before the final outcome.

Summative evaluation assesses the effect or quality at the end conclusion of the treatment. Results describe the overall outcome of the investigated variable because it is an end assessment process or an after-the-fact procedure (Popham, 1988). Formative evaluation methods are used to *improve* and not to prove. Formative teacher evaluations should be intended to identify weaknesses or deficiencies that hinder the quality and effectiveness of teaching and to make modifications while the process is in progress. Summative evaluation represents an end or final assessment, after formative evaluation has taken place, and the results are used for dismissal, reassignment, pay increases, tenure, and promotion. Popham makes clear the function of summative evaluation methods for assessing teacher performance when he states: "Summative teacher evaluation has as its primary function the determination of a teacher's competence—not the augmentation of that competence. Summative evaluation makes no pretense about helping a teacher get better. Improving the teacher's performance is the job of formative teacher evaluation" (p. 282).

Clearly, the job of remediation falls within the scope of formative evaluation. Castetter (1996) relates that performance ineffectiveness should be identified on measures before any final decision about reemployment or end decisions about performance are made. It is essential that assistance be provided in areas deemed ineffective to allow the employee a fair opportunity to improve *before* a final decision on performance capability is made.

Appraiser Styles

Those evaluating performance should approach the task objectively. Unfortunately, personality conflicts and appraiser styles can obscure objectivity. Letton et al. (1977) have identified appraiser styles of those rating performance. Their model maintains that appraisers have certain expectations about the purpose of evaluation and the performance behaviors they expect to see. These expectations make up their performance appraiser style. The model, based on leadership and conflict management research, maintains that an appraiser can display a variety of appraiser styles at different times, but that one style is predominant and most repetitive.

The four basic appraiser styles are as follows:

(1) *Dominant–hostile.* People work best when they are scared and results are best achieved when they feel insecure or afraid. Appraisers are very rigid in their duties, they discourage ideas or suggestions from subordinates, they make decisions independently and expect subordinates to do as they are told, and they deal with conflict or dissent by using their positional authority.

(2) *Dominant–warm.* People perform at their best in a supportive environment where they can match their work efforts with their own goals. Ideas are sought from subordinates and their creativity and initiative for job improvement are valued. Appraisers look for ways to help subordinates improve by matching personal goals with job goals. Decisions are based on subordinate input, and open communication exists for candid feedback from subordinates. Conflict is resolved by investigating facts and is resolved openly and personally.

(3) *Submissive–hostile.* People have an inherent dislike for work and lack self-motivation, and little can be done to motivate them to achieve. Reminding people of job requirements and expectations are the best motivators, and little input from subordinates is sought. Little communication exists between superordinate and subordinate. The appraiser is overly concerned about the expectations of the appraiser's own "boss" and what evaluation results the boss expects from the appraiser's work. Decisions are made primarily with the expectations of the boss in mind, and conflict is ignored or the appraiser assumes that it will go away.

(4) *Submissive–warm.* People perform best in a cheerful and friendly envi-

ronment and making sure that subordinates are satisfied and happy are primary concerns. Appraisers expect good work and loyalty from people, and they work hard to satisfy their expectations and maintain good relationships with subordinates. Suggestions and ideas are encouraged, and those that are most appealing or have most merit are implemented. Decisions are made primarily on the basis of popular appeal with conflict resolved through compromise or appeasement.

Appraisers who consistently display a dominant–warm style promote consistently high outcomes from subordinates. Having a dominant behavior, the appraiser exercises control and lets subordinates know that the appraiser is in charge of the situation. The appraiser shows respect for others' rights, opinions and ideas and has a basic trust in subordinates' desire to improve and to perform at their maximum capabilities. The other three styles provide average or mediocre outcomes depending on the situation and/or the superordinate-subordinate relationship.

The following case study illustrates the effect of appraiser style on the evaluation process:

> The principal conducts an unannounced formal observation that lasts twenty minutes, as mandated by state and local policy, in a eleventh grade social studies classroom. The class is composed of students with a wide range of abilities. The principal observes the teacher lead into a reading strategy known as a graphic organizer to help students formulate an overall picture of the reading material that they have been assigned. All the students work on the assignment. Within ten minutes at least seven of the twenty-five students complete the assignment. The remainder of the students continue to work on the assignment for the duration of the observation. The students who have completed the assignment begin to talk to one another as they wait for the other students to finish. The teacher asks the students to be quiet while their classmates are working. One of the performance criteria on the state-mandated instrument the principal is using calls for the teacher to optimize the use of instructional time by techniques such as focusing on objectives and providing sufficient instructional activities. By failing to provide additional instructional activities for the students who finished their original assignment early, the teacher has not met this performance criteria. There are four different methods of handling this situation based on the four basic appraiser styles.

THE DOMINANT–HOSTILE STYLE

The principal gives the teacher a rating of "unsatisfactory" on the performance criteria related to the effective use of instructional time. Because the state-mandated procedures do not require the principal to meet with the teacher after an observation, the principal places a copy of the scored instrument in an envelope in the teacher's mailbox. When the teacher reviews the scored instrument, he becomes angry. The teacher believes that the principal is unaware of extenuating circumstances in the classroom that justify students' having completed their work early—that is, the wide range of abilities of the students. He believes that if he has the opportunity to explain, the principal will understand and rescore the instrument. On his way back to class, he runs into the principal in the hall and explains what he believes will resolve the issue. The principal tells the teacher that the justification the teacher offers is unsatisfactory and that the instrument will remain as originally scored. The teacher believes that the principal does not understand his explanation—if he had understood, he would have agreed with him. The teacher continues to build up anger and resentment toward the principal, who, in the teacher's opinion, has no concept of what "teaching is really like." The principal feels he did what he "had to do."

THE DOMINANT–WARM STYLE

The principal gives the teacher a rating of "unsatisfactory" on the effective use of instructional time and makes an appointment to discuss the rating with the teacher. During the conference the teacher explains that the students have a wide range of abilities and that the students who finished their work early had met the instructional objective and that it was "unfair" to expect the students to do extra work. The principal has a long discussion with the teacher during which he tries to get the teacher to see that if anything is "unfair," it is the teacher's unwillingness to provide instructional activities for students who have the ability to go beyond minimal requirements. The teacher promises to think about what they have discussed over the next few days and makes an appointment to discuss the issue further. At the next appointment, the teacher brings in a proposal for "social studies labs." The teacher explains that he would like to discuss the proposal with his department members and perhaps implement it throughout the social studies department. The proposal provides detailed descriptions of what would be teacher-prepared learning centers for students on a variety of social studies topics. Students would be required to move to a learning center upon completion of a class assignment. The principal encourages the teacher to pursue the idea. Both parties leave the conference with a feeling that the instructional program will be changed for the better.

THE SUBMISSIVE–HOSTILE STYLE

The principal gives the teacher a rating of "unsatisfactory" on the effective use of time and places a copy of the scored instrument in the teacher's mailbox. The teacher requests a conference during which he offers his explanation. The principal decides that he has accomplished his purpose by getting the teacher's "attention" and as he does not want the rating appealed "higher up," he agrees to change the "unsatisfactory" rating to "satisfactory." The principal cautions the teacher to pay particular attention to this criteria in the future. The teacher leaves the conference feeling vindicated. The principal leaves feeling as if he had escaped a close call.

THE SUBMISSIVE–WARM STYLE

The principal gives the teacher a rating of "satisfactory" on the effective use of time and makes an appointment to discuss the observation with the teacher. During the conference, the principal praises the teacher on the use of the reading strategy activity and makes no mention of the loss of instructional time for some students. The principal believes that praise for what the teacher did best will lead to more effective outcomes. Both parties leave the conference feeling good about their relationship.

PERFORMANCE CRITERIA AND ASSESSMENT

In evaluating teacher performance, the performance criteria will be the individual's job requirements or other mutually agreed-upon criteria; for example, the performance criteria will be that of other teachers' or the average performance of a large group of teachers (norm referenced); or the performance criteria will be geared to a specific standard that fits teachers' actual job responsibilities (criteria referenced). Valentine (1992) relates that the criteria for evaluating job performance will come from state and/or local policies that vary in their level of specificity. States regulating the evaluation of teachers vary from states with strict mandates addressing all aspects of assessing teacher performance to states that allow local boards to adopt their own teacher evaluation policies. Figure 9.1 provides an example of criteria for assessing teacher performance (Georgia Department of Education, 1993). These criteria were state mandated in Georgia until approximately three years ago when Georgia revised state law to allow local school systems to establish their own performance criteria.

In addition to the teaching performance criteria listed in Figure 9.1, the Georgia evaluation instrument also includes a teacher's duties and responsibilities component that includes criteria for evaluation other than teaching.

School systems that wish to use supplemental evaluation instruments or to develop their own to meet state or local mandates for evaluating teacher performance should consider three common criteria types. Ginsberg and Berry (1990) relate that *trait, results,* and *performance-based* criteria are the three most often used types for performance assessment. *Trait* criteria describe what a teacher is

TEACHER PERFORMANCE CRITERIA

Teaching Task I: Provides Instruction

<u>Dimension A</u>: Instructional Level—The amount and organization of the lesson content are appropriate for the students based on their abilities and the complexity and difficulty of the material.

<u>Dimension B</u>: Content Development—Content is developed through appropriate teacher-focused or student-focused activities.

<u>Dimension C</u>: Building for Transfer—Lesson includes initial focus, content emphasis or linking, and summaries that build for transfer of learning.

Teaching Task II: Assesses and Encourages Student Progress

<u>Dimension A</u>: Promoting Engagement—Instructional engagement is promoted through stimulating presentations, active participation, or techniques that promote overt or covert involvement.

<u>Dimension B</u>: Monitoring Progress—Progress, understanding, and bases of misunderstanding are assessed by interpreting relevant student responses, contributions, performances, or products.

<u>Dimension C</u>: Responding to Student Performance—Students are provided reinforcement for adequate performances when appropriate and specific feedback or correctives for inadequate performances.

<u>Dimension D</u>: Supporting Students—Support for students is conveyed by using techniques such as providing encouragement, lowering concern levels, dignifying academic responses and by using language free of sarcasm, ridicule, and humiliating references.

Teaching Task III: Manages the Learning Environment

<u>Dimension A</u>: Use of Time—Use of instructional time is optimized by techniques such as providing clear directions and using efficient methods for transitions, materials distribution, and other routine matters and by techniques such as focusing on objectives and providing sufficient instructional activities.

<u>Dimension B</u>: Physical Setting—The physical setting allows the students to observe the focus of instruction, to work without disruption, to obtain materials, and to move about easily. It also allows the teacher to monitor the students and to move among them.

<u>Dimension C</u>: Appropriate Behavior—Appropriate behavior is maintained by monitoring the behavior of the entire class, providing feedback, and intervening when necessary.

FIGURE 9.1. Teacher performance criteria formerly state-mandated in Georgia (Georgia Department of Education, 1993).

or the attributes of a teacher and not what a teacher does. For example, dependability, punctuality, and honesty are traits. *Results criteria,* the second criteria type, focus on the achievement of objectives and the degree to which they are met. *Performance-based* criteria are those that identify specific performance-based criteria that are linked to effective teaching outcomes. Valentine (1992) notes that performances must be research based and focus on what teachers *actually do* to promote student learning. In other words, performance criteria should address the specifics of the job and assignments associated with the job function. A job description and a job analysis of actual, as opposed to desired, teacher tasks are a prerequisite for performance-based evaluation criteria. One or all three types of assessment criteria can be used to evaluate teacher performance.

The type of performance criteria to be used for assessment and the level to which the criteria are determined to have been met are two separate considerations. Standards or levels of performance indicate the degree to which the performance criteria are achieved. Levels of implementation must be clearly stated and placed in sequential order.

An example of a criterion and its designated levels are discussed next.

CRITERION: PLANS LESSONS FOR DAILY INSTRUCTION

The different levels of implementation are dealt with in the following:

(1) Lessons have goals and objectives.
(2) Lessons have goals and objectives correlated with teaching methods.
(3) Lessons have goals, objectives, correlated teaching methods, and appropriate technology for instruction.
(4) Lessons have goals, objectives, correlated teaching methods, appropriate technology, and are referenced to the textbook or curriculum guide.

Teachers must be informed of the criteria and the designated levels of performance on the instrument that will be used for teacher performance evaluation. Pre-assessment conferences allow principals and teachers to discuss each of the performance criteria and to resolve confusing issues before performance appraisal occurs. Principals will also inform teachers of the methods that will be used to gather data in the appraisal process. The most common methods are classroom observations, self-evaluation, peer appraisals, parent and student appraisals, and portfolios.

Classroom Observations

Classroom observation, either announced or unannounced, is the most commonly used method of appraising teaching performance. Criteria vary and observations can assess a narrow to broad range of behaviors. Observations for formative evaluation should be spaced throughout the year, with summative evaluation being conducted at the conclusion of the year. Stiggens and Duke (1988) maintain that observations should have a specific purpose, that teachers should be aware of the purpose, and that written feedback on the results of the observations should be provided to the teacher within one or two days of the observation in a post-observation conference. Classroom observations should be used as only one measure of performance assessment, with other methods being used to supplement performance appraisal.

Classroom observations are usually recorded on rating scales that assess behaviors observed by a trained appraiser. Criteria being assessed are often placed on a Likert-type scale with a numerical range of one to six. Summary judgments are made by total score, and some criteria may be weighted more heavily than others. Even with trained observers, rating can be subjective and influenced by the halo effect that results from the appraiser's overall impression of the appraisee (Medley, 1992). Halo effects can be minimized by training and experience, by having more than one rater, and by making several observations. Many principals see rating scales as a quick way to assess teacher performance, but unless teacher shortcomings are addressed, the value in using these scales to enhance teacher performance is highly questionable. Some argue that rating scales are most beneficial when used for self-evaluation as a means to improve performance.

Self-Evaluation

Self-evaluation instruments are an effective and important source of information and should be used in conjunction with other appraisal instruments. Castetter (1996) and Stiggens and Duke (1988) report that teachers have important information about themselves that is valuable to the overall performance appraisal profile. Koehler (1990) notes the positive psychological effect that self-evaluation has on teachers and its value as a foundation for developing self-improvement plans. Teachers perceive the reporting of their strengths and weaknesses on a self-evaluation instrument as a nonthreatening approach to performance appraisal. When self-evaluations are used only for self-improvement, teachers are more likely to be candid in their responses and are more open to improvement suggestions.

Self-evaluations also provide a degree of ownership in the appraisal process when the instruments become a part of the total evaluation package. Other benefits of self-appraisal include the following: (1) it provides a data source that may conflict with a possible halo effect, especially if the effect is not a "true" representation of performance and (2) self-appraisal instruments become an official part of decisions on promotion, salary, tenure, and retention. When conflicts occur between self-evaluation results and data obtained by other means, principals should discuss the evaluation findings objectively with teachers, pointing out the possibility that an error in judgment has occurred. Should conflict result, principals can apply a conflict resolution model to resolve the dispute or use a third party evaluation to appraise the teacher's performance and resolve the conflict. Popham (1988) notes that conflict usually occurs over inflating one's own competence and effectiveness. If evaluators realize this fact, they can make adjustments in their evaluation findings.

Peer Appraisals

Peer appraisals are valuable and important in providing a holistic model for appraising teacher performance. Seyfarth (1996) relates the value of master teachers who evaluate beginning teachers or those with identified deficiencies from previous evaluations. Castetter (1996) and McCarthy and Peterson (1988) place high value on peer review as "expert judgment" and state that teachers judging other teachers on performance criteria may have more credibility because principals cannot be "experts" in all areas. Moreover, with some principals, their own teaching may not fall within the criteria of the master teacher or expert. When a mentoring or coaching program exists in the school, mentors are a natural choice for peer evaluation responsibilities. Here, objective analysis is provided from a recognized expert who can provide immediate feedback and modeling of desired behaviors.

Critics of peer evaluation maintain that cost is a factor with peer review. Getting substitutes to cover peer classes during the evaluation may be worth the expense, however, if teacher improvement is the ultimate goal and if peer evaluation, feedback, and modeling are highly valued by the principal. Additional criticism lies with the possible lack of objectivity in peer evaluation. Teachers usually work closely together and friendships exist. Principals will have to weigh the advantages and disadvantages of this possibility, but when peer review programs are properly designed, professionalism usually promotes an objective analysis (McCarthy and Peterson, 1988).

Parent and Student Appraisals

Evaluation of teacher performance should not be conducted by either parents or students as a part of the formal teacher appraisal process. There is debate over whether either population has the background to assess the knowledge and skills necessary to be an effective teacher. Both parents and students *can* assess certain behaviors of teachers such as interpersonal relationships and human relations skills.

Student evaluations have been criticized as being popularity contests. Students cannot know the specific requirements for good or effective teaching, nor can they assess the teacher's command of subject matter. For these reasons, caution should be exercised before using student evaluations in these areas. Should student and parent input be desirable, questions should be carefully written to address areas deemed important, and questions should be written so that they can be answered objectively (Murphy, 1987; Ginsberg and Berry, 1990). Popham (1988) also cautions against the use of student evaluations in assessing teacher performance. He states that "the students' estimates of a teacher's instructional skills are often contaminated by the teacher's popularity or the student's interest in the subject matter being taught" (p. 278). Moreover, the question arises as to how mature students should be to provide valid information on teacher effectiveness or teacher competence. Popham notes that should student evaluations be used to appraise teacher performance, care should be taken to weigh these evaluation results and to ensure student's anonymity because poor teacher evaluations may lead to low grades.

Others argue that students are capable of providing valuable input about their teachers with regard to their teaching capabilities. In fact, many colleges and universities regularly employ student feedback as a vital part of their formal appraisal of professors, and many public school administrators at the high school level point to the unerring accuracy of students in their ability to pinpoint the strengths and weaknesses of their teachers. Whether students' opinions are based on the "popularity" of their teachers may be missing the point. A teacher's lack of "popularity" in many cases may very well be a result of poor teaching skills.

However, the weakness in the argument of those who support the use of student feedback in the appraisal process is that the "popularity" issue can always be raised by teachers who may not want to hear what their students have to say. Teachers are fearful of the power their students wield when their input becomes a part of the formal evaluation of teachers, and students may not be able to handle this power well or maturely.

How then can the information that students have about their teachers be elicited from them and be used to improve teaching in a way that reassures teachers that their professional fate is not in the hands of students who may "carry a grudge" against them and see the evaluation process as a way to even the score? One way to do this is to make student input a prerogative of the teacher and to place such input safely in the hands of teachers. In other words, remove student input from the formal evaluation process and provide teachers with a mechanism to use student input for professional development. Teachers will feel much safer when they know that student feedback is to be seen only by the teacher being evaluated. Such a method also causes students to offer their feedback with different motives in mind. When such feedback instruments are used by teachers they should let their students know that the results will be used only to improve their teaching. Presented in Figure 9.2 is a proposal for a staff-development course for teachers interested in using student feedback to improve teaching.

As seen in the proposal, teachers explore effective teaching practices and create their own instrument, testing it themselves for validity and reliability. The process of creating such an instrument is an excellent vehicle for the review of effective teaching practices and ensures that the teacher has confidence and an interest in the results.

Parent evaluations of teachers should also be used with care. Parents who have frequent contact with teachers may be in a better position than those with little teacher interaction to assess *traits* of teachers. Parents usually do not have the background to assess either teaching skills or content mastery, and they are not present in the classroom during the process of teaching. An assessment of interpersonal skills and human relations skills, however, may be useful. Principals should realize, however, that results may be influenced by the halo effect, by personality, or by other confounding variables. Selected samples can also bias results and provide misleading information. Objective criteria should be used for parent input with the most reliable results coming from parent conversations over time. Summaries of these conversations can be analyzed and they may present the most valuable parent feedback available.

Portfolios

Appraising teacher performance through portfolios is similar to evaluating student performance through the "authentic" assessment approach to evaluation of performance. Seyfarth (1996) provides a model that is document focused, assembled by the teacher, and evaluated by the principal. Portfolio documents create a mental image of the teacher's effectiveness and provide documented evidence for principals to evaluate. Portfolio assessments allow teachers more control over what is to be assessed, but the task is time consuming and requires organized record keeping. Guidelines should be prepared to assist teachers concerning the types and the amount of documentation required. Bird (1990) relates that videotapes of class sessions are useful in assessing teacher performance, and when accompanied with copies of lesson plans, tests, and so forth, their value can surpass the classroom observation method. Bird recommends a portfolio that consists of the following documentation:

(1) Sample of lesson plans over a specified time period

(2) Sample of student tests, handouts, and projects

(3) Grade distributions

STAFF DEVELOPMENT PROPOSAL

Program Title: Using Student Evaluation and Feedback to Improve Instruction

Description: This ten-hour course will focus on the use of student feedback to improve teacher instruction, appropriate date-gathering instruments to obtain student feedback, validity and reliability of such instruments, and the use and design of professional development plans based on student input. Student feedback will be gathered by and available only to the involved teacher. No other party will have access to the data.

Goals Addressed:
(1)   To emphasize continual professional growth.
(2)   To use student input as the basis for improving instruction.
(3)   To develop a data-gathering instrument.
(4)   To formulate individualized professional improvement plans based on data.

Improvement Practices to be Implemented:
Participants will:
(1)   Review literature on student feedback to improve instruction.
(2)   Design a data-gathering instrument.
(3)   Field test the instrument.
(4)   Use the data gathered from the use of the instrument to formulate an individualized professional improvement plan.

Total Hours:
Participants will meet for a minimum of ten hours for one Staff Development Unit (SDU). Sessions will begin during pre-planning, will be held approximately once every six weeks, and will continue until the end of the school year.

Session 1 (90 minutes):   What Makes a Good Teacher? Part I
Session 2 (90 minutes):   What Makes a Good Teacher? Part II
Session 3 (90 minutes):   What Can Your Students Tell you About Your
                                 Teaching?
Session 4 (90 minutes):   Data-Gathering Instruments
Session 5 (90 minutes):   Designing an Instrument
Session 6 (90 minutes):   Field-Testing an Instrument
Session 7 (90 minutes):   Interpretation and Use of Data

Persons Responsible for Training Activities:
Assistant Principal for Curriculum and Instruction

Projected Costs:
None

Principal _____ Date_____

School Staff Development Coordinator _____ Date_____

Curriculum Coordinator _____ Date_____

FIGURE 9.2. Sample staff development proposal for a course for teachers on the use of student feedback to improve instruction.

(4) Parent comments and student evaluations (if appropriate)

(5) List of workshops and/or staff development sessions that list new ideas or information and their application to teaching

(6) Professional improvement plans and progress toward meeting stated goals

(7) Peer or mentor evaluations

Some argue that principal-made checklists should not be used for developing assessment portfolios because they restrict the kinds of material that teachers may feel contribute to classroom effectiveness (Wolf, 1991). Wolf also argues that quantitative scoring of portfolio content should be discouraged because of the diversity of documentation found in portfolios. Portfolios allow the teacher to exercise professional judgment on what promotes student learning and the necessary knowledge and skills that are required to be effective. This broad-based approach to demonstrate job effectiveness does not lend itself to quantification. The goal of teacher portfolio assessment is like authentic assessment for students; that is, it gives a complete and clear picture of what happens in classrooms. According to Wolf, portfolio assessment is as authentic and holistic as any teacher evaluation method can get because it allows one to actually see teaching and learning ". . . as they unfold and extend over time" (p. 136).

The evaluating of portfolios is time consuming, calls for subjective judgment, and can give rise to teacher-principal conflict when no clear evaluating criteria have been established. Questions of validity and reliability frequently arise and unless a well devised, mutually agreed-upon evaluation plan for assessing portfolios is determined between principal and teachers, conflict will surround the teacher portfolio appraisal practice. However, as Wolf (1991) and Collins (1991) point out, if agreement is reached on what documents are needed in a portfolio and what weights (if any) are to be assigned to these documents and if teachers support the portfolio appraisal practice, then this evaluation process can be of high value to teachers and principals alike.

Using Student Achievement Tests as a Part of the Appraisal Process

Debate exists over using student achievement scores in appraising teacher performance. Some believe student test scores should be a part of the overall teacher evaluation data because the bottom line for assessing teacher effectiveness is increased student test scores. This is a popular view held by many parents, community members, and government officials. Findley and Estrabrook (1991), however, argue that the use of achievement tests for formative or summative evaluation would give too much credibility to norm- or criterion-referenced tests. Standardized tests have several shortcomings, they add, which lay people fail to realize. The use of test results without due consideration of their weaknesses would provide an inaccurate representation of teacher performance.

Major weaknesses of standardized tests are discussed by Popham (1988). Whether tests are norm-referenced or criterion-referenced, there is the possibility of *cultural bias*. Another weakness is "that unrecognized mismatches will occur between testing and teaching" (Popham, 1988, p. 108), a mismatch between what the test measures and what is being taught in the curriculum. A third weakness is the "high generality" of the tests that test makers build into the test for selling their product. This "reduces the likelihood of providing effective formative evaluation guidance" (p. 109). Also test items often omit key concepts or content deemed important by the teacher or state or local curriculum guides and include items not deemed essential by these same guides. In such cases lack of coverage or partial coverage of tested concepts cannot be attributed to teaching performance in such cases when students do poorly on standardized tests. Consequently, standardized instruments do not adequately measure what is taught, standardized tests cannot relate the effectiveness of a teacher (there is great variation among students and comparing one teacher with another teacher on standardized tests without consideration of mitigating variables lacks foundation), and some students naturally perform poorly on standardized measures, regardless of their knowledge and skills. Stiggens (1989) supports Popham's arguments (1988) against using student standardized test scores to evaluate teacher performance but notes that a quandary exists for educators. On the one hand, student learning must be assessed, and learning is correlated with teacher performance. On the other hand, standardized tests have inherent weaknesses for assessing teacher performance. Tests of this kind, Stiggens maintains, cannot provide an accurate appraisal of teacher performance.

What then should be used to assess teacher performance? Stiggens (1989) suggests that teacher-made measures of classroom performance may be the best way to assess student learning. If pre- and post-testing is used, if content measured directly correlates to content taught, and if teachers have the essential knowledge of how to make valid and reliable tests, a more accurate and reliable assessment of teacher performance can be made based on these measures.

DEVELOPING AN EFFECTIVE APPRAISAL MODEL

In the absolute sense, effective performance is really a situation-specific variable that can only be defined by local standards and expectations. In essence, effectiveness is what each school expects its teachers to do to promote student learning as defined by the school system. Stronge and Helm (1991) relate that state evaluation criteria for teachers may or may not coincide with local school goals and objectives on their conceptualization of effective teaching. When state evaluation criteria do not match those deemed important at the local level, supplemental evaluation procedures should be developed to provide a more adequate reflection of teacher performance. Discontent over the criteria to assess effective teacher performance often stems from a lack of agreement among teachers and administrators regarding the key components that promote effective classroom performance *and* how these key components can best be assessed and by whom. Until there is mutual agreement between the appraiser and the appraisee over these matters, the traditional approach of having several classroom observations and/or using different assessment instruments during these observations will do little to resolve the problem.

Three other considerations are central to developing an effective, holistic performance appraisal model. These are (1) instruments used for appraisal must be both valid and reliable; (2) legal standards must be met to ensure the requirements of due process exist and are followed; and (3) the evaluation process must be free from race and sex discrimination practices.

Reliability and Validity of Instruments

Test reliability is defined as the consistency with which an instrument measures what it is purported to measure (i.e., "Will the assessment measure the same variable over time?") [Popham, 1988]. For teacher assessment instruments, reliability means that if different appraisers use the same evaluation instrument, the results will be the same or will be so similar that a close and recognizable pattern of performance exists. When evaluators are trained in instrument use and there are multiple scores for assessing different behaviors, subjectivity in evaluating performance is substantially reduced (Stronge, 1991).

Test reliability is an extremely important concern for test developers. Constructs must perform their measurement function consistently and must measure what they are designed to measure, over time. Reliability does not guarantee validity, but is a necessary condition for test validity. This concern for consistency of measurement over time is called test *stability* and can be achieved through the *alternate form* method, the *split-half* technique, and a *test-retest* process. The alternate form method is accomplished by giving two forms or tests with the same content to the same group on the same day and by correlating the test results. The split-half technique divides the test into two separate instruments, usually by odd and even numbers, and then administers the test to one group with the two sets of scores then being correlated.

The test-retest is perhaps the most frequently used method to assess test reliability, with the instrument administered to one group one day and then again to the same group ten to fourteen days later. The Pearson correlation coefficient yields scores on each construct of ±1, with a strong correlation ranging from 0.80 to 1. Ideally, test items that have strong correlation coefficients should have coefficients not lower than 0.70. Reliability for instrument item constructs is relatively easily computed by using one of the Kuder–Richardson formulas. Either of the two formulas, the K-R20 or the K-R21, can be used. The K-R21 is easier to use than the more complicated K-R20, but is also less accurate. Principals are referred to any standard statistics text for formulas and methods for computation.

The validity of a test focuses on the issue of whether a test actually measures what it is purported to measure. Three methods are common to establishing test validity:

(1) *Face validity* or *content-related validity* is assessed by a panel of experts or judges who have knowledge of the areas being assessed. Content for assessment can come from textbooks, journal articles, or from other research-based sources.

(2) *Criterion-related validity* is established through correlating performance on the test with another criterion known to have high validity.

(3) *Construct-related validity* is accomplished through a series of studies to compile evidence, over time, on hypothetical constructs, such as behaviors in the affective domain, using empirical methods such as correlations.

Thus, heuristic measurements serve to guide and discover information that administrators can use to make sound, data-based decisions.

Types of Appraisal Instruments

The instruments selected to assess teacher performance should reflect the specific purpose of appraisal. As mentioned before, teacher performance instruments should be objective in scope, have high reliability and validity, and be criterion- or performance-based in nature to make sound decisions on retention, tenure, and salary and promotion. Assessment instruments can also be used to evaluate the effectiveness of the teacher selection process and to assess knowledge and skill areas for planning staff development programs. Leap and Crino (1992) discuss several appraisal measures and their uses, and they emphasize the importance of using multiple assessment measures that have been selected based on the specific goal(s) of the assessment process.

Subjective Instruments

Subjective assessments call for the use of rater judgment on a scale of general or normed descriptive traits or behaviors or on specific behaviors of another like group. Frequently, traits are assessed using rating scales, forced distributions, and descriptive critiques. These assessment-type instruments are most valuable when self-report instruments are used to supplement the data (Leap and Crino, 1992).

Self-report instruments are questionnaires and attitude scales and are used in teacher appraisal to reveal the teacher's feelings and perceptions but not ability or actual performance behavior. The more truthful the teacher's responses, the more helpful they are for diagnosis and for comparing the responses with the data from other assessment instruments.

Rating scales are used to assess behaviors on the job compared with general normed behaviors, literature-based behaviors, or local criteria. Essential interpersonal skills to promote effective classroom management is an example of a behavior suitable for a rating scale. In this example, descriptors of essential behavior are provided, along with performance indicators (such as *almost never, seldom, frequently, almost always*) that have been assigned numerical values of one to four. Rater judgment assesses the degree of observed behavior and assigns values for each behavior observed. Total scores represent an overall assessment, with individual values identifying areas for remediation.

The forced distribution method can be used to assess teacher performance through the use of a normal distribution curve. Using a variety of behaviors and four or five performance percentage categories (such as 10 percent, Poor; 20 percent, Fair; 40 percent, Average; 20 percent. Above Average; and 10 percent, Excellent), the rater "forces" the performance of each individual teacher into one of the predetermined categories. Decisions on merit pay, promotion, and staff development could be based, in part, on the results of forced distribution data. Data from a self-report instrument should be used to measure each teacher's *perception* of his or her performance on the same criteria used on the forced distribution instrument.

Descriptive critiques or anecdotal records call for written descriptions of a teacher's strengths and weaknesses as observed in the classroom or another assessed environment. Behaviors important to the assessment goal are noted using facts and specific examples. When compiled over time, they represent a more accurate pattern of behavior than that obtained from one or two observations using other assessment techniques. This process is time consuming and open to the rater's interpretation of observed behavior. Skill in writing exact behavior descriptions and the difficulty in quantifying observed behaviors are drawbacks of the descriptive critiques method.

Objective Instruments

Objective instruments, referred to as *absolute standards* by Leap and Crino (1992), are based on valid and reliable criteria (as discussed earlier). With objective measures, such as *checklists* and *goal setting*, certain local standards are determined and used as assessment variables.

Checklists are used to capture specific data in a systematic way and can be made up of a collection of categories. Data can be raw facts or behaviors and can be grouped to make decisions. Checklists can also be used to assess progress or progressive steps in meeting criteria. Items can be weighted or forced-choice or have numerical ratings. Rater bias through the halo effect or perceptual bias can influence recorded information. Also, forced-choice checklists allow little variance for recording highly specific behaviors, especially when descriptor statements are limited to three to four in number.

Goal setting relates to the goal-setting theory models and can assess behavior and stimulate motivation. Goal setting is more commonly used after weaknesses have been identified by other evaluation methods. At this point, goals for improvement are jointly developed, and criteria are determined to assess goal achievement. Usually behavioral objectives are stated and time frames are agreed-upon for assessment conferences or observations. Formative evaluation is essential in making goal setting a successful performance assessment method.

AVOIDING CHARGES OF DISCRIMINATION IN PERFORMANCE APPRAISAL

Charges of discrimination can be brought against a principal when teachers perceive that negative ratings of teaching performance are a result of evaluator bias, the judgments were subjective in scope, or the evaluation instrument was not valid or reliable. Valid and reliable assessment instruments are the essential first step in capturing accurate, objective data in evaluating teaching performance. Next, using two or more trained peer evaluators, with the teacher being fully informed about the evaluation procedures and the criterion evaluation instrument(s), can provide a check on the evaluation results of the principal's observation(s). Third, conferences following evaluation observations and the development of signed and dated plans for professional development, mutually agreed-upon, are other safeguards against charges of discrimination. Fourth, having a mentoring or coaching model in place to allow for immediate demonstration and assistance is another way to ensure fair and equal treatment. Finally, legal standards to ensure due process must be followed with teachers, who know their rights and procedural steps. *Procedural* due process guarantees teachers fair and equal treatment through procedures prescribed by law. *Substantive* due process is designed to protect teachers from discriminatory, arbitrary, and unreasonable acts from the administration. In the latter case, the concept of "just cause" is central to the process and means that teacher dismissal cannot result unless a clear violation of law or policy is proved.

Procedural due process focuses on issues denying "life, liberty, or property" to a teacher by the school board. Property and liberty issues of the Fourteenth

Amendment are the ones most often in question in teacher evaluation disputes. *Property* has been interpreted by the courts to mean a "legitimate entitlement" to the continuation of employment. *Continuation* does not mean a desire on the part of the teacher to remain employed. Tenured teachers, however, have a vested interest or property right to remain employed. *Liberty* has been held by the courts to mean actions that affect one's reputation. Serious damage to one's reputation usually means damage that causes the lack of other employment opportunities or damage to one's standing in the community. Damage has to be of such magnitude that the reputation is damaged through public ridicule or scorn. Liberty interest also has been interpreted as a violation of one's constitutional rights or those rights pertaining to marriage, personal privacy, or family (McCarthy and Cambron-McCabe, 1992).

Due process procedures for dismissal usually include notice of dismissal by a specific date, a specific list of reasons for the action, and the opportunity for a hearing to discuss the reasons listed. When states have laws pertaining to teacher dismissal, they must be specifically followed to make the dismissal legal (Lunenburg and Ornstein, 1996). McCarthy and Cambron McCabe (1992) note that courts generally hold that procedural due process comprises the following steps:

(1) Notification of [specific] changes

(2) Opportunity for a hearing

(3) Adequate time to prepare a rebuttal to the charges

(4) Access to evidence and names of witnesses

(5) Hearing before an impartial tribunal

(6) Representation by legal counsel

(7) Opportunities to present evidence and witnesses

(8) Opportunities to cross-examine adverse witnesses

(9) Decision based on the evidence and findings of the hearing

(10) Transcript or record of the hearing

Substantive due process procedures are somewhat more difficult to ensure. In substantive due process, the courts have not set guidelines that are as clear as those for procedural due process, and decisions are often made on a case-by-case basis. Because substantive due process involves both individual and state interests, courts seek a balance between the two when investigating to determine if school administrators sought to deprive the teacher of "life, property, or liberty." A pattern does seem to emerge in substantive due process cases. That is, the criteria on which the teacher evaluation is based needs to be (1) consistent with state or local statutes; (2) clearly defined, observable, and job related; (3) made known to all employees; (4) fairly and equally applied;

(5) developed in cooperation with employees; (6) and compiled through multiple sources with sufficient objective documentation (Webb et al., (1994).

Based on the pattern emerging from case law, the following five steps should be implemented by principals to ensure that substantive due-process procedures are followed.

(1) *Avoid appraiser bias:* Appraisers can often be influenced by their own bias and personality differences between themselves and appraisees. Tension can exist and negative feelings can influence ratings. Some appraisers have high standards that they themselves cannot meet, and others are victims of the halo effect or "rose-colored glasses" complex. Some appraisers are lenient by nature, whereas others are not. Proper training on the use of assessment instruments and the use of multiple evaluators can supplement anecdotal records and self-reporting instruments as a means of negating rater bias.

(2) *Allow time for appraisals and remediation:* Opinions vary, but having both announced and unannounced classroom observations allows fair and equal treatment for the teacher and observer(s). Allowing teachers some choice as to the time of day and which class will be observed provides teachers with an opportunity to present their best performance. Formative assessment procedures and methods should precede summative evaluation with adequate time and resources to remediate deficiencies. Mutually developed and agreed-upon improvement plans, with goal setting or other agreed-upon appraisal techniques, should be used.

(3) *Review assessment criteria:* Performance criteria used for assessment should be carefully reviewed with teachers and confusing terms or behaviors should be explained and/or demonstrated before assessment. For locally developed instruments, high validity and reliability should be established, and criteria not appropriate for some teachers should be noted as nonapplicable. Criteria should clearly reflect the goals of the assessment purpose and standards should be challenging, but attainable. High standards stimulate motivation to excel, whereas excessively high standards serve to cause frustration and resentment.

(4) *Use composite ratings and peer evaluations:* Rarely will results from one evaluation instrument or one observation provide a comprehensive picture of performance capability. Using multiple raters reduces the probability of rater bias but opens the possibility of *generosity error* (too lenient a rater) and *severity error* (too strict a rater). Popham (1988) notes the best one can do for fairness is to average the scores.

Peer evaluators allow teacher choice in classroom evaluations when principals and teachers jointly select peer teachers to observe and evaluate performance. When mentoring or coaching is used, peer coaches or mentors should be included as raters, and cumulative assessment records of the teacher's performance and professional development should supplement instrument appraisal results.

(5) *Pilot study the appraisal model.* Performance appraisal systems should be pilot tested with teacher volunteers to identify weaknesses or inequities in the assessment process. Teacher feedback is essential in refining any evaluation of classroom performance, and results should be presented to the entire faculty for consideration and approval. When two or more teacher assessment processes seem viable, principals and teachers can pilot test these evaluation processes during a single year, with different volunteers being assessed on different processes, or principals and teachers can implement one evaluation process one year and the succeeding evaluation process the following year.

REFERENCES

Bennis, W. G. 1990. *Why Leaders Can't Lead: The Unconscious Conspiracy Continues.* San Francisco: Jossey-Bass.

Bird, T. 1990. "The School Teacher's Portfolio: An Essay on Possibilities;" in *The New Handbook of Teacher Evaluation.* J. Millman and L. Darling-Hammond, eds., 241-256. Newbury Park, CA: Sage.

Castetter, W. B. 1996. *The Human Resource Function in Educational Administration.* Sixth edition. Englewood Cliffs, NJ: Prentice-Hall.

Collins, A. 1991. "Portfolios for Biology Teacher Assessment." *Journal of Personnel Evaluation in Education,* 5:147–167.

Cunningham, W. G. and D. W. Gresso. 1993. *Cultural Leadership: The Culture of Excellence in Education.* Needham Heights, MA: Allyn and Bacon.

Darling-Hammond, L. 1986. "A Proposal for Evaluation in the Teaching Profession." *Elementary School Journal,* 86:532–551.

Deal, T. E. and K. D. Peterson. 1990. *The Principal's Role in Shaping School Culture.* Washington, DC: Office of Educational Research and Improvement.

Duke, D. and R. Stiggins. 1993. "Beyond Minimum Competency: Evaluation for Professional Development" in *The New Handbook of Teacher Evaluation.* J. Millman and L. Darling-Hammond, eds., 116–132. Newbury Park, CA: Sage.

Findley, D. and R. Estrabrook. 1991. "Teacher Evaluation: Curriculum and Instructional Considerations." *Contemporary Education,* 62:294–298.

Georgia Department of Education 1993. *Georgia Teacher Evaluation Program: Evaluation Manual.* Atlanta, GA.

Ginsberg, R. and B. Berry. 1990. "The Folklore of Principal Evaluation." *Journal of Personnel Evaluation in Education,* 3(3):205–230.

Greetz, C. 1973. *The Interpretation of Culture.* New York: Basic Books.

Heckman, P. E. 1993. "School Restructuring and Practice: Reckoning with the Culture of the School." *International Journal of Educational Reform,* 2(3):263–272.

Herzberg, F., B. Mausner, and B. Snyderman. 1959. *The Motivation to Work.* New York: Wiley.

Hoenack, S. and D. Monk. 1990. "Economic Aspects of Teacher Evaluation" in *The New Handbook of Teacher Evaluation.* J. Millman and L. Darling-Hammond, eds., 390–402. Newberry Park, CA: Sage.

Koehler, M. 1990. "Self-Assessment in the Evaluation Process." *National Association of Secondary School Principals Bulletin,* 74(527):40–44.

Leap, T. L. and M. D. Crino. 1992. *Personnel/Human Resource Management.* Second edition. New York: Macmillan.

Letton, R. E., V. R. Buzzotta, M. Sherberg, and D. L. Karraker. 1977. *Effective Motivation through Performance Appraisal.* New York: Wiley.

Lunenburg, F. C. and A. C. Ornstein. 1996. *Educational Administration: Concepts and Practices.* Second edition. Belmont, CA: Wadsworth.

Medley, D. M. 1992. "Teacher Evaluation" in *Encyclopedia of Educational Research.* M. C. Akin, ed., Vol. 4, 1345–1352. New York: Macmillan.

McCarthy, S. J. and K. D. Peterson. 1988. "Peer Review of Materials in Public School Evaluation." *Journal of Personnel Evaluation in Education,* 1:259–267.

McCarthy, M. M. and N. H. Cambron-McCabe. 1992. *Public School Law: Teachers' and Student's Rights.* Third edition. Boston: Allyn and Bacon.

Murphy, J. 1987. "Teacher Evaluation: A Comprehensive Framework for Supervisors." *Journal of Personnel Evaluation in Education,* 1:157–180.

Popham, W. J. 1988. *Educational Evaluation.* Second edition. Englewood Cliffs, NJ: Prentice-Hall.

Rebore, R. W. 1995. *Personnel Administration in Education: A Management Approach.* Fourth edition. Englewood Cliffs, NJ: Prentice-Hall.

Seyfarth, J. T. 1996. *Personnel Management for Effective Schools.* Second edition. Boston: Allyn and Bacon.

Stiggens, R. J. 1989. "A Commentary on the Role of Student Achievement Data on the Evaluation of Teachers." *Journal of Personnel Evaluation in Education,* 3:7–15.

Stiggens, R. J. and D. L. Duke. 1988. *A Case for Commitment to Teacher Growth: Research on Teacher Evaluation.* Albany, NY: State University of New York Press.

Stronge, J. and V. Helm. 1991. *Evaluating Professional Support Personnel in Education.* Newbury Park, CA: Sage.

Stronge, J. H. 1991. "The Dynamics of Effective Performance Evaluation Systems in Education: Conceptual, Human Relations, and Technical Domains." *Journal of Personnel Evaluation in Education,* 5:77–83.

Valentine, J. W. 1992. *Principles and Practices for Effective Teacher Evaluation.* Boston: Allyn and Bacon.

Weller, L. D. 1996. "The Next Generation of School Reform." *Quality Progress,* 29(10):65–70.

Webb, L. D., P. A. Montello, and M. S. Norton. 1994. *Human Resources Administration: Personnel Issues and Needs in Education.* Second edition. New York: Macmillan.

Wolf, K. 1991. "The School Teacher's Portfolio: Issues in Design, Implementation, and Evaluation." *Phi Delta Kappan,* 73:129–136.

CHAPTER 10

The Beginning Teacher: Maximizing Potential

Helping beginning teachers to assimilate into the school's culture quickly and easily is a goal of effective principals. Schools that are quality oriented and promote effective outcomes have systematic induction programs to assist beginning teachers in adjusting to their new assignments. These programs are designed to provide immediate personal and professional satisfaction through a peer support network designed to provide guidance and friendship. The goal of this induction process is to help beginning teachers become self-motivated, secure, and confident employees. Comprehensive induction programs provide the necessary *socialization* process needed to learn about the school's vision and culture, to develop a sense of belonging and acceptance, and to become familiar with those with whom they will interact on a personal and professional basis. These programs assist in retaining personnel, increasing morale, and making teaching a personally rewarding profession.

THE NEED FOR INDUCTION PROGRAMS

Research suggests that more voluntary resignations occur in schools without comprehensive induction programs than in schools with such programs (Costello, 1991, Seyfarth, 1996). Rebore (1998) notes that induction processes have a cause-and-effect relationship with employee retention, job performance, and personal satisfaction. Early resignations are costly to the school system in terms of time and money invested in the recruiting, selecting, and hiring processes.

New teachers and staff members often feel apprehensive about demonstrating competence and being accepted by others. New personnel lack the knowledge of how things "get done" within the organization, as well as its traditions, rituals, taboos, and unwritten standards of conduct. Those who enjoy early personal satisfaction and job success are products of induction programs that focus attention on meeting the needs of the individual first and then meeting the goals of the organization.

Successful induction programs have two goals: (1) short-range goals designed to facilitate adjustment, acceptance, security, and confidence and (2) long-range goals designed to assimilate the teacher as an accepted social member of the school and to assist the teacher in becoming a self-motivated, self-directed professional pursuing quality outcomes.

Effective principals establish peer coaching and mentor-protégée programs that assist beginning teachers in gaining confidence, taking the initiative, and becoming valued additions to the school. The induction program should be designed around the needs of beginning teachers, the needs and expectations of veteran teachers, and the vision and goals of the school. This personalized approach to induction is a key factor in making such a program successful. The importance of a strong induction program is illustrated in the following case study.

Ms. Wilson is a first year teacher in South High School's social studies department. The department has fourteen faculty members, all of whom are tenured and experienced teachers and are highly personable. The department is well known for their camaraderie, parties, and daily jokes that are played on one another. Many teachers in other departments sometimes wish they were certified in social studies that so they could be involved in this highly productive, dedicated, and yet "fun loving" department. Mr. Hadley, the principal, was extremely proud of the department because South's students continuously rated in the ninety-eight percentile on the state's achievement test in social studies. In fact, Mr. Hadley was proud of hiring Ms. Wilson in mid-August, two weeks before the school started, with the sudden resignation of Mrs. Field, who had taught at South for ten years but decided to work on a Ph.D. in history in another state. A fully paid fellowship was difficult to resist, and Mrs. Field always wanted to focus her energies on research and writing.

Mr. Hadley recalled the day Ms. Wilson came for the interview. The other two applicants were weak, at best, but Ms. Wilson had credentials that were excellent in his opinion. Ms. Wilson had just completed a Master's Degree in American history and was elected to Phi Beta Kappa at her undergraduate school where she majored in psychology and minored in history. Ms. Wilson was outgoing, mature beyond her age, well read, and had letters of recommendation of exceedingly high caliber. That afternoon, Mr. Allen, the head of the social studies department for the past eighteen years, interviewed Ms. Wilson and was equally impressed with her academic preparation and human relations skills. Mr. Allen commented that, "On such short notice, we'll be lucky if she signs the contract."

But now, five months later, Mr. Hadley is in a quandary. Mr. Jamison, the school's technology coordinator, has just shared some disturbing information about Ms.

Wilson. At Ms. Wilson's request, Mr. Jamison was to meet her after school, at 3:30 in her classroom, to provide updated information on the use of new computer software for American history. Mr. Jamison, who was late for the appointment, arrived at 4:15 and found Ms. Wilson at her desk in tears. According to Mr. Jamison, students and parents were not the problem, and Mr. Hadley reflected that over the past five months both student and parent feedbacks had been highly positive. In fact, no discipline referrals or parent telephone calls were brought to his attention during this time frame. He continued to listen to Mr. Jamison.

The gist of Mr. Jamison's conversation focused on the following. Ms. Wilson was discouraged and disillusioned. She felt she was not fully accepted by the other members of the department. She was not asked to be a part of the "lunch crew" that usually ate together, she was not included in the frequent practical jokes played on others, nor was she the brunt of any jokes or puns. Ms. Wilson also felt her views on departmental issues were not well received at department meetings and although her suggestions for improving the curriculum were acknowledged, they were never seriously considered. She also believed that she was excluded from several weekend parties and that her efforts to develop good, positive working relationships with department members were not successful. She felt estranged and that she was not accepted as a colleague and as an equal.

Mr. Jamison's concluding remark to Mr. Hadley was, "Jim, I don't feel I'm in a position to give advice, but there seems to be a real problem here and good teachers are difficult to find. Maybe Mr. Allen can shed some light on what's going on."

In a discussion with Mr. Allen, the principal sense that Ms. Wilson is an above-average first-year teacher is reinforced. She has a strong command of the subject, is well liked by students and parents, has no classroom discipline problems, and is creative, pleasant, and professional, all of which are key qualities Mr. Allen looks for in faculty members. However, he believes the custom of hiring new staff members was violated in the case of Ms. Wilson. In the past, all department members interviewed each prospective candidate and all candidates' qualifications were then discussed in a department meeting, with each member having a voice and vote regarding their selection of new personnel. In the case of Ms. Wilson, many department members felt the administration (both principal and department head) tried to "pull one over" on them. In fact, five members of the department expressed this concern to Mr. Allen at the beginning of the school year. When Mr. Allen explained the circumstances of the situation, four of the five members asked why they were not called immediately to interview Ms. Wilson and the two other candidates as they lived close to the school. Mr. Allen perceived that his re-explanation of the tight time frame for hiring a replacement (two weeks) was accepted and understood. Unfortunately, Mr. Allen's perceptions were wrong. In addition, there was no induction program in place for new teachers.

Despite efforts made by Mr. Allen with his staff, Ms. Wilson was not fully accepted as a member of the department. At the end of the year, Ms. Wilson took another job in another high school and three years later became the school's Teacher of the Year and a state semifinalist for that award.

Building an Induction Program

Induction programs have three major components: (1) assessing beginning teacher needs, concerns, and expectations; (2) providing information to beginning teachers about the community and the school system, and (3) facilitating personal and professional adjustment within the school, the school system, and the community.

Assessing the Needs of Beginning Teachers

New teachers need essential information about the school, the school system, and the community in which they live. Preemployment literature traditionally focuses on the school and usually includes a school map, a salary scale, and a list of curricular offerings. This information is helpful for the interviewing phase but is inadequate for newly hired personnel. Most helpful are the following pieces of information that should be contained in induction packets: copies of student and faculty handbooks, community and school maps, insurance and real estate information, pay periods, salary scale, sick and professional leave policies, and dates for inservice and professional opportunities for growth within the school system.

Induction programs should begin with a preemployment questionnaire designed to ascertain the type of information and assistance each new teacher requires. Questions may be school focused and may center around employment regulations and responsibilities such as discipline, inservice requirements, planning periods, and instructional materials. Some questions may pertain to insurance coverage, housing, and community resources. Many principals make lists of questions and concerns presented over the year by beginning teachers and use these lists to develop their preemployment surveys. Support staff and supervisors are another information source to gather survey information. Space should be provided for respondents to ask questions not covered in the questionnaire or not made clear by information in the preemployment packet. Results of the survey form the nucleus of the induction program that then becomes "personalized" for each new group of beginning teachers.

Providing Information about the Community

A knowledge and understanding of the community's social, political, and economic structure are important to new teachers. Knowing the community's cultural heritage, ethnic composition, customs, traditions, and religious composition helps new teachers better understand parents, students, and the educational expectations held by the community for their schools. Knowledge of community resources, such as libraries, civic and cultural organizations, and museums, is important to beginning teachers for personal enrichment purposes as well as for instructional resources. Representatives from the community's social, economic, and political structures should be involved in planning the induction process and be available to provide first-hand information about the community and to extend personal invitations for teacher involvement.

Providing Information about the School System

The school system itself significantly influences new teachers through its organizational structure and policies. New teachers need time to become knowledgeable of the rules and regulations affecting their work and to become familiar with school policies. The induction program should include orientation in areas of curriculum and instruction, business, and personnel. Orientation sessions should be conducted by central office personnel in their areas of expertise and should inform new teachers of laws, codes, and regulations that affect assignments and provide specific information on insurance coverage, retirement packages, salary schedules, supervisory practices, and the like. Board of education members and the superintendent should welcome new teachers, present their expectations of teachers, and share their own educational goals for the school and the school system.

Providing Information about the School

The principal and administrative staff of the school play the most important role in the induction process, and every effort should be made to personalize their interaction with new teachers. Introducing new teachers to the school's professional and support personnel is an essential first step. A breakfast or luncheon provides a nonthreatening, sociable atmosphere. Department heads, supervisors, team leaders, or lead teachers should act as hosts or hostesses for seminars designed to acquaint beginning teachers with school policies. Explaining administrative procedures; introducing new teachers to procedures for completing reports, ordering materials, and requesting technology; and discussing extracurricular responsibilities, attendance policies, and legal responsibilities of teachers are salient information areas.

Role modeling is used by effective principals through the pairing of new personnel with veteran teachers for a three- to six-month time period. This mentor relationship influences morale and job satisfaction. As a resource person, friend, and coach, the mentor provides daily assistance and support to new personnel. Peers, more so than supervisors or administrators, are successful in this role because they are not responsible for evaluating job performance and pose little threat to the beginning teacher.

Providing Immediate Involvement for Beginning Teachers

Assigning new teachers to committees and teams allows beginning teachers to develop new relationships, experience early successes, and build self-confidence early in their careers. These assignments bring them into contact with support staff, parents, and community members and increase their acceptance as valued members of the school. Through informal conversations, coffees, and social events, principals can build close working relationships with new teachers while exploring their personal interests and expectations. When principals know teachers on a personal basis they can match teachers with committee assignments and can understand their job motivators and satisfiers. When principals have this knowledge early in a teacher's career, experiences can be made personally rewarding and challenging. Building close working relationships with beginning teachers also builds trust and reduces the anxiety often associated with subordinate-superordinate relationships.

SHORT-RANGE GOALS

Short-range goals for induction programs should be achieved within a four- to six-week time frame. The first two weeks of induction are critical, as perceptions are formed early about the school, the support and teaching personnel, and the administration during this time period. Beginning teacher success, report Riches and Morgan (1989), is based more often on the quality of the induction process and the types of experiences new teachers have with peers and administrators than on their professional preparation and desire to achieve. Creating positive first impressions and providing personalized helpful information and assistance help to foster the existing enthusiasm and the desire to succeed in first-year teachers.

Induction programs vary, but generally begin with a two or two and one-half day orientation session that is planned and coordinated by school personnel and developed around the results of the preemployment survey. Table 10.1 presents an abbreviated two and one-half day orientation session for beginning teachers with suggested activities, persons responsible, time periods, and evaluation methods. Before induction orientation activities, however, extracurricular assignments should be made to allow beginning teachers time to clarify questions regarding their responsibilities with peers and administrators. Duties, such as hall, cafeteria, and parking lot monitoring, should be assigned on a rotating basis and should pair beginning teachers with veteran teachers.

TABLE 10.1. *Example of an outline for an induction orientation for beginning teachers.*

INDUCTION ORIENTATION

DAY ONE

	ACTIVITY	WHEN	RESPONSIBILITY	TASK/ASSIGNMENT
1.	Welcome and school orientation a. Discuss rules and regulations of school system. b. Present vision and goals of school system. c. Explain relevant personnel policies (e.g., contract obligations, employment periods, insurance, retirement pay scale, and so forth).	8:00–9:30	Superintendent, Board of Education Chair, Principal	Evaluate process and content of information. Solicit participants' oral feedback.
2.	Welcome to the school. a. Discuss school vision and goals. Describe responsibilities of administrators and go over important information in school handbook. b. Discuss school calendar, extra curricular programs and activities, and extra duties of new personnel. c. Discuss teacher evaluation process, staff development programs, and advancement opportunities. d. Introduce department heads, lead teachers, team leaders, and so forth.		Principal and Assistant Principal(s)	Solicit participants' oral feedback.
3.	Welcome of instructional team and overview of their responsibilities	9:30–10:30	Department Heads, Team Leaders, Lead Teachers, Athletic Directors, Media Specialist, and so on.	Solicit participants' oral feedback.
4.	Break	10:30–10:45	Principal	
5.	Small group orientation. a. Discuss specific school rules and regulations (e.g., absenteeism, personal and sick leave, insurance, pay roll, and inservice). b. Discuss extra curricular assignments. c. Discuss specific concerns. d. Discuss school reporting forms, and so on.	10:45–12:00	Relevant Department Heads, Lead Teachers, and Peer Mentors	Solicit staff members' and participants' oral feedback.

255

	ACTIVITY	WHEN	RESPONSIBILITY	TASK/ASSIGNMENT
6.	Lunch (Cafeteria). a. Welcome to community – community background, cultural and civic opportunities, and clubs and organizations.	12:00–1:00	Principal, Assistant Principal, Chair of Chamber of Commerce and City Council Representative	Solicit participants' oral feedback
7.	Department and instructional rules, responsibilities, and goals. a. Introduce teachers to other department or grade-level members. b. Discuss course/level goals and objectives, team teaching, textbooks, guest speaker and field trip policies, lesson planning, grading system, parent contact and conference procedures, and so on.	1:00–2:30	Department Head, Team Leaders, Lead Teachers, and Mentors.	Solicit staff members' and participants' oral feedback.
8.	Break (Refreshments)	2:30–2:45	Principal, Assistant Principals	
9.	Introduction to technology (Media Center).	2:45–4:00	Technology or Media Specialist	Solicit staff members' and participants' oral feedback.
10	Concluding remarks	4:00–4:15	Principal	Provide evaluation instruments designed to evaluate content of day one orientation to participants.

DAY TWO

	ACTIVITY	WHEN	RESPONSIBILITY	TASK/ASSIGNMENT
1.	Extra curricular programs and clubs. a. Discuss the types of programs and clubs, their goals and policies. b. Procedures for fund raising, meeting times, and parent/community involvement.	8:30–9:30	Directors and Advisors	Solicit participants' oral feedback.
2.	PTA and auxiliary programs, goals and purposes.	9:30–10:30	President of PTA and heads of other parent-oriented committees.	Solicit participants' oral feedback.
3.	Breaks (refreshments)	10:30–10:45		
4.	Teacher evaluation instrument and procedures. a. Scheduling observations, who evaluates, post evaluation conferences, and so on.	10:45–12:00	Principal, Department Heads, Lead Teachers, and Team Leaders.	

	ACTIVITY	WHEN	RESPONSIBILITY	TASK/ASSIGNMENT
5.	Lunch	12:00–12:30	Principal, Assistant Principal(s) and Staff	
6.	Role Play teacher classroom evaluation. a. Step-by-step example of teacher evaluation process. b. Explain evaluation instrument(s) and scheduling of observations; conduct an actual assessment of a peer teacher. c. Critique the teaching performance as compared to the evaluation criteria. d. Conduct post-evaluation conference and critique conference based on criteria.	12:30–2:30	Principal, Department Heads, Peer Teachers	Solicit staff members' and participants' oral critique.
7.	Break (refreshments)	2:30–2:45	Principal and Assistant Principal(s)	
8.	Small groups. a. Discuss teacher evaluation instrument(s) and example provided in the role-playing evaluation demonstration. b. Address questions and concerns. c. Discuss inservice program to strengthen teacher weaknesses from evaluation observations.	2:45–4:00	Department Heads, Team Leaders, Lead Teachers, and Mentors.	Solicit staff members' and participants' oral feedback.
9.	Concluding Remarks	4:00–4:15	Principal	Administer evaluation instrument for content of day two orientation.

DAY THREE

1.	Mentoring program a. Overview, purpose, examples of mentor–protégée program.	8:30–10:30	Principal, Department Heads, Mentors	
2.	Break (refreshments)	10:30–10:45	Principal and Assistant Principal(s)	
3.	Small groups. a. Discuss mentoring program's goals and objectives, provide handouts of duties and responsibilities, provide case studies of how the program works.	10:45–12:15		Administer evaluation instrument for content of day three orientation

Coaching assignments and club sponsorships should be on a volunteer basis to free beginning teachers so that they can concentrate on instruction and teaching performance.

FACILITATING PERSONAL AND PROFESSIONAL ADJUSTMENT THROUGH MENTORING

A strong mentoring program can provide immediate and long-term support for beginning teachers. Friendliness, objectivity, and patience are essential characteristics of mentors. A mentoring program provides valuable assistance in the following areas:

- Provides first-hand information and personal experiences about the policies, procedures, and power structure of the community, school system, and the school. For new teachers, information about the social and economic factors of the community are important for understanding the needs of students and expectations of parents.
- Provides immediate introduction to school staff and community members that helps new teachers feel accepted in the school and community.
- Provides personal and emotional support that increases self-confidence and morale and assists in reducing anxieties associated with new demands and environments.
- Provides personal assistance to strengthen instructional and human relations skills. Webb, Montello, and Norton (1994) note that when mentors provide ongoing assistance and meet the special needs and interests of teachers, their classroom effectiveness increases.

Mentors and Beginning Teachers

The selection of mentor teachers should involve input from department heads, team leaders, and others who have first-hand knowledge of faculty members having superior teaching and human relations skills. Experienced, competent, and enthusiastic teachers who express an interest in serving as mentors should be given top priority during selection. Huling-Austin (1987) relates that a mentor teaching the same discipline as the protégée, having the same planning period, and having a similar personality make mentoring more effective. Activities that are most helpful to new teachers include providing assistance in developing lesson plans, helping in the selection of curriculum materials, providing experienced-based knowledge about classroom management and instructional techniques, and serving as a resource person for community information. Mentors should observe beginning teachers' classroom performance and provide assistance in strengthening their teaching skills. Anderson and Shannon (1988) pointed out that mentors provide valuable political information and advice, and help beginning teachers understand how things "get done" in the community, school, and school system. Ganser (1993) observed that mentors also benefitted from this relationship through personal and professional satisfaction by helping new teachers develop and in learning new knowledge and skills.

Some negative aspects are associated with mentoring. Ganser (1993) relates that mentors can receive insufficient recognition from principals or supervisors; that a lack of adequate resources is a source of discontent; and that a lack of scheduled observing, planning, and meeting times detracts from their potential effectiveness. Unclear job descriptions also cause mentor dissatisfaction and lead to early dropout rates. Anderson and Shannon (1988) report that mentors express concerns over inadequate training and being paired with new teachers who have different interests, personalities, and teaching and learning philosophies. Comprehensive training programs, planned and conducted by the principal, do much to alleviate the many negative aspects associated with mentoring programs.

Preparing Mentors

Programs to help experienced teachers become effective mentors may vary in content and length. Mentoring programs should be comprehensive in scope and encompass the following skills and knowledge areas:

(1) Knowledge of the latest research on improving classroom instruction and increasing student learning

(2) Classroom management and student motivation techniques

(3) Conflict resolution

(4) Listening skills

(5) Stress management

(6) Preparing both essay and objective-type classroom tests (Web, Montello, and Norton, 1994; Thies-Sprinthall, 1986; Norton, 1988)

Each of the knowledge and skill areas just mentioned is essential for obtaining good classroom performance and in developing effective, productive working relationships with parents, students, peers, and administrators. Mentors may also serve as instructors for in-service programs. When new teachers are diagnosed as having deficiencies, mentors can conduct special in-service programs to strengthen these identified weaknesses. Principals should provide the necessary time, support, and resources for these mentor-conducted programs.

The Principal's Role in Mentor Programs

Principals are the initiators, facilitators, coordinators, and resource people in designing and conducting mentoring programs. The goal of the short-range induction process is to facilitate the adjustment of new teachers as they gain acceptance, confidence, and a feeling of security in their surroundings. The most important role principals play in the induction program is by providing leadership through establishing program initiative and by sustaining the necessary moral and fiscal support.

In mentoring, the key responsibilities of the principal are (1) to select mentors with the necessary skills, knowledge, and enthusiasm and (2) to establish a comprehensive program to train teachers for their mentoring role. Zahorik (1987) points out that mentoring programs achieve greater success when the school's culture focuses on high instructional standards, values teacher collegiality, and emphasizes the importance of student learning and quality instruction.

Principals also have the responsibility of meeting with mentors and beginning teachers on a regular basis to answer questions and address concerns. Regular meetings reinforce the support for and commitment to the mentoring program and allow for timely intervention in problem areas. Meetings should be structured, have an agenda composed jointly by all parties who will be in attendance, and be action focused. This means that meetings should serve as a forum to share experiences and discuss new and different ways to solve problems or strengthen weaknesses. Some sessions may be devoted to role playing, reading, and sharing research, while others may focus on learning new skills and knowledge provided by consultants. Work by Veenman (1984) relates that beginning teachers have concerns about classroom discipline and student motivation, parent conferences, and planning instruction to meet individual student differences. Regularly scheduled meetings, conducted in a collegial-type atmosphere, foster openness and acceptance of new teachers learning new knowledge and skills as professionals seeking continuous improvement.

Mentors, however, cannot replace principals as formal evaluators of personnel. Seyfarth (1996) relates that effective principals use mentor or peer evaluations as a resource or check on their own findings, but realize that these evaluations cannot replace those of the principal. For new teachers who work closely with their mentors, written critiques of their performance should be carefully examined by principals before they make a summative report about a beginning teacher's competency. For weak or marginal first-year teachers, principals should reexamine their class assignments and extracurricular responsibilities. When mentors assess that more time is needed to strengthen deficiencies of new teachers, principals may need to add an additional planning period, provide duty-free lunch, reassign classes to reduce the number of low achievers or those with discipline problems, or temporarily transfer club or organizational assignments. Saving and cultivating human potential is a major concern for effective principals.

CALCULATING CLASS LOADS

Equity in class load assignments is essential for promoting effective instructional outcomes. Principals in quality-oriented schools calculate class load assignments to maximize teacher effectiveness, not to maximize the pay-for-work ratio that prevails in many schools. Pay-for-work ratio thinking is a scientific management artifact that maintains that employees' work assignments should fully reflect the dollars earned for their labor. The more work assigned, the more the organization gets for its dollar. Quality is merely a by-product of this thinking, whereas full work schedules and quantity outcomes represent management's success in justifying pay checks. In professions such as education, the pay-for-work ratio fails to recognize the creative and individual initiative elements and the reflective and planning time needed to apply these elements toward innovative and continuous progress. In teaching, when teachers are loaded with auxiliary responsibilities, time is taken away from instructional effectiveness. Moreover, many principals give little thought to teacher time dedicated to parent interactions, conferences with teacher aides, work with student teachers, and the demands placed on them to personalize student instruction and address the complex problems of their students. When assignments, such as lunchroom and parking lot duty and serving as advisors to clubs or organizations, are placed on top of the list of demands for effective teaching outcomes, quality outcomes become extremely difficult to achieve.

Interviewing teachers, practicing management by walking around, attending team meetings and teacher advisory meetings, and discussing teacher workloads with supervisors will provide principals with a more realistic picture of what teachers do than examining class schedules or constructing an extracurricular assignment matrix. Some principals ask teachers to keep daily logs of work activities over a two- or three-month time period and then compute the average time spent per activity for workload computations. Both teacher logs and first-hand information provide a good index for understanding teacher workloads. Workload information can be used to request additional teachers or teacher aides and can provide the data often required by central office personnel for adding teacher slots.

ASSISTANT PRINCIPAL INDUCTION

Inducting new assistant principals into school administration is akin to an apprenticeship situation. Although little research on this topic exists, assistant principals are crucial to overall school effectiveness and in the efficient and effective daily operation of the school's programs. Orientation for new assistant principals usually begins in the summer, a time that can be developed into the most important phase of the induction process. Summer allows time for principals to concentrate fully on training new administrators with minimum external distractions. Orientation approaches vary, but generally include the following components:

(1) A thorough review of school system and school policies is conducted.

(2) The school's vision and mission are discussed, and expectations of job requirements and performance are reviewed from the principal's and assistant principal's perspectives.

(3) Relevant forms and personnel procedures are reviewed and discussed. This includes teacher contracts, requisition forms, policies on illness and professional leave days, and the school schedule and calendar.

(4) Student discipline codes and policies regarding suspension, search and seizure, vandalism, drugs, and fighting are thoroughly covered.

(5) Specific auxiliary duties, such as expectations for lunchroom, bus, and extracurricular assignments, are discussed.

(6) A priority checklist of the most important duties for future reference is made. This list provides direction and lets the assistant principal know the salient work priorities.

Principals need to view an assistant principal as a principal-in-training, as a junior colleague under the tutelage of a senior colleague. Therefore, an assistant principal should not be looked upon as one who assumes all the responsibilities that are personally repugnant to the principal. Principals need to continue their share of student and teacher discipline problems, lunch and bus duties, and supervision of extracurricular events. Assistant principals need experience in all administrative areas if they are to be effective principals in their own schools. Principals who mentor future principals effectively enjoy a coveted reputation among their peers, and recommending and supporting assistant principals for a principalship becomes a major responsibility of their job. Mentoring future leaders is demanding, but this role remains the most valuable contribution a principal can make to a school system.

LONG-RANGE INDUCTION PLANNING

Long-range induction planning focuses on providing continued support for new teachers after orientation activities are concluded through an expansion of the mentor-protégée program that is the keystone for helping beginning teachers become effective teachers. The teacher improvement model presented next focuses on mentors providing direct continuous assistance and is a variation of models used in clinical supervision and evaluation of teaching performance. Planning with the principal, mentors take the leadership in developing programs, with input from their respective protégées, to personalize the support and improvement plan. The support and improvement model has five basic phases that are as follows:

Phase one. Lesson plans are jointly developed with goals, objectives, and student evaluation methods clearly stated. Teaching strategies, instructional materials, and needed technology are identified and their applications to instruction are specified. Each of these variables is correlated to the academic levels and special needs of the students. Observation times are determined and beginning teacher and mentor agree on the observation instrument to be used. It is suggested that the criteria of assessment closely resemble those found on the assessment instrument used for contract renewal.

Phase two. Mentors observe and evaluate lessons on agreed-upon performance criteria. Additional comments are also made for future reference.

Phase three. Post-observation interviews immediately follow each observation within the following format:

(1) Beginning teachers self-critique their performance with suggestions on how perceived weaknesses could be improved. Self-critique is a valuable learning experience and assists mentors in strengthening areas of weakness.

(2) Mentors begin by stressing the positive aspects of the lesson and then discuss perceived weaknesses of the lesson by providing specific examples from the observation instrument.

Phase four. A plan for improvement is mutually developed with specific activities and time frames for improvement that have been agreed upon. Remediation activities and methods must coincide with adult learning theories to maximize effectiveness. Knowledge and learning activities must have personal value and interest, must be action oriented, must provide immediate satisfaction, and must provide reinforcement and evaluation of teacher progress that is direct and ongoing.

Phase five. At the conclusion of Phase four, the activities and procedures found in Phase one through four are recycled until beginning teachers reach satisfactory performance levels.

Learning activities beneficial to beginning teachers include direct observation of exemplary teaching, viewing videos, and reading specific materials relative to improvement areas. Post-observation interviews and discussions should immediately follow video and reading assignments to promote effective outcomes. Beginning teachers can benefit by observing an array of teaching styles and techniques. Scheduling new teachers to observe veteran teacher practices provides additional insight and allows new teachers to gain important knowledge and skills quickly. This "intern-type" approach for beginning teachers is personally and professionally rewarding for all parties involved.

Principals also play a direct role in long-range induction activities. The modified long-range plan for induction activities that includes the school's faculty and administrative team is presented next. The plan begins at week five *after* the initial orientation activities are concluded and beginning teachers have a brief period for adjustment.

Week five

(1) The principal meets with beginning teachers individually to address concerns and questions and to review initial progress reports from mentors and supervisors. Early attention to problems assists in the successful development of new teachers.

(2) With each beginning teacher, the principal discusses grading and reporting policies and procedures for parent-teachers conferences.

(3) The principal reviews student discipline and attendance procedures and practices required for ordering materials, scheduling field trips and guests speakers, and reserving rooms and technology.

Week six

(1) The principal meets with new teachers in group sessions to review procedures of formal classroom evaluation observations. Department heads and mentors discuss the observation instruments in small groups and answer specific questions. Role playing, which is a micro-evaluation situation, should be a part of the small group session(s).

Week seven

(1) In a group session, the principal reviews procedures for making parent contacts, and department heads and mentors role play parent-teacher conferences in which beginning teachers participate. Written guidelines are prepared and given to new teachers and the simulated parent-teacher conferences are conducted and critiqued.

(2) The principal provides individual assistance to beginning teachers based on supervisors' and/or mentors' recommendations.

Week eight

(1) The principal meets with new teachers individually to schedule formal evaluation observations that will occur during weeks ten and eleven. The principal reviews mentor and supervisor progress reports and makes specific suggestions for improvement or the principal and teacher jointly agree on a remediation plan.

Week nine

(1) The principal individually discusses special problems or concerns raised by parents, students, mentors, and supervisors.

(2) The principal discusses special interests, creative projects or ideas, or innovative practices new teachers have for improving instruction, school policy and procedures, or other areas that can promote new teacher effectiveness.

Weeks ten and eleven

(1) The principal conducts formal classroom evaluations and post-observation interviews.

(2) The principal shares observation results with mentors and schedules a meeting with both the mentor and the new teacher to develop a joint plan for remediation. Conferences should be as nonthreatening as possible and emphasis should be placed on evaluation as a learning and strengthening exercise.

Weeks thirteen and fourteen

(1) The principal schedules and coordinates special seminars or staff development programs for new teachers based on classroom observation results, new teacher survey results, and mentor recommendations. (It may be that some programs need to be conducted earlier based on new teacher needs and interests).

Week fifteen

(1) The principal individually discusses new teacher progress, concerns, and problems encountered during the first semester. Information from interviews should be noted for the next year's induction plan.

(2) The principal provides a schedule of teacher induction program events for the second semester and scheduled times for "drop-in" formal evaluation classroom observations.

(3) The principal requests new teachers to provide ideas for the second semester improvement seminars and in-service programs and other ideas for school improvement that may be related to school policies and procedures, mentoring activities and practices, and the like. Second semester induction activities are similar to those conducted during the first semester. However, the following deviations, by week, take place:

Weeks four and five

(1) The principal and mentors begin to analyze, in detail, new teacher strengths, weaknesses, and their progress toward remediating deficiencies. Feedback is sought from department heads, team leaders, parents, and other teachers for contract-renewal consideration.

(2) The principal schedules formal classroom evaluations for weeks six and

seven that allow time for an additional formal assessment during week nine if additional assessments are needed for marginal or weak teachers.

Weeks six and seven

(1) The principal conducts formal classroom evaluations and post-observation interviews.

(2) The principal helps each teacher identify weaknesses and develop plans for improvement.

Weeks eight and nine

(1) The principal conducts or coordinates the required seminars or staff development sessions.

(2) The principal meets with each new teacher individually to discuss progress and employment status, frankly and professionally, using written comments from mentors and supervisors and other information gained to this point.

Weeks ten and eleven

(1) The principal offers teaching contracts for the next year or assists the teacher in finding other employment. (In states where "No Cause" laws exist, principals are not required to provide reasons for nonrenewal of contract.)

Weeks fourteen and fifteen

(1) The principal conducts exit or end-of-year interviews with beginning teachers to gather information for topics for next year's in-service programs and teacher induction plan.

END-OF-YEAR OR EXIT INTERVIEWS

Information from exit or end-of-year interviews is valuable for strengthening future induction and staff development programs. Information can be obtained through principal-teacher interviews and through surveys that allow teachers to express freely their concerns and suggestions regarding administrative practices. Questions for the interview should be prepared well in advance and should target specific areas such as the mentor program, enrichment seminars, and the overall quality of the support network. Other questions designed to elicit more specific information are as follows:

(1) "What is your overall impression of the school, faculty, students, and academic program?"

(2) "What do you think of the school's policies and procedures?"

(3) "How do you feel about the subjects you were assigned to teach and the overall student make up of your classes?"

(4) "Do you feel the induction program met your specific needs and expectations?"

(5) "What were the most helpful aspects of the induction program?"

(6) "What were the least valuable aspects of the induction program?"

(7) "How can the induction program be designed to make it more personalized?"

INDUCTION FOR SUPPORT PERSONNEL

Essential to the overall operation of the school is the support staff, which includes secretaries and clerical personnel, custodians, and food service workers. According to a 1992 U.S. Department of Education report, support personnel account for thirty-one percent of the full-time employees in public schools. Principals hire many support personnel whose job descriptions are developed by central office administrators who have little knowledge of an individual school's needs and goals. Job descriptions are often lists of generic responsibilities associated with positions, such as those of a secretary or a custodian, and contain the rudimentary essentials of the job. Job descriptions frequently serve as the basis for questions while interviewing candidates for support positions and for any induction or evaluation process at the school level (Denis and Austin, 1992).

In effective schools, principals modify job descriptions to fit the needs of their teachers and students and hire support personnel whose behavior and performance reflect the values and norms of the school's culture. Rebore (1998) emphasizes the importance of support personnel in fostering the school's culture and maintains that their beliefs and behavior should complement those of instructional and administrative personnel. Cascio (1987) observed that principals who understand the important contributions support staff make in sustaining school environments modify job descriptions to meet the mission and goals of the school. Job descriptions are modified through information obtained from teacher requests and surveys, from observation, and from previous employee behavior.

The turnover rate among support personnel is high and costly. The lack of job training and adjustment programs is a major cause of high turnover rates, which can be reduced through induction programs that help support personnel to adjust to their work environments (Castetter, 1996). Turnover can cause hostility in the school and lower morale. Support staff turnover usually results more from frustration over job expectations and inadequate interpersonal skills rather than from a lack of job-related skills. Principals concerned about retaining support staff use mentoring to induct new personnel into their schools.

Induction programs are designed to train, educate, and infuse employees into the school's culture. Principals play a dominant role in making new personnel feel a part of the school's community and a valued member of the instructional team. With cooperative planning from supervisors, effective principals develop and conduct many personal and professional growth programs and provide training in new technology and human relations skills. Some principals, for example, arrange or conduct seminars on goal setting, time and stress management, conflict resolution, and work efficiency planning. As with certified personnel, initial employment surveys and exit interviews form the basis for planning induction programs. When needs and expectations of new support staff match those of beginning teachers, both sets of new inductees can attend staff development sessions. Webb, Montello, and Norton (1994) relate that effective principals are concerned over high rates of absenteeism and provide counseling services and wellness programs for support personnel. They pointed out that problems resulting from family tension and poor diet and health habits contributed to excessive absenteeism and early turnover.

Principals in quality-oriented schools are both firm and caring. They carefully review the school's policies and procedures with support personnel and clearly define expectations of job performance and personal conduct. Employee handbooks are provided and rules governing absences, lateness, and sick leave are fully discussed. At the same time, staff members are encouraged to share problems and work concerns with the principal and request additional resources or assistance in performing their work assignments. Essential to assisting employees perform their tasks is the mentoring program that is designed similarly to the one for beginning teachers. Mentors are supervisors or peers who provide support and guidance to new support personnel as they become productive and valued members of the school's community.

The most salient part of support staff induction programs is stressing personal behavior and dress expectations. Behaviors are expected to reinforce the school's culture. Support staff perpetuate and model the culture of the school and, in effect, assist teachers and administrators in meeting the goals and mission of the school's instructional program. Employee behaviors are observed by others and can serve as a positive or negative source of public relations for the external public entering the school. Flippo (1980) relates that when support personnel know their job expectations and the accepted codes of conduct, their morale remains high, their job performance increases, and employee turnover is low.

Evaluation of noncertified staff is primarily the responsibility of the principal, and the principal should hold periodic conferences with supervisors and the new employee. This is essential to promoting high-performance outcomes. Conferences conducted on a regular basis allow principals to praise work accomplishments personally and to provide individual assistance in areas of concern or need. Swan et al. (1988) provide a comprehensive performance appraisal instrument for noncertified personnel. The instrument can be used to assess periodic performance or as an end-of-the year assessment. Swan et al. recommend that principals conduct orientation sessions over the performance criteria and that copies of evaluation outcomes be presented to staff members at the conclusion of each evaluation session. Results on performance evaluation instruments should be used for merit pay, promotion, job requirement modification, and disciplinary action. When performance improvement is required, evaluation results will serve as the basis for developing "personalized" improvement plans. Should dismissal be required, exit interviews or questionnaires can provide valuable information to assist mentors and principals in refining staff induction programs.

REFERENCES

Anderson, E. M. and A. L. Shannon. 1988. "Toward a Conceptualization of Mentoring," *Journal of Teacher Education,* 39:38–42.

Cascio, W. F. 1987. *Applied Psychology in Personnel Management.* Third edition. Englewood Cliffs, NJ: Prentice-Hall.

Castetter, W. B. 1996. *The Human Resource Function in Educational Administration.* Sixth edition. Englewood Cliffs, NJ: Prentice-Hall.

Costello, R. T., ed. 1991. *School Personnel Administration: A Practitioner's Guide.* Boston: Allyn and Bacon.

Denis, J. and Austin, B. 1992. "A Basic Course in Job Analysis." *Training and Development,* 46(7):67-70.

Flippo, E. B. 1980. *Personnel Management.* Fifth edition. New York: McGraw-Hill.

Ganser, T. 1993. *"How Mentors Describe and Characterize Their Ideas About Mentor Roles, Benefit, and Mentoring."* Paper presented at the annual meeting of Association of Teacher Educators, Los Angeles (ERIC Reproduction Service NO. ED 251438).

Huling-Austin, L. 1987. "Teacher Induction," in *Teacher Induction: A new beginning.* D. M. Brooks, ed., 3–23. Reston, VA: Association of Teacher Educators.

Norton, M. S. 1988. "Employee Assistance Programs—a Need in Education," *Contemporary Education,* 60:23–26.

Rebore, R. W. 1998. *Personnel Administration in Education: A Management Approach.* Sixth edition. Englewood Cliffs, NJ: Prentice-Hall.

Riches, C. and C. Morgan. 1989. *Human Resources Management in Education.* Bristol, PA: Open University Press.

Seyfarth, J. T. 1996. *Personnel Management for Effective Schools.* Boston: Allyn and Bacon.

Swan, W. W., C. T. Holmes, C. L. Brown, M. L. Short, and L. DeWeese. 1988. "A Generic Performance Appraisal System for Classified Personnel," *Journal of Personnel Evaluation in Education,* 1:293–310.

Thies-Sprinthall, L. 1986. "A Collaborative Approach For Mentor Training: A Working Model," *Journal of Teacher Education,* 37:13–20.

U. S. Department of Education, National Center for Educational Statistics 1992. *The Condition of Education,* Washington, DC: Government Printing Office.

Veenman, S. 1984. "Perceived Problems of Beginning Teachers," *Review of Educational Research,* 54:143–178.

Webb, L. D., P. A. Montello, and M. S. Norton. 1994. *Human Resources Administration: Personnel Issues and Needs in Education:* New York: Macmillan.

Zahorik, J. A. 1987. "Teachers' Collegial Interaction: An Exploratory Study," *Elementary School Journal,* 87:385–396.

CHAPTER 11

Developing Teachers as Leaders

Teachers constitute the largest group of potential leaders and are the greatest, unlimited resource for school change and innovation. However, little is being done to capitalize and to enhance their leadership capabilities or to offer them competent leadership roles. Principals can take the initiative to maximize human resource potential by identifying teacher leaders and then providing them with opportunities to lead others to achieve quality educational programs within their schools or school systems.

THE NEED FOR TEACHERS AS LEADERS

Teachers as leaders are central to effective school change. Little is being done in providing teachers with leadership knowledge and skills, even though many effective school reforms result from the work of teachers who demonstrate initiative, creativity, and perseverance. Empowered teachers and teacher teams provide a viable and proven vehicle for teacher leadership and effective school reform.

The idea of a "community of leaders" is the foundation for the teacher-as-leader concept. Many teachers are enrolled in leadership programs to attain leadership certification, but remain in the classrooms to which they are dedicated. These teachers develop leadership expertise and their talents should be utilized to contribute to the overall improvement of school programs. As peers leading peers, teacher leaders can promote collaboration among peers and facilitate the improvement of instruction without the fear of retribution associated with administrative positions.

The truism "that nothing has more credibility to one teacher than the word of another teacher" has particular application for principals seeking school reform. Principals can promote the teacher-as-leader concept by expanding leadership opportunities and responsibilities for teachers, by providing seminars and workshops on leadership, and by establishing a school culture that values teacher leaders. Teacher leadership begins with teachers realizing their leadership potential as leaders of instruction and as role models for their students. Through their own behavior, teachers influence student conduct and attitudes by leading the learning process in their classrooms. Schargel (1995) points out that schools which practice the total quality management (TQM) theory for school reform provide leadership opportunities to teachers daily through the application of the continuous improvement principle to make decisions and solve problems that affect their classrooms. Classrooms become the practical proving ground for leadership theory, and effective school reform begins with and is measured by the outcomes in classrooms.

TEACHERS AS LEADERS DEFINED

Definitions of teachers as leaders abound in the literature. For example, Whitaker (1995) and Smylie (1995) broadly define teachers as leaders as those who undertake those activities associated with the leadership definition in general and apply them in classrooms, schools, and the community to influence others to improve educational outcomes. Schlechty (1990) defines teachers as leaders when they strive to influence peers to become more effective in classrooms and when they themselves become active in school governance committees, especially when they chair committees or teams that undertake educational renewal or reform efforts. Vance (1991) defines teacher leadership as performance that affects the behavior of their students both in and outside classrooms. Wilson (1993) relates that teacher leadership can be evidenced in the future behaviors and successes of their students.

Teachers' influence on students can be judged in their students' behaviors and attitudes in later life through their vocational achievements, lifestyles, and contributions to society. Successful teachers motivate, challenge, and encourage creativity and risk taking in their students, all of these being attributes of effective leaders. With these functions, Wilson points out, teachers are to students what principals are to teachers.

Site-based managed schools, especially those practicing TQM, view students as clients deserving of ongoing service by professional knowledge brokers who facilitate student achievement on a continuous basis. Motivating and satisfying students' quest for personal development and intellectual growth require leadership skills. Sizer's Coalition of Essential Schools (1989) describes students as knowledge workers and teachers as leaders of this knowledge industry. Fay (1990) relates that teachers are daily using the leadership skills of planning teaching strategies and concepts, conducting action research, supervising student teachers, serving as peer tutors or mentors, and leading empowered teams to improve others and the overall effectiveness of the school.

Finding ways to help others to improve and influencing others' behavior to enhance job performance are also leadership attributes. Whitaker (1995) discusses teacher *influence* as a leadership quality and notes their ability to change the behavior of others, both peers and students, through overt and subtle ways. Teachers serve as catalysts for change and as innovators and have spheres of influence within their schools and community. Many teachers hold leadership positions in community and civic organizations and exercise many of the same skills as do principals and superintendents. Formal positions or titles do not make leaders. Boles and Troen (1994) report that teacher leaders have good human relation skills, are people centered, and take the initiative in solving problems or in trying something new or different. Rosenholtz (1989) notes that teacher leaders have high credibility among their peers, seek to develop personally and professionally, and share a mutual quest for learning. Weller and Hartley (1994) note that teachers who have high credibility among their peers act as "power agents" in their schools (i.e., as leaders who influence the actions of other teachers). These "influentials" establish ways of how things "get done" in the school, they reinforce the school's culture, they initiate new staff in the ways of the school's power structure, and they apply "pressure" to those engaging in behaviors outside the standards of practice. Principals seeking change or school reform practices seek their early cooperation as an essential element to promote successful outcomes.

Further, teachers who are likely to support school reform efforts, such as TQM, are "influentials" among their peers. That is, many teachers who actively support changes in school governance procedures are known as school "power agents" and provide both quiet moral support and active frontline leadership by chairing committees, leading discussion groups, and supporting the move to shared governance through community member discussions (Weller and Hartley, 1994; Weller, 1996). Principals who seek to make change less difficult and to enhance the probability of success know their teacher power agents and request their assistance and council.

TEACHER LEADERSHIP ROLES

Viewing teachers as leaders requires a paradigm shift in the concept of leadership. Senge (1990) discusses "mental models," assumptions based on previous experiences, as a major deterrent to progressive and innovative thinking. For effective progress to take place, principals must first change their assumptions and then approach problems from a different perspective or a renewed mental model. Duke (1993) and Robinson (1985) see educational problems as being more of the same, but with different terms and different people. New remedies are but old solutions in disguise, and the proof lies in the continuously existing problems. The adage that "the more things change, the more they stay the same" is an apparent truism in education. However, Confucius said that the best time to plant a tree is ten years ago. The second-best time is now.

In this context, principals must first be willing to view teachers as leaders rather than as subordinates under contract with specific duties and responsibilities to perform in the traditional and sometimes antiquated manner. Principals who are receptive to this initial step in making a paradigm shift can facilitate the process by recalling their years as teachers and the frustrations and anxieties they experienced with their attempts to lead improvement initiatives in their schools or classrooms. Reflecting on colleagues with similar frustrations and unfulfilled innovative ideas and recalling the leadership potential and creativity of peers can help speed the paradigm shift along. Finally, when principals reflect on the leadership characteristics of their own teachers the paradigm shift is brought into focus and new mental models are formed to replace old assumptions that teachers cannot lead nor make positive, creative contributions to education.

Conventional Leadership Roles

Traditional leadership roles for teachers include department heads and administrative assistants in high schools, team leaders in middle schools, and lead teachers in elementary schools. Leiberman (1992) notes that the master teacher and career ladder concept, when implemented, provide formal leadership roles for teachers. Other traditional leadership roles include those of chairpersons of standing or ad hoc committees or chairpersons of instructional or curricular design teams. Some of these leadership positions carry positional power, whereas others are functional positions that necessitate the use of a teacher's referent power, expert power, or both. Both *referent power,* which is the ability to lead through personality characteristics, and *expert power,* which is the ability to lead or influence others through special skills or knowledge, are needed by teachers in leadership positions who lack positional or legitimate power that comes from organizational authority. French (1993) presents research that proves that effective leaders use five sources of power to influence the behavior of others to accomplish tasks. *Referent power* and *expert power* were found to be more effective, overall, than *coercive power* (use of punishment), *reward power* (ability to reward), and *legitimate* or *positional power* (authority from the organization) in influencing subordinates to achieve organizational goals.

Teacher Collegial Groups

The teacher-as-leader concept can be promoted through teacher collegial groups (TCGs), which have been used effectively in some TQM schools to develop teacher leadership and to foster teaching excellence. Weller and Weller (1997) found that principals who promote the TQM principle of continuous improvement implement TCGs by forming teams of teachers to identify individual year-long goals for improvement in instruction or professional development. Groups meet once a month for half a day, elect their group leader, and devise strategies to achieve their goals. Release time is provided by the principal, with staff development units being awarded at the completion of the program. Each group evaluates its own progress, based on its goals and objectives, and modifies learning strategies as needed. Successes and failures are shared with peers who make suggestions on how each team member can better meet the individual goals of the team members.

For example, one team may choose the overall goal of becoming more effective in reducing classroom discipline problems. After setting specific goals and objectives, teachers may decide to use videos, books, and journal articles to identify new approaches to solving discipline problems. Teachers will choose different methods, implement and evaluate them, and report back to the team on their successes and failures. Suggestions for improvement are then made by team members, and the process is repeated until teachers reach a predetermined level of success. Teams practicing the TCG method use the leadership skills of planning, organizing, coordinating, decision making, evaluating, budgeting (managing staff development monies for needed resources), and leading instructional improvement projects.

Some principals practice the teacher-as-leader concept by establishing peer coaching networks where peers supervise peers to provide leadership in instruction. Other principals encourage teachers to serve as trainers in staff development programs, to lead discussions in personal and professional improvement seminars, and to serve as hosts for visiting dignitaries, new teachers, and community visitors. Rotating committee or team chair responsibilities, appointing teachers to serve on the schoolwide governance council or on systemwide committees, and appointing teachers as administrative assistants are additional ways principals promote the teacher-as-leader concept.

In TQM schools where action research is a major component of the continuous improvement principle, principals form action research committees that function at the grade, department, or school level. Focusing on instructional and curricular improvement, these teams develop and conduct research projects to improve the educational programs of the school, thereby undertaking an important responsibility that has long been attributed solely to the school principal.

THE PRINCIPAL'S ROLE IN DEVELOPING TEACHER LEADERS

Whether leaders are born or made, has been the subject of an ongoing debate. The "Great Man" theory of leadership states that leaders are born. Those of the right breed are natural leaders, whereas others are not. The "Big Bank" theory of leadership maintains that events make leaders and that situations allow certain people to take charge of and command others. Neither theory provides a satisfactory explanation of leadership. Other theories, such as "leadership is a *rare* skill," is debunked by the existence of respected and talented people in millions of leadership positions and roles today (e.g., military personnel and local, state, and federal government officials). The "cream rises to the top" theory holds that leaders exist only at the top of organizations and that only the most skilled and qualified are recognized and appointed. However, leadership occurs at every level of the organization, and it is the quality of this leadership that is central to making top leaders look good. Talent and skill are not always recognized and rewarded, and some of the best leadership material is lost because of the political or jealous nature and entanglements between people and organizations.

What is now recognized and less disputed is that leadership exists in all kinds of organizations, at all levels, and without regard to knowledge or skill level or base (Bennis and Nanus, 1985). In this context, principals who view teachers as leaders can promote leadership in a variety of ways. In fact, lack of creativity on the part of the principal remains the greatest impediment to promoting the concept of teacher leadership. In site-based managed schools, empowered teacher teams allow all teachers to practice essential leadership skills. Little (1993) observed that many school-based problems are solved by teachers when they are given the opportunity to provide a solution. Deming (1986) admonishes leaders to allow those closest to the problem to solve the problem because they know it the best. Weller (1996) notes that teacher teams, in solving problems of an instructional and curricular nature, become active learners and researchers, and their body of knowledge and expertise continuously expands. The acquisition of new knowledge contributes to self-growth and personal satisfaction and enhances classroom expertise.

Principals can promote leadership in teachers through staff-development activities. Glickman (1990) relates that effective staff-development programs are teacher developed and teacher conducted (see Chapter 5). These programs call for teachers to plan, make decisions, coordinate, and manage resources. Program content is practical in nature, is easily applied to classroom situations, and promotes success which, in turn, enhances self-concept, self-esteem, and work attitude. These findings concur with those of McLaughlin (1990) who states that when teachers become interested in information they deem useful, they become motivated to expand this knowledge and to work collaboratively to apply new and different strategies to increase student learning.

Schools are learning communities and staff development programs are designed as "pump primers" to extend the learning community concept and facilitate teacher leadership. Pump priming occurs when seminars or other type activities serve to extend teacher knowledge or development in a structured and sustained way. Having teachers organize reading and discussion groups, for example, allows further exploration into a topic or subtopic of interest to teachers and extends learning initiated by the staff development program. These activities allow teachers to reflect, gain new information and understanding, and promote creative and innovative ways to meet students needs better.

A LEADERSHIP DEVELOPMENT MODEL FOR TEACHERS

Who has the responsibility for teaching leadership attributes to teachers? Some argue that teacher preparation programs should infuse leadership training into their undergraduate curriculum and graduate courses. Others argue that central office staff should provide leadership training through workshops or staff development. We believe that principals have the responsibility to provide training and opportunities for teacher leadership. Further, principals have the responsibility to facilitate opportunities for teacher leadership in the school system, the central office, and in professional organizations. Figure 11.1 presents a leadership development model for principals to promote the teacher-as-leader concept.

As seen in Figure 11.1, the principal has the primary responsibility for developing teacher leaders through this seven-stage process.

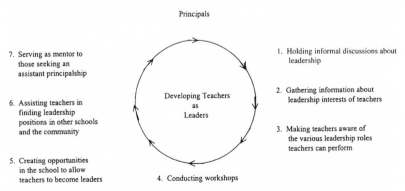

FIGURE 11.1. Leadership development.

Stage One: This deals with the principal informally talking with teachers about their interest in leadership positions and how they feel about taking on additional duties and responsibilities. Here, principals point out that many of their daily classroom interactions with students are leadership behaviors; for example, planning daily lessons, organizing instructional material, teaching through group work and peer tutoring strategies, seeking student input on preferred learning activities, and practicing the leadership styles of democratic, situational, and authoritarian leadership are all leadership behaviors.

Stage Two: This concerns developing questionnaires and other survey instruments to assess teacher interest in becoming school leaders and in assessing their current and future leadership aspirations. Information gathered through informal discussions and surveys forms the basis for principals to develop structured leadership development programs that allow teachers to explore leadership opportunities and acquire the skills and knowledge associated with leadership behavior.

Stage Three: This relates to conducting seminars and workshops that identify leadership roles for teachers, paths to leadership positions, and the knowledge and skills that are essential for their positions. Informal seminars and individual counseling sessions help teachers identify leadership positions that are more closely aligned with their current and future aspirations.

Stage Four: This provides leadership training to teachers, both from a theoretical and practical perspective, and grounds teachers in the basic knowledge and skill areas that are essential to maximize their chances for success as teacher leaders.

Stage Five: This establishes positions or provides opportunities in the school to allow teachers to practice newly acquired leadership knowledge and skills. Providing teachers with student teachers, establishing a peer coaching network, instructional lead teacher positions, and placing teachers as chairs of committees and teams introduces teachers to leadership responsibilities.

Stage Six: This deals with actively helping teachers find leadership positions in other schools, in the school system's central school office, and on committees within the community and the school system.

Stage Seven: This entails serving as mentor to teachers who hold promise and aspire to become assistant principals. This also provides release time for teachers to "shadow" principals and delegate administrative responsibilities to these teachers as they practice the craft of building level leadership and preparing for a school principalship.

One principal in a suburban high school in Georgia regularly teaches a course entitled "Teachers as Leaders." The following case study describes how this course evolved and how the principal uses the course as a part of the Stage Four process.

The principal's leadership philosophy changed over a period of several years from that of a top-down leader to one who began to understand the benefits of teacher empowerment. During this change he began to seek ways to use the expertise of staff members in decision making through empowered teams.

The first team formed was the *leadership team,* a team made up of department heads, at-large faculty members, and administrators. Led by the principal, this team met at least once a month and dealt with a wide variety of issues, including things such as rule and procedural changes at the school level, recommendations for policy changes at the system level, the dissemination of information to and from departments, and topics requested by staff members which are placed on the agenda by leadership team members.

Through the leadership team process, which allowed key faculty members to monitor various school situations, make recommendations for improvement, and then see the results of their problem solving, the concept of continuous improvement began. As these changes were implemented, team members received feedback from teachers and gathered data. Evaluation of this information called for further changes and further monitoring. Their decision to act on this continuous flow of data led them away from what is typical of such groups. Instead of monitoring to maintain the status quo once the major problems had been dealt with, they began to monitor and use data to make continual improvements.

As the team's responsibility grew and positive outcomes were evidenced, other teams began to form as natural offshoots of the leadership team. Teams of teachers, students, and community members were formed to address discipline and attendance issues. Computerized records in these areas made it easy to analyze the outcomes of policy and procedural changes designed to remedy problems. In the area of discipline, for example, the computerized data bank of all discipline referrals to administrators allowed for easy identification of students who had chronic behavioral problems. This led to a recommendation by the student management committee to the leadership team for new procedures for dealing with such referrals. The recommendation was accepted and administrators automatically contacted parents of students upon their referral to an administrator for the third time.

Over a three-year period, and in conjunction with similar improvements the school reduced violent acts by 67 percent and reduced total discipline referrals by 35 percent. The review of data also led to further improvements in the support offered to these identified at-risk students.

As a result of the successes in this area, the principal began to focus on ways to empower teachers in the area of instruction, including staff development for teachers. The principal had always required that all certified staff attend the school-based staff development offered each year. Topics focused on areas that applied to all teachers, such as classroom management, reading across content areas, or stress management.

As the school evolved into an organization, which made the continual learning and professional development of its staff a top priority, teachers began to request more personalized staff development. Many teachers were assuming increased leadership responsibilities, such as training other teachers and acting as facilitators of peer groups, and these teachers needed or would benefit from staff development related to teachers as leaders. Other teachers had expressed interests in several other areas.

The principal requested the systemwide staff development coordinator to allow the school to offer several different staff development courses to teachers. From this selection of courses taught by teachers and administrators, teachers were required to take one course of their choice.

One of the courses offered was a "Teachers as Leaders" course developed and taught by the principal. Figure 11.2 presents the proposal submitted by the principal to the systemwide staff development coordinator for approval.

As seen in Figure 11.2, teachers who wish to develop skills for assuming more leadership responsibilities may opt for the course. The goals for participants are to understand better the principles of leadership development; to use leadership skills and principles on the job; to design, implement, and evaluate a leadership improvement plan; and to present the results of the plan to class members.

SITE-BASED MANAGED SCHOOLS AND TEACHER LEADERSHIP

Site-based managed schools provide teachers with excellent opportunities to lead and practice leadership skills for obtaining the assistant principalship. Walling (1994) and Warwick (1995) note the importance of delegating authority to teachers to solve problems and make decisions, both of which are central leadership skills. Warwick (1995) relates that in schools practicing Deming's quality management principle of continuous improvement (Deming, 1986), teachers solve problems that affect the efficiency of classroom instruction and teacher teams address problems and make decisions about instruction and curriculum at the grade or department level. Weller and Hartley (1994) and Fullan (1993) observed that principals who encourage teachers to carry out action research provide them with the opportunity to be creative and innovative and encourage them to practice the leadership skills of planning, coordinating, decision making, and evaluating. Principals in quality-oriented schools realize that progress and innovation require risk taking and autonomy, and principals in these schools reward teacher success through extrinsic and intrinsic means.

STAFF DEVELOPMENT PROPOSAL

Program Title: Teachers as Leaders

Description: This ten-hour course will focus on the skills necessary for teachers and department heads to become more effective leaders in their classrooms, as department heads, and in the school setting.

Goals Addressed
To emphasize continual professional growth.
To develop leadership skills.
To understand better the principles of leadership development.
To use leadership skills and principles in the workplace.

Improvement Practices to be Implemented:
Participants will:
(1) Read three books on leadership.
(2) Design a leadership improvement plan.
(3) Implement a leadership improvement plan.
(4) Evaluate the leadership plan at the end of the year.

Performance Indicators Suitable for On-the-Job Assessment.
Participants will demonstrate attainment of course objectives through completion of activities listed below:
1. Participants will apply leadership principles learned in the course.
2. Participants will receive input from faculty and students on their leadership development skills.
3. Participants will use feedback to continue professional growth.

Total Hours:
Participants will meet for a minimum of ten hours for one SDU. Sessions will begin during preplanning, will be held approximately once every six weeks, and will continue until the end of the school year.

Session 1 & 2 (90 minutes each):	Literature Review/Leadership
Session 3 & 4 (90 minutes each):	Literature Skills Plan
Session 5 & 6 (90 minutes each):	Implementation and Feedback
Session 7 (2 hours):	Presentation to group on project implementation and evaluation.

Persons Responsible for Training Activities:
Principal

Project Costs:
None:

Principal_____ Date_____

School Staff-Development Coordinator_____ Date_____

Curriuculum Coordinator_____ Date_____

FIGURE 11.2. Staff-development proposal for a teacher-as-leader course.

ENCOURAGING RELUCTANT TEACHERS TO LEAD

Some teachers are reluctant to assume leadership responsibilities or to undertake initiatives to improve. Whitaker (1995) encourages principals to have such teachers observe respected peer behavior and to discuss the benefits and satisfaction these teachers derive from their leadership initiatives. These dialogues provide insight into why some teachers are more respected than others, have more success with their students, and experience greater job satisfaction levels. Observing peer models often promotes reluctant teachers to take initiatives especially when they are teamed up with their respected peers and receive moral support from principals.

Sometimes reluctant teachers will share innovative or creative ideas with the principal or others, suggesting someone else to take the lead in introducing the innovative practice. Here, principals can personally motivate these teachers to undertake their own ideas and to provide the essential support necessary for successful outcomes. Whitaker (1995) noted that reluctant teachers can become motivated to assume responsibilities when principals actively seek their ideas and opinions. Soliciting teacher ideas increases their self-esteem and provides motivation to undertake leadership responsibilities. For example, getting teachers involved in writing grant proposals, attempting new teaching methods, introducing new technology, and developing new curricular materials are leadership activities that are essential to promoting quality educational outcomes. Projects such as these begin as individual efforts and then expand into group work or involve a large portion of the school's faculty. Leadership experience in these cases allows teachers to practice many of the skills used by department heads or assistant principals.

SCHOOL CULTURE AND TEACHERS AS LEADERS

A school's culture, which comprises its values, beliefs, norms, customs, and traditions, influences its policies, its expectations, and the *modus operandi*. Deal and Kennedy (1982) emphasize the importance of culture in perpetuating shared beliefs and values that form the organization's goals and norms. It is through the school's culture that principals foster the teacher-as-leader concept. Wilson (1993) reported that when a school's culture does not support the teacher-as-leader concept, teachers explore outside options, such as civic or service organizations, to fulfill their leadership needs. Schools that tend to prevent teacher leadership from taking root are those characterized as the traditional school culture and have the following characteristics:

- Leadership style is authoritarian where teachers are expected to follow rules and regulations with little or no input into policy making.
- Teachers have little or no input into matters affecting curriculum and

instruction and little or no incentive to acquire new knowledge or skills outside the principal-prescribed staff development programs.

* Teachers receive little, if any, recognition or rewards for their accomplishments or initiatives.
* Teachers having few interactions among themselves and rare and unsupported collaboration about professional matters.
* Communication within the school is top-down with little open or candid communication among teachers and administrators.

Central to a school's culture is its organizational structure. Site-based management models incorporate many recognized aspects of leadership into their organizational processes. Teamwork, shared decision making, and joint policy making provide teachers with the opportunity to take initiatives to improve the school's educational programs. Bolman and Deal (1990) refer to these activities as being essential in the development of teacher leadership. Providing teachers with the opportunity to take risks, try new methods, and have autonomy are leadership-promoting variables. Collegiality and collaboration among teachers also promote teacher leadership. Hart (1990) maintains that in schools where friendly relationships exist among teachers, there is an environment that stimulates professional dialogue and encourages the experimentation of new ideas and programs. Weller and Weller (1997) report that in schools practicing the site-based management principles of TQM, teachers are encouraged to practice action research, to share their results through seminars or discussion groups, and to expand their work into staff development programs or schoolwide research projects.

Teachers also act as leaders by influencing team or group members. Hart (1990) observes that teachers who facilitate activities, engage in debate with peers, or try new educational methods are leaders. Some teachers are "idea" people, some are naturally creative, and some are gifted at resolving conflict. When these attributes are provided opportunities to materialize, teachers become appliers of leadership functions. Hart also points out that team leadership can be exhibited by chairpersons, timekeepers, recorders, and parliamentarians. Each serves an important purpose in accomplishing team or group goals.

A PERSONAL PHILOSOPHY ON TEACHER LEADERSHIP

A personal philosophy is a very general belief and attitude toward life, a group, or the individual. Principals have a general philosophy of education and teachers, as a group. Different philosophies lead to different practices. O'Neill (1990) noted that having a philosophy and implementing that philosophy are not the same because what one may espouse publically may not always be practiced. The proof of advocating one's values, beliefs, and attitudes lies in the actual application of one's philosophy while performing life's activities—

there is no other "acid test." A principal's philosophy of education is composed of the personal beliefs, attitudes, and values the principal holds about teachers, the mission of education, school governance, curriculum, and classroom instruction. The sum is the total of its parts.

As leader of the school, the principal and his or her philosophy greatly affect the school's culture, its curriculum, its instructional practices, and its organizational structure. Teachers are influenced by the principal's philosophy in their attitudes toward education, students, parents, and classroom performance. The three prevailing philosophies are (1) *behavioral,* (2) *progressive,* and (3) *humanistic.* Howard (1992) reports that a behavioral philosophy emphasizes compliance and standards. Central to this philosophy is the idea of control and that management by well-defined objectives is the best way to achieve predetermined ends. Behavior modification through the use of authority and threats ensures compliance to standards.

A progressive philosophy holds that people are responsible by nature, that they can resolve their own problems, and that they tend to work cooperatively. Principals holding this philosophy, claims Howard (1992), incorporate site-based management models, rely on teacher teams for school improvements, and believe that teachers can best solve their own classroom problems with adequate moral support from administrators.

A humanistic philosophy supports freedom, trust, and autonomy. Emphasizing individualism, principals with a humanistic philosophy believe that teachers are rational, self-motivated, inclined to grow personally and professionally, and are capable of solving professional problems that influence their job effectiveness. Elias and Merriam (1995) point out that trust, respect, friendship, cooperation, and sincere regard for teachers as valued people are essential elements of humanistic philosophy.

Principals who practice the teacher-as-leader concept may have a progressive philosophy, a humanistic philosophy, or a combination of the two. The behavioral philosophy is too traditional to maintain that teachers can lead, use autonomy wisely, be productive without tight supervision, or work cooperatively in team or group situations. Teachers also have their own philosophies, and work effectiveness can be maximized when the teachers' and the principal's philosophies coincide. Each philosophy has its own merits given the organization, its mission, and its employees. However, the people-positive approach to leadership and organizational policy yields more efficient and effective outcomes than do approaches that entail viewing the capabilities people possess in a more negative light.

REFERENCES

Bennis, W. and B. Nanus. 1985. *Leaders: The Strategies for Taking Charge.* New York: Harper Collins.

Boles, K. and B. Troen. 1994. "Teacher Leadership in a Professional Development School." Paper presented at the Annual Meeting of the American Educational Research Association, New Orleans, LA.

Bolman, L. G. and T. E. Deal. 1990. *Reforming Organizations,* San Francisco: Jossey-Bass.

Deal, T. E. and A. A. Kennedy. 1982. *Corporate Cultures: The Rites and Rituals of Corporate Life.* Reading, MA: Addison-Wesley.

Deming, W. E. 1986. *Out of the Crisis,* Cambridge, MA: MIT Press.

Duke, D. L. 1993. "Removing Barriers to Professional Growth," *Phi Delta Kappan,* 74: 702–704, 710–712.

Elias, J. L. and S. B. Merriam. 1995. *Philosophical Foundations of Adult Education.* Second edition. Melbourne, FL: Kreiger.

Fay, C. 1990. *Teaching and Leading: The Teacher's Voice.* Paper presented at the Annual Meeting of the American Education Research Association, Boston, MA

French, J. R. 1993. *A Formal Theory of Social Power.* New York: Irvington.

Fullan, M. G. 1993. *Change Forces.* New York: Falmer Press.

Glickman, C. 1990. "Pretending Not to Know What We Know," *Educational Leadership,* 48(8):4–10.

Howard, C. C. 1992. *Theories of General Education: A Critical Approach.* New York: St Martin's Press.

Leiberman, A. 1992. "Teacher Leadership: What Are We Learning?" in *Teachers as Leaders: Evolving Roles* C. Livingston, ed., 159–165. Washington, DC: NEA.

Little, J. W. 1993. "Norms of Collegiality and Experimentation: Workplace Conditions of School Success," *American Educational Research Journal,* 19(3):325–340.

McLaughlin, M. W. 1990. "The Rand Change Agent Study Revisited: Macro-Perspectives and Micro-Realities," *Educational Researcher,* 19(9):11–16.

O'Neill, W. F. 1990. *Educational Ideologies: Contemporary Expressions of Educational Philosophy.* Dubuque, IA: Kendall/Hunt.

Robinson, G. E. 1985. *Effective Schools Research: A Guide to School Improvement.* ERS Concerns in Education, Arlington, VA: Educational Research Services.

Rosenholtz, S. J. 1989. *Teacher's Workplace: The Social Organization of Schools.* New York: Longman.

Schargel, F. 1994. *Transforming Education through Total Quality Management: A Practitioner's Guide.* Princeton, NJ: Eye on Education.

Schenkat, R. 1993. *Quality Connections: Transforming Schools through Total Quality Management,"* Alexandria, VA: Association for Supervision and Curriculum Development.

Schlechty, P. C. 1990. *Schools for the Twenty-First Century: Leadership Imperative for Educational Reform.* San Francisco: Jossey-Bass.

Senge, P. 1990. *The Fifth Discipline.* New York: Doubleday.

Sizer, T. R. 1989. "Diverse Practice, Shared Ideas: The Essential School," in *Organizing for Learning: Toward the 21st Century,* H. J. Walberg and J. J. Lane, eds., Reston, VA: National Association of Secondary School Principals.

Smylie, M. A. 1995. *"New Perspectives on Teacher Leadership,"* The Elementary School Journal, 96(1):3–8.

Vance, P. S. 1991. *"Pre-Initiating Extended Role Teacher: Exploring Facets of Teacher Leadership," Dissertation Abstracts International,* 53:01A–60.

Walling, D. R. 1994. *Teachers as Leaders: Perspectives on the Professional Development of Teachers.* Bloomington, IN: Phi Delta Kappa Educational Foundation.

Warwick, R. 1995. *Beyond Piece-Meal Improvements: How to Transform Your School Using Deming's Quality Principles.* Bloomington, IN: National Education Service.

Weller, L. D. and S. H. Hartley. 1994. Teamwork and cooperative learning: An educational perspective for business. *Quality Management Journal,* 2(2), 18–25.

Weller, L. D. 1996. Benchmarking: A paradigm for change in quality education. *The TQM Magazine,* 8(6), 24–29.

Weller, L. D. and S. J. Weller. 1997. "Quality Learning Organizations and Continuous Improvement: Implementing the Concept," *National Association of Secondary School Principals Bulletin,* 18(591):62–70.

Whitaker, T. 1995. "Informal Teacher Leadership: The Key to Successful Change in Middle Level Schools," *National Association of Secondary School Principals Bulletin,* 79(567):76–81.

Wilson, M. 1993. "The Search for Teacher Leaders," *Educational Leadership,* 50(6): 24–27.

ABOUT THE AUTHORS

L. David Weller earned his Ph.D. in educational administration from Iowa State University. Currently, he is a professor in the Department of Educational Leadership at the University of Georgia. He has been a high school teacher, a middle school principal, a marketing representative for Xerox Corporation, and Department Head of Middle School Education at the University of Georgia. He serves as a consultant to public and private schools and universities in the areas of organizational development and Total Quality Management. He has been a visiting lecturer at several British universities teaching in the areas of leadership theory and Total Quality Management.

Sylvia J. Weller earned her Ed.D. in educational administration from the University of Georgia. Currently, she is an assistant principal for curriculum and instruction at Winder-Barrow High School in Winder, Georgia. She has been a high school teacher of gifted and advanced placement English, personnel director, and director of secondary curriculum and gifted. She has won many awards for her teaching and was recently named Assistant Principal of the Year for District L in Georgia.